MATHS

*Curriculum*Bank

**KEY STAGE ONE
SCOTTISH LEVELS A-B**

SHAPE, SPACE AND MEASURES

JAN WORDEN

Published by Scholastic Ltd,
Villiers House,
Clarendon Avenue,
Leamington Spa,
Warwickshire CV32 5PR
Text © 1996 Jan Worden
© 1996 Scholastic Ltd
67890   012345

AUTHOR
JAN WORDEN

EDITORS
RUTH NASON
CLARE GALLAHER

SERIES DESIGNER
LYNNE JOESBURY

DESIGNER
TOBY LONG

ILLUSTRATIONS
PAT MURRAY

COVER ILLUSTRATION
GAY STURROCK

INFORMATION TECHNOLOGY CONSULTANT
MARTIN BLOWS

SCOTTISH 5–14 LINKS
MARGARET SCOTT AND SUSAN GOW

Designed using Adobe Pagemaker

British Library Cataloguing-in-Publication Data
A catalogue record for this book is available from the
British Library.

ISBN 0-590-53393-2

Contents

INTRODUCTION	5
Overview grid	9
THREE-DIMENSIONAL SHAPE	13
TWO-DIMENSIONAL SHAPE	23
POSITION AND MOVEMENT	31
LENGTH	41
MASS	49
CAPACITY	57
TIME	65
ASSESSMENT	71
PHOTOCOPIABLES	79
USING AND APPLYING	139
IT links	142
Cross-curricular links	144

Introduction

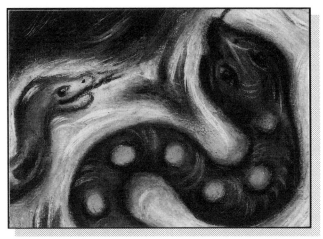

Scholastic Curriculum Bank is a series for all primary teachers, providing an essential planning tool for devising comprehensive schemes of work as well as an easily accessible and varied bank of practical, classroom-tested activities with photocopiable resources.

Designed to help planning for and implementation of progression, differentiation and assessment, *Scholastic Curriculum Bank* offers a structured range of stimulating activities with clearly-stated learning objectives that reflect the programmes of study, and detailed lesson plans that allow busy teachers to put ideas into practice with the minimum amount of preparation time. The photocopiable sheets that accompany many of the activities provide ways of integrating purposeful application of knowledge and skills, differentiation, assessment and record-keeping.

Opportunities for assessment are highlighted within the activities where appropriate. Ways of using information technology for different purposes and in different contexts, as a tool for communicating and handling information and as a means of investigating, are integrated into the activities where appropriate, and more explicit guidance is provided at the end of the book.

The series covers all the primary curriculum subjects, with separate books for Key Stages 1 and 2 or Scottish Levels A–B and C–E. It can be used as a flexible resource with any scheme, to fulfil National Curriculum and Scottish 5–14 requirements and to provide children with a variety of different learning experiences that will lead to effective acquisition of skills and knowledge.

SHAPE, SPACE
AND MEASURES

SCHOLASTIC CURRICULUM BANK MATHEMATICS

The *Scholastic Curriculum Bank Mathematics* books enable teachers to plan comprehensive and structured coverage of the mathematics curriculum and pupils to develop the required skills, knowledge and understanding through activities that promote mathematical thinking and ways of working.

There are two books for Key Stage 1/Scottish Levels A–B and two for Key Stage 2/Scottish Levels C–E reflecting the sections of the programmes of study:
▲ Number (including Handling Data);
▲ Shape, Space and Measures.

Using and Applying Mathematics is integrated into these contexts as required by the National Curriculum and these links are highlighted on the grid on pages 139 to 141.

Bank of activities

This book provides a bank of activities that can be used in many different ways – to form a framework for a scheme of work; to provide breadth, variety or extension to a core scheme; to supplement a mathematical or cross-curricular topic; or they can be set as tasks to answer specific, individual learning requirements.

Range

The range of activities provided will enable pupils to develop mathematical language. They will need to select and use a variety of materials, and they will have appropriate contexts for measuring and using IT.

Communication skills

The activities aim to develop mathematical language and communication skills by encouraging children to:
▲ use mathematical vocabulary, diagrams and symbols;
▲ describe and discuss their work, and respond to questioning;
▲ present their work using a variety of mathematical forms;
▲ use and apply mathematics in everyday situations and within mathematics itself.

Lesson plans

Detailed lesson plans, under clear headings, are given for each activity and are set out in a standard way so that the material is easy to follow and can be readily implemented in the classroom. The structure for each activity is as follows:

Activity title box

The information contained in the title box at the beginning of each activity outlines the following key aspects:
▲ *Activity title and learning objective.* Each activity has a clearly stated learning objective given in bold italics. These learning objectives break down aspects of the programmes of study into manageable, hierarchical teaching and learning

chunks, and their purpose is to aid planning for progression. These objectives can be easily referenced to the National Curriculum and Scottish 5–14 requirements by using the overview grids at the end of this chapter (pages 9 to 12).
▲ *Class organisation/Likely duration.* Icons †† and 🕑 signpost the suggested group sizes for each activity and the approximate amount of time required to complete it. Small groups will generally mean up to four to six children whereas larger groups could be ten to twelve children, or half the class. Timing arrangements are by their very nature arbitrary as so many factors are involved. Sometimes teachers may wish to extend the time spent on practical work and discussion and at other times children may find the task easier or harder than expected, which will in turn affect the time taken to complete it.

Previous skills/knowledge needed

The information given here alerts teachers to particular knowledge or skills that pupils need prior to carrying out the activity.

Key background information

The information in this section is intended to set the scene and provide helpful guidance for teachers. The guidance may relate to pupils' learning, teachers' knowledge of mathematics, or both.

Preparation

Advice is given for those occasions where it is necessary for the teacher to orientate the pupils to the activity or to collect and prepare materials ahead of time.

Resources needed

All the equipment, materials and photocopiable sheets needed to carry out the activity are listed here, so that the pupils or the teacher can gather them together easily before the beginning of the teaching session.

What to do

Easy-to-follow, step-by-step instructions are given for carrying out the activity, including, where appropriate, suggestions for suitable points for discussion. Issues of classroom management are raised where relevant.

Suggestions for extension/support

Where possible, ways of modifying or extending tasks, for easy differentiation, are suggested. Thus the activities are accessible to less able pupils and the more able.

Assessment opportunities

Each activity has clearly staged assessment opportunities which relate directly to the learning objectives for that activity and provide the framework for ongoing assessment. By taking advantage of these assessment opportunities teachers can reassure themselves that the stated learning objectives have been achieved. Where appropriate, teachers' questions for eliciting information from pupils are also included.

Opportunities for IT

Where opportunities for IT present themselves, these are briefly outlined with reference to particularly suitable types of program. The chart on page 143 presents specific areas of IT covered in the activities, together with more detailed support on how to apply particular types of program. Selected lesson plans serve as models for other activities by providing more comprehensive guidance on the application of IT, and these are indicated by the bold page numbers on the grid and the ⬦ icon at the start of an activity.

Display ideas

In this section ideas for displays in the classroom and the maths corner are incorporated into activity plans.

Reference to photocopiable sheets

Where activities include photocopiable sheets, small facsimiles of the relevant sheets are included in the lesson plans, with notes describing how they can be used.

Summative Assessment

There will be key points in time when teachers wish to take an overview of each pupil's achievement in mathematics. The final chapter contains assessment activities which enable teachers to address a number of the learning objectives contained within each chapter of the book. Assessment activities are indicated by the ⬦ icon.

Using and applying mathematics

Aspects of using and applying mathematics are integral to each activity. Using and applying mathematics cannot be taught separately from the other areas of mathematics. It must be set in the context of mathematical content. It should be thought of more as a teaching methodology and a mathematical process than as a distinct and separate content area. The teaching methodology relies strongly on the ability to challenge pupils through questioning and extending tasks. Pupils need to be encouraged to ask questions and follow alternative suggestions to support the development of reasoning. Therefore, on pages 139 to 141 a grid relating each activity to using and applying mathematics is provided. This grid will enable teachers to ensure that sufficient time and attention is paid to this central area of mathematics.

Photocopiable sheets

Many of the activities are accompanied by photocopiable sheets. For some activities, there may be more than one version; or a sheet may be 'generic', with a facility for the teacher to choose the appropriate task in order to provide differentiation by task. Other sheets may be more open-ended to provide differentiation by outcome. The photocopiable sheets are ideal for assessment and can be kept as records in pupils' portfolios of work.

Cross-curricular links

Cross-curricular links are identified on a simple grid (on page 144) which cross-references particular areas of study in mathematics to the programmes of study for other subjects.

SHAPE, SPACE AND MEASURES AT KEY STAGE 1

We live in a three-dimensional world. It is full of shapes. Children need to learn the language for describing their surroundings, not only to make sense of the world, but also so that they can communicate with others. In talking and listening, we depend heavily on language that describes shapes and their positions, or how their positions change in relation to other people and objects. As our vocabulary broadens and our use of language becomes more refined, so we are able to describe and visualise in greater detail, deepening our understanding of the spatial world and thus gradually moving into a more abstract way of thinking.

Working on the geometrical aspects of the mathematics curriculum, children will be involved initially with the naming and describing of shapes in two and three dimensions. Later, they will come to an awareness of the location and movement of shapes within space, and will acquire the language associated with position and movement. They will then be able to recognise different types of movement and this will result in their studying other features: for example, whether there has been a straight-line or a turning movement, what measure of turn has been taken (which leads ultimately to measuring angle), and whether the movement has resulted in a shape with reflective symmetry.

Geometry, therefore, is more than just the utilitarian naming of shapes and properties. It is a dynamic subject involving movement, manipulation of structures, measurement, discussion, language and communication. And this enables pupils to create images of their own and develop

ways of thinking geometrically, so that they come to a better understanding of shape and space.

Measurement sometimes seems to fit more comfortably in the mathematics curriculum as an extension of number, rather than as an extension of shape and space. However, counting is used in measuring activities. For example, to measure the length of a desk, children may lay straws across it and count the number of straws; or to find the weight of an object, they may balance it against conkers and count the number of those required.

As children progress and start to use standard measures such as centimetres or grams, measurement begins to feel distinctly different from number. Measurement includes practical activities, discussion and communication. Like geometry, it is a dynamic aspect of mathematics.

Daily, in real-life situations, we are naturally involved in measuring. We can estimate just the right amount of milk to pour into a saucepan for a cup of coffee, or the length of ribbon required to tie around a present, or the time needed to reach the shops before they close. At other times we need to be much more precise in our measurements, perhaps to make three-dimensional objects or to record details on two-dimensional plans. Accurate measurement depends on the accuracy of the tools being used, but even the most sophisticated tools have an error limit or a 'tolerance factor'.

The always approximate nature of measurement makes it seem further removed from number. When we count in whole numbers, each one is exact and remains so, regardless of what is being counted. The number 6, for example, is the same number whether you are counting eggs, cows, trees or people. The number 6 does not become more or less accurate each time it is counted. Nor does it change if the items being counted change position.

It is necessary to know the degree of accuracy required before embarking on a measuring task. As children progress through the educational system, they should develop their understanding that there are times when it is important for measuring to be as accurate as possible, as, for example, when they are making a box-lid with a good fit, or constructing a regular polygon; and that there are other occasions when measuring 'by eye' or handfuls or strides is perfectly adequate.

When looking at Shape, Space and Measures the children will need to be taught the following:

Three-dimensional shape
▲ That three-dimensional shapes have patterns and properties that can be used to describe them;
▲ How to make common three-dimensional models;
▲ To begin to classify shapes according to mathematical criteria;
▲ To recognise and use the geometrical features of cubes, cuboids, cylinders and spheres;
▲ To recognise simple reflective symmetry.

Two-dimensional shape
▲ That two-dimensional shapes have patterns and properties that can be used to describe them;
▲ How to make common two-dimensional shapes;
▲ To begin to classify shapes according to mathematical criteria;
▲ To recognise and use the geometrical features of rectangles, squares, circles, triangles, hexagons and pentagons;
▲ To recognise simple reflective symmetry.

Position and movement
▲ To use common words to describe position;
▲ To recognise movements in a straight line (translation) and turning movements (rotation) and to combine them;
▲ To copy, continue and make patterns;
▲ To understand that angle is a measure of turn and recognise quarter-turns, half-turns and right angles.

Length
▲ To measure the length of objects and make comparisons, using appropriate language;
▲ To use non-standard and standard units for measuring and estimating length;
▲ To choose simple instruments for measuring length;
▲ To read and interpret scales when using simple measuring instruments.

Mass
▲ To measure the mass of objects and make comparisons, using appropriate language;
▲ To use non-standard and standard units for measuring and estimating mass;
▲ To choose simple instruments for measuring mass;
▲ To read and interpret scales when using simple measuring instruments.

Capacity
▲ To measure the capacity of different containers and make comparisons, using appropriate language;
▲ To use non-standard and standard units for measuring and estimating capacity;
▲ To choose simple instruments for measuring capacity;
▲ To read and interpret scales when using simple measuring instruments.

Time
▲ To recognise special times on a clock-face which can be linked to daily routines;
▲ To use arbitrary units and, later, standard units, to measure and compare intervals of time;
▲ To recognise that time is continuous throughout the day, week, month, seasons, and the year;
▲ To tell the time using analogue clocks.

SHAPE, SPACE AND MEASURES

Overview grid

Learning objective	PoS/AO	Content	Type of activity	Page
Three-dimensional shape				
To describe three-dimensional everyday shapes and use the mathematical language of shape.	2a, b. *Range of shapes: Level A.*	Sorting and classifying a collection of everyday items. Describing shapes through touch.	Small group. Discussion. Sorting. Describing and classifying shapes.	14
To make three-dimensional shapes with flat and curved faces.	2b. *Range of shapes: Level A.*	Making mathematical shapes with clay, dough or Plasticine.	Small group. Making common shapes.	15
To recognise and use the geometrical features of shapes when making and when recording three-dimensional models.	2b, c. *Range of shapes: Level B.*	Building with blocks from a two-dimensional representation. Drawing and labelling.	Individuals or pairs. Recognising and using geomentrical shapes with reference to shapes of buildings. Recording.	16
To understand that cuboids have six faces and to begin to identify the vertices and sides/edges.	2c. *Range of shapes: Level B.*	Decorating a face on a cuboid with repeating patterns.	Individuals and groups. Recognising vertices, sides/edges and surfaces of cuboids.	18
To use geometrical criteria when classifying and recording a range of three-dimensional shapes, including everyday items.	*2c. Range of shapes: Level B.*	Sorting three-dimensional shapes by similar features.	Small group. Discussion. Sorting solids. Recording.	19
To use mathematical terms when sorting from a collection of three-dimensional shapes.	2c. *Range of shapes: Level B.*	Sorting shapes and guessing the mystery criterion.	Game using clue cards played by small or large groups. Recording.	21
Two-dimensional shape				
To recognise and describe two-dimensional shapes and patterns within a classroom environment.	2a, c. *Range of shapes: Level B.*	Discussing edges and their length. Recording squares and rectangles found in floor patterns.	Whole class or groups listen to a story. Discussion. Making coloured patterns with shapes. Individual recording.	24
To recognise two-dimensional shapes within a pattern.	2c. *Range of shapes: Level B.*	Colouring shapes found in a mosaic pattern.	Large group. Investigation of polygons. Recording.	25
To make simple patterns which have reflective symmetry.	2c. *Symmetry: Level B.*	Making reflecting patterns with right-angled triangles.	Large or small groups and individuals. Recognition of symmetrical pattern. Recording.	26
To investigate geometrical features of triangles and classify triangles according to mathematical criteria.	2b, c. *Range of shapes: Level B.*	Finding different-shaped triangles within a hexagon.	Pairs. Investigation of triangles.	27

Learning objective	PoS/AO	Content	Type of activity	Page
To investigate patterns and find which shapes best cover an area.	2a, 3a. *Range of shapes: Level B.*	Printing with various shapes.	Small group. Understanding regular patterns.	28
To investigate reflective symmetry in everyday items.	2c. *Symmetry: Level B.*	Discussion and exploration of patterns in a collection of socks with reflective symmetry.	Teacher-directed group discussion followed by individual exploration. Matching symmetrical designs.	29
Position and movement				
To follow instructions and use appropriate language to describe position and movement.	3a. *Position and movement: Level A.*	Story followed by playing a game during a PE lesson.	Whole class/large group listen to a story. Use of positional language.	32
To use instructions about going left and right to follow a route.	3a. *Position and movement: Level A.*	Drawing routes and following instructions, using a flow chart.	Pairs. Discussion. Work on mazes. Use of direction. Recording.	33
To use a regular non-standard linear measure to construct straight line movement and repeat the action.	3a. *Position and movement: Level A.*	Using a programmable toy to estimate distance and describe movement.	Small groups. Recognition of movement in a straight line.	35
To understand and use quarter- and half-turns.	3b. *Position and movement: Level B.*	Using a programmable toy to describe movement and build up a procedure involving turns.	Pairs. Understanding angle as a measure of turn. Gauging degree of turn.	36
To follow and give instructions for position.	3a. *Position and movement: Level A.*	Giving instructions to fill three shelves. Guessing game, using positional descriptions.	Large group. Use of common words to describe positions.	38
To explore and recognise rotating shapes.	3a. *Position and movement: Level B.*	Discussing and manipulating rotating objects. Creating patterns which rotate.	Large group discussion and introductory practical session. Individual recording.	39
Length				
To use comparative language associated with linear measurement.	4a. *Measure and estimate: Level A.*	Story followed by making animals/objects in different sizes and comparing sizes directly.	Whole class listen to a story. Smaller groups. Observation and use of appropriate language. Recording.	42
To compare the lengths of objects by measuring with a non-standard measure and counting the number of repeats.	4a. *Measure and estimate: Level A.*	Measuring animals/objects using non-standard units and indirect comparison.	Pairs within small groups. Measuring length. Recording.	43

SHAPE, SPACE
AND MEASURES

Overview grid

Learning objective	PoS/AO	Content	Type of activity	Page
To understand the need for standard units.	4a, b. *Measure and estimate: Level A.*	Making a large animal/object, deciding what measure to use, measuring, recording and comparing.	Large group/pairs. Measuring length. Group review.	45
To refine estimating skills and use standard units.	4a, b. *Measure and estimate: Level B.*	Estimating the length of a train, measuring with a metre stick and a trundle wheel.	Pairs and groups. Estimation of length. Recording.	47
Mass				
To use language, including comparatives, associated with measuring mass.	4a. *Measure and estimate: Level A.*	Handling packages to investigate and compare directly whether they are heavier or lighter than one another.	Small groups. Use of appropriate language when comparing the mass of objects.	50
To compare the mass of objects using non-standard units and a simple measuring instrument.	4a. *Measure and estimate: Level A.*	Measuring the mass of teddy bears/animals with irregular non-standard units and pan balances.	Whole class and groups. Use of scales for balancing objects correctly. Recording.	51
To understand the need for using a standard unit when measuring mass.	4a, b. *Measure and estimate: Level A.*	Measuring the mass of four parcels with a variety of regular non-standard units using pan balances.	Small groups. Use of different measuring units. Large group discussion. Recording.	53
To begin using standard units of mass and calibrated scales.	4a, b. *Measure and estimate: Level B.*	Ordering parcels by weight and measuring their mass with standard units, using metric weights and a calibrated scale.	Pairs. Investigation using scales. Sorting. Recording.	55
Capacity				
To use comparative language when measuring the capacity of two or more containers.	4a. *Measure and estimate: Level A.*	Comparing the capacity of two containers which hold the same, then comparing three containers which do not hold the same.	Pairs. Using appropriate language to make comparisons when measuring capacity.	58
To compare the capacity of containers by measuring with non-standard units and counting the number required.	4a, b. *Measure and estimate: Level A.*	Comparing and ordering the capacity of containers by counting the number of non-standard measures required to fill them.	Small groups. Measuring capacity by filling containers differentiated by size. Recording.	59

SHAPE, SPACE
AND MEASURES

Learning objective	PoS/AO	Content	Type of activity	Page
To use simple measuring instruments when measuring capacity/volume and understand the need for a standard unit.	4a, b. *Measure and estimate: Level A.*	Using a range of non-standard units as simple measuring instruments and share the data for a common purpose.	Two groups of four children listen to a story. Measuring of capacity. Recording.	61
To refine estimating skills and use standard units.	4a, b. *Measure and estimate: Level B.*	Estimating the capacities of a range of containers using a standard unit, followed by measurement to check their accuracy.	Rotating groups. Estimation. Checking of accuracy of measurement.	63
Time				
To compare and order events using language associated with time.	4a. *Time: Level A.*	Comparing the length of time taken to complete two tasks.	Four pairs. Timing of different activities to understand and use appropriate language.	66
To use arbitrary units when measuring time and understand the need for a standard unit.	4a, b. *Time: Level A.*	Participating in a range of activities and measuring the time taken by counting.	Rotating groups. Use various methods for counting and recording.	67
To begin using standard units of time.	4a, b. *Time: Level B.*	Playing a game using a clock-face and the hour-hand.	Large group listen to a story. Accurate placing of hour-hand in learning to tell the time.	68
To refine the use of standard units of time.	4a, b. *Time: Level B.*	Playing a game using dice. Recording by writing and drawing both hands of the clock.	Small groups or pairs. Use standard units of time. Recording.	69

Entries given in italics relate to the Scottish Mathematics 5–14 National guidelines.

SHAPE, SPACE
AND MEASURES

Three-dimensional shape

By the time they start school, children have already had many experiences which have helped to build up their knowledge about shape and the spatial world in which they live. They can recognise and name many shapes, both natural and man-made. Many children can identify a range of three-dimensional shapes belonging to the same set. That is, they will know that cats, dogs, horses and rabbits all belong to a set called animals. They can recognise not only the actual items but also two-dimensional representations of them. This all means that they have the ability to select and classify according to some learned criteria and to extract the finer details that make an animal a cat, rather than a dog.

We should make good use of this background experience by providing activities which involve handling, sorting and classifying common three-dimensional shapes. Children can thus begin to build up a knowledge of the properties of these shapes and learn their names. It is important to recognise that although we may wish to teach children about three-dimensional shape, there will inevitably be some 'blurring of the edges': opportunities will arise at the same time to introduce language associated with two-dimensional shape, position and movement. This is advantageous, as spatial awareness means seeing the whole rather than fragmented parts. By relating shapes and their changing positions within space, we come to an understanding of our immediate environment. And it is from these early beginnings that we build up a complex image of the wider spatial framework in which we live.

SHAPE, SPACE AND MEASURES

UNPACKING THE SHOPPING

To describe three-dimensional everyday shapes and use the mathematical language of shape.

†† *Group of six to eight children.*

🕐 *20–30 minutes.*

Previous skills/knowledge needed

Children should be used to listening to and providing descriptions.

Key background information

It is essential for children in the early stages of learning to gain confidence in understanding and using appropriate language to describe three-dimensional shapes. From this base they can progress to more refined descriptions of more complex shapes. It is important early on to identify any terms that are being used incorrectly such as 'side' instead of 'edge'. The edges of a solid are formed where two faces meet: a cube... has 12 edges. Their continued misuse will lead to greater confusion as the subject becomes more difficult.

Preparation

Collect different items which are familiar to the children and can be found in the local shops or supermarket. They should include cans, boxes and packets of varying sizes, as well as something spherical. Two of each item is required. The shapes chosen should provide for a range of descriptive language to be used: straight, flat, curved, round, pointed, corner, top, bottom, edge, taller, shorter, fatter, thinner.

Resources needed

A collection of cans, boxes, packets, something spherical (two of each item) as described in 'Preparation', a shelf or table on which to display half the collection (one of each pair of items), a large covered shopping bag (or a basket with a tea towel) packed with the other half of the collection.

What to do

Discuss the items of shopping you have on display with the children. Encourage the children to describe individual items. Initially, they are likely to describe items in a visual or personal way, referring, for example, to the colour, whether the packaging is shiny or dull, what the item is used for, whether they have it at home and if they like it or not. Gradually introduce the words that can be used to describe a shape, as suggested under 'Preparation'. Allow the children to feel the articles as you are describing them, so that they have a tactile perception of what it is to be curved or flat as well as a visual one. Tell the children that they are going to help you unpack the shopping, but without looking at it. Ask them to take it in turns simply to feel one item in the basket and describe it to the group. The shopping on display is left out to help the group classify and match the items mentally to one of the shapes on display. The children take it in turns to guess from the description. If they are right, it is placed alongside its partner on display. If wrong, the next child tries to guess. When a correct guess is given, that child feels the next item and provides the description. This activity can be repeated daily so that all the children in the class are able to have a turn both at describing and at guessing which shape is being described. New items can be added to the shopping to extend pupils and to keep interest going.

Suggestion(s) for extension

Some pupils may be able to cope with mathematical terms such as cube or cylinder, progressing from the specific, such as a tin of cat food, to the general shape – in this case, a cylinder.

Suggestion(s) for support

For children who are struggling with their descriptions, ask questions such as: 'What does the top feel like? Is it flat or pointed?' or 'Does your shape have straight edges?'

Assessment opportunities

Assess the language used by the pupils. Is it to do with mathematical properties or is it more generally descriptive (red, shiny, favourite)? Do the pupils use the mathematical language correctly and with confidence? Are some pupils able to differentiate between edges and faces? Do they use mathematical terms such as 'cube', or do they use everyday language such as 'shaped like an Oxo'?

Opportunities for IT

Children could extend their work on shape recognition and the development of the language of shape by using a

SHAPE, SPACE AND MEASURES

branching database. This type of software works like a key, asking the children a series of questions which have only a yes/no answer until it arrives at the name of the shape that the child has selected.

Questions to identify a cuboid might be:

▲ Does it have six faces?

Answering yes might lead to:

▲ Are all the edges the same length?

Answering yes might lead to:

▲ You have chosen a cube.

Answering no might lead to:

▲ Are some of the faces rectangular?

Answering yes might lead to:

▲ You have chosen a cuboid.

The initial database could be set up in advance by the teacher, or even older pupils, and used by the children. After some practice, they could add shapes of their own to the database by forming their own questions to be added into the software.

The children will probably need initial support in the use of this software, particularly in framing questions which have a yes or no answer to arrive at new shapes. They will also need basic reading skills or support from an adult to read the text of questions on the computer screen.

Display ideas

Have a supermarket shelf or classroom shop where each item is labelled with its name and one of its properties: for example, 'The cornflakes box has all straight edges.'

The display could include a feely bag containing one item, which is changed daily, for children to guess. And another game could involve children in working out from the pictorial clues provided which of several items should go in an empty space you have left on the shelf. You could make some pictorial clue cards for this, perhaps mounting them on card and laminating them. The 'empty space' item could be changed daily.

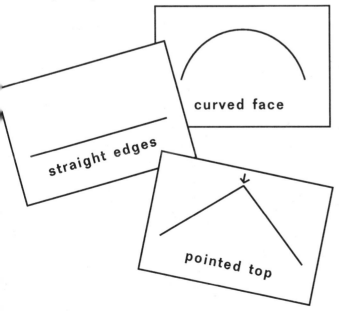

MAKING SHAPES

To make three-dimensional shapes with flat and curved faces.

†† Group of six to eight children.

🕐 20–30 minutes.

Previous skills/knowledge needed

Children should be used to handling and shaping clay, dough or Plasticine.

Key background information

Using 'face' as a mathematical term may cause confusion for young children as they are not used to common terms being used mathematically. The faces of solids are formed by plane shapes. Therefore a cube has six square faces, a sphere has one curved face, and a cylinder has three faces – two are circles and one is a curved face (formed from a rectangle).

Preparation

Decide which resource you wish to use: clay, dough or Plasticine. If children have had no experience of using the chosen medium, try to give them an opportunity to become familiar with its feel and texture, in a period of play one or two days before the lesson.

Resources needed

Clay, dough or Plasticine; pastry cutters (or similar) which are square, rectangular and circular; a covered table to work on – thick polythene or a vinyl-coated cloth is useful and makes the clearing up much easier. If this is not available, then rolling boards will do.

What to do

Demonstrate how to roll the clay, dough or Plasticine in the palm of your hand, or in a circular motion on the flat of the table. Children will probably wish to follow suit with their own piece of material, but, if not, encourage them to do so. Use this opportunity to begin discussing and describing the shapes they are making. To start with, they are likely to describe them in a personal way – mentioning a smell they recognise or whether the material is sticky or not. As children offer you their descriptions, pick up on those which have a mathematical flavour and introduce the word 'face'. For example, a child might liken his or her shape to 'an orange without the bumpy bits on it'. Talk about what the face feels like: smooth, curved, for instance. Move on to rolling the material flat (as you would for pastry) and again discuss the feel of its surface. Allow the children plenty of opportunities to hand-mould the following shapes: sphere, cylinder, cuboid. Each time discuss the faces, including the edges, as appropriate. After they have described their experiences and any difficulties they have encountered (when trying to obtain

straight or curved faces, and straight or curved edges), the children can be shown how to use the pastry cutters for greater precision. The final collection of solid shapes the children make should include different-sized spheres, cylinders (short and fat, tall and thin) and cuboids, so that children do not build up a narrow view of what these solids look like.

Suggestion(s) for extension

Some pupils may be able to cope with making a cube. This requires more precise modelling skills and an awareness that a cube's faces are all the same size and its edges all the same length.

Suggestion(s) for support

Pupils who find rolling or shaping difficult may find it easier to make shapes with only curved faces, or it may be better for them to move on quickly to using the cutters and at this point describe the faces and edges.

Assessment opportunities

Assess the language used by the pupils. Are some still using only general descriptive vocabulary? Are they using the term 'face'? Do they know which faces are flat and which are curved? Which children are extending their mathematical vocabulary to include 'sphere', 'cylinder', 'cube' and 'cuboid'?

Display ideas

When clay or dough shapes have dried, they can be decorated and kept for display. Later the collection of decorated shapes can be used as a resource for mathematics.

BUILDINGS

To recognise and use the geometrical features of shapes when making and when recording the names of three-dimensional models.

†† *Individuals or pairs.*

🕐 *20 minutes.*

Previous skills/knowledge needed

Children should be able to make the links between two-dimensional representation and three-dimensional construction. They need to know the mathematical names of common three-dimensional shapes and their visual properties. They should also be able to sort, using Venn and Carroll diagrams.

Key background information

In everyday life we are surrounded by three-dimensional objects, but pictures represent this reality in two dimensions. This causes confusion for many children when it comes to naming shapes correctly. Two-dimensional shapes do not exist in real life, and yet, in a picture a sphere appears to be a circle and a cube may look more like a square. It is important to identify any confusion among the pupils, stemming from two-dimensional representation, so that they do not build up incorrect information.

Preparation

Photocopy one or both of photocopiable sheets 80 and 81 and also photocopiable sheets 82 and 83 for children doing the extension work. Collect together all the required equipment. Make sure that all the buildings illustrated can be made from the three-dimensional shapes you have available.

Resources needed

A collection of Poleidoblocs or similar three-dimensional solid shapes: cubes, cuboids, cones, cylinders, spheres; blank paper and pencil for each child; copies of photocopiable pages 80 and/or 81; and 82 and 83 for extension work.

What to do

Give out the photocopiable sheets (80 or 81) and discuss the pictures with the children. What buildings do the shapes represent? Point to a shape in the picture and ask the children to pick out the corresponding three-dimensional shape from the collection. Ask them to name the shape. Repeat this two or three times. Explain to the children that they should choose (with their partners if you want them to work in pairs) which of the buildings in the picture they would like to copy; and then use the three-dimensional shapes to build it. After they have built it, each child should draw a picture of it and label the shapes used.

SHAPE, SPACE
AND MEASURES

Suggestion(s) for extension

Once all discussion of their finished buildings has been completed, ask the children to sort the three-dimensional shapes according to some of their properties, using a Venn diagram (as shown in figure 1).

Also, ask the pupils to sort the three-dimensional shapes using a Carroll diagram and to give their reasons for sorting them in this way. Their reasons should relate to the criteria on the Carroll diagram. If the children have difficulty reading across and down the diagram to all four segments, then it often helps to label all the diagram's edges (as shown in figure 2). The children can record their sorting either on plain paper or on photocopiable sheets 82 and 83.

Suggestion(s) for support

For children who have difficulty representing three-dimensional models as two-dimensional pictures, exchange that part of the task with discussion and open-ended questioning about the shapes they used for their buildings.

Assessment opportunities

Assess pupils' knowledge of the names and properties of three-dimensional shapes by asking them about their buildings. What shape did you use most? What shape is on top of...? Is it a good shape for a building? Why? What isn't a good shape for a building? Why? Can you use the shape any way up? Their pictures should provide evidence of their ability to label the shapes correctly. Have the children who were involved in the sorting tasks used mathematical criteria correctly?

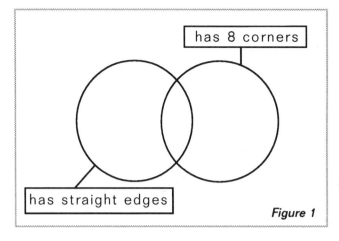

Figure 1

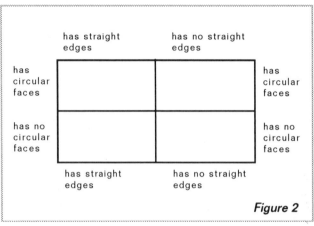

Figure 2

Display ideas

The children's drawings could be mounted on the wall above a small table containing the three-dimensional shapes (once they are no longer needed), with an invitation for pupils to try to use the shapes to make one of the buildings in the pictures. Further discussion with the class will allow them to verbalise any difficulties they might encounter. A Carroll diagram showing some shapes already sorted could provide an interesting puzzle: children should try to work out the criteria used for sorting the shapes. The sorting arrangement can be changed on a regular basis. Spare pieces of card and a felt-tipped pen alongside would enable children to write down their own suggestions for what the labels to the Carroll diagram might be.

Reference to photocopiable sheets

Photocopiable sheets 80 and 81 are designed to give pupils some ideas for building three-dimensional models. They may not be needed for the more able pupil. Photocopiable sheets 82 and 83 may be helpful for some pupils to record their sorting activities.

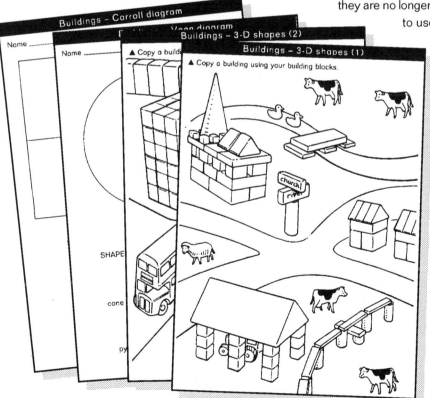

SHAPE, SPACE AND MEASURES

PAINT A FACE

To understand that cuboids have six faces and to begin to identify the vertices and sides/edges.

†† *Individuals and groups.*

🕐 *10–30 minutes (depending on the child's creativity).*

Previous skills/knowledge needed
Children should have some experience in using the painting medium chosen and in making repeating patterns.

Key background information
All three-dimensional shapes have faces. A cuboid may have only rectangular faces, only square faces, or a mixture of square and rectangular faces. Depending on the two-dimensional shapes of the faces, cuboids may also be known by other, more specific names: for example, cube, square prism, rectangular prism.

Preparation
Collect a variety of cuboid-shaped boxes (with lids, or closed on all sides) – for example, a single-bottle wine box, a shoebox, a copier paper box capable of holding a ream of paper. Cover them with strong paper. Collect together some shapes suitable for printing. They could be commercially produced or ones you have made from pieces of sponge,

vegetable or cotton reels and so on. Squares, rectangles and triangles would give further experience in naming two-dimensional shapes, but this is not a requirement of the task. The shapes could be animals, flowers or abstract if you wish. Decide whether one box at a time will be decorated by six children (each child taking responsibility to complete one face) or whether to have groups of children working on a class collection. For example, in a class of 30, five boxes and five groups (containing six children in each group) would be needed. If the children in each group are given a number from one to six, all the number one children can work on the boxes at the same time around the art table. They would be responsible for decorating the first face on their group's box. Later, it would be the turn of all the number two children to decorate the second face of the box belonging to their group, and so on until all five boxes have had the six faces decorated. A completed box would be a collaborative effort from a group of six children.

Resources needed
Cuboid-shaped boxes covered with paper (see 'Preparation'); three colours of paint, in shallow dishes, for each group; shapes suitable for printing.

What to do
Show the children the boxes and ask them to count the faces. Help them by marking each face as it is counted so that they do not count that face again. Demonstrate the printing technique and how to make simple repeating patterns using a maximum of three shapes. Explain to the children that you want them to decorate the boxes, each child being responsible for putting a different pattern on each face. They are to start by painting just one face. Stress that they must keep their pattern to just that face. It must not continue across an edge or corner to another face. Point out the edges and corners to avoid any misunderstanding. Other children from their group will be working on the other faces later. You must make sure that you leave enough time for the paint to dry after the children have painted the first (and subsequent) faces of the boxes. Then continue the activity by getting the children to print a pattern on a second face of a box and so on. Each time, before setting the children to decorate the next face, discuss how many faces have already been decorated and how many are still left to be completed. This will reinforce the message that cuboids have six faces.

Suggestion(s) for extension
Provide more able pupils with additional three-dimensional shapes to decorate. Get them to record the number of faces, vertices and edges on these shapes.

Suggestion(s) for support
Some children may need to make their patterns, not directly on to the boxes, but on pieces of paper cut to the same size

SHAPE, SPACE AND MEASURES

as the faces of the box. These can be glued into place later. Pupils who have difficulty making repeating patterns should be given only two shapes and two colours.

Assessment opportunities

Assess pupils' knowledge of the names of the faces and the number of faces required for different solids through discussion. Are they able to count the corners of the cuboids accurately? Are they beginning to devise a systematic approach to counting the edges, without any repeats?

Opportunities for IT

The children could use a simple art or graphics package to create repeating patterns for each face of the cuboid. The resulting patterns could be printed out and cut to fit the face being decorated. They can then be stuck on to the cuboid itself.

This activity would give children opportunities to create and repeat different shapes; select and alter the colours; move shapes around the screen, using a mouse or cursor keys to create a repeating pattern; and use the printer to print out their finished pattern.

More able children might be able to use a graphics package to create the net of a cuboid and go on to decorate each face with a different repeating pattern. They will need to know how to draw squares or rectangles for this work, and will find it useful to have a background grid on the screen with the 'snap to grid' option set so shapes automatically fit on to the background grid (with right-angled corners and with no gaps between the different parts of the net).

Display ideas

The completed boxes can be displayed. Children could be asked to see how many patterns are the same. If appropriate, as an aid to their understanding, you could open up a further box to show the net of a cuboid, with its faces clearly numbered one to six.

SORTING SOLIDS

To use geometrical criteria when classifying and recording a range of three-dimensional shapes, including everyday items.

†† *Group of six to eight children.*

🕐 *20–30 minutes.*

Previous skills/knowledge needed

The children need to be familiar with using two-dimensional representations of three-dimensional objects.

Key background information

Two-dimensional representation can be a very difficult concept for some pupils to grasp. Using and feeling the solid objects should not be rushed. Children need plenty of experience in handling objects so that eventually they are able to develop clear images of them in their minds which they can manipulate.

Preparation

Collect together a set of mathematical shapes and a range of solid shapes from everyday life. Try to include spheres, cubes, cuboids, cylinders, prisms, pyramids, cones, an ovoid and a half-sphere. Shapes such as cuboids and cylinders should be represented with items of varying dimensions, so that children get used to handling tall, thin shapes as well as short, flat shapes. Make photocopies of sheets 84 and 85 for all the children, and some labels with a space for the children to write in the number of faces that each shape has.

Resources needed

A set of mathematical solid shapes, a collection of everyday solid shapes, labels (see 'Preparation'); pencils, scissors, glue, photocopies of sheets 84 and 85.

What to do

Set out the solid shapes and the everyday items as two separate groups. Introduce the task by looking at all the solid

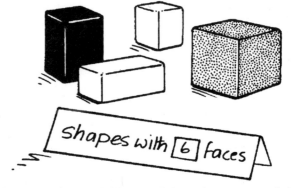

shapes with the children and describing some of their features. Each child should then choose an item from the everyday group and be given the opportunity to talk about it and describe its features (for example, curved surface, two

SHAPE, SPACE AND MEASURES

flat faces and so on) with the others in the group. While they are feeling the curves and the edges, direct their discussion towards the faces and how many faces their shape has. Then let one child choose a solid shape and see if the remainder of the group can find other shapes, from both collections, which have the same number of faces as the solid. The set should then be labelled (see 'Preparation') to confirm what they have all done. Let each child have at least one go at choosing a solid shape in this way for the others to match. When you feel sufficient choosing and matching has been done and there are several collections of solids labelled, it is likely that you will need to recap on what has been found out before children start recording. Finally, return all the shapes to the central pool.

Provide the children with copies of photocopiable pages 84 and 85. Tell them to cut around the pictures using the dotted lines. They will need to cut one picture at a time from photocopiable page 84 and also one from photocopiable page 85 which matches it in shape. The two pictures should be stuck into their workbook side by side so that a short sentence about the number of their faces can be written below: for example, 'The orange and the sphere have one face each.'

Suggestion(s) for extension

Use the full range of solid shapes collected, with some more complex additions such as pyramids with a variety of bases, including hexagonal ones. Although learning the names of a wide range of shapes is not a requirement for this task, don't miss this opportunity to extend the knowledge base of more able children. These pupils may be able to draw some of the shapes rather than cutting them out from the photocopiable sheets.

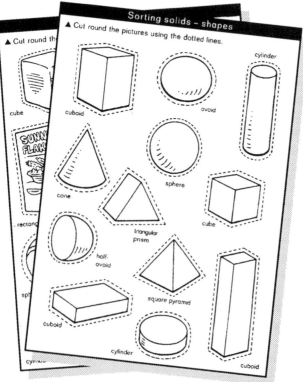

Suggestion(s) for support

Reduce the number of solid shapes. Add one new one at a time when you are sure that the children understand the difference between faces and edges.

Assessment opportunities

As the children sort the solids, are there pupils who still get confused by faces and edges? Do some pupils find curved faces particularly difficult to distinguish? Observe how different pupils go about counting the faces. Are they systematic? Do they have a method for keeping track of which faces they have counted and which they have not?

Display ideas

Display the final set of items that the children sort, with its label. A larger display on solid shapes could include the children's recorded work together with appropriate pictures from magazines.

Reference to photocopiable sheets

Photocopiable pages 84 and 85 are provided for the children to cut out the pictures, using the dotted lines for guidance, and then to group the pictures according to numbers of faces. The children can stick them, in these groups, on paper or in their books. Below each set of pictures they should record how many faces the objects have.

GUESS THE CLUE

To use mathematical terms when sorting from a collection of three-dimensional shapes.
†† *Small group or large group.*
🕐 *30–45 minutes.*

Previous skills/knowledge needed
Children need to know how to sort and record using Venn diagrams.

Key background information
Although we are surrounded by a variety of three-dimensional shapes in everyday life, we are often unaware of the similarities and differences between their properties. A greater depth of understanding can be obtained by sorting and classifying shapes according to different criteria. For example, children will become aware that although a cube and a cuboid have differences in the shapes of their faces and lengths of their edges, they also have similarities: both have six faces and eight square corners.

Preparation
Decide whether you are working with a small or large group so that you can organise enough space for children to work in. This task can be done successfully at a table or on the carpet area, as long as the children can see everything that is going on and have space to change places when it is their turn. Use photocopiable sheets 86 to 89 to make a set of playing-cards. It is worth mounting them on card and laminating them or covering them with self-adhesive plastic film for durability. Collect together all the equipment required. Try out the card game yourself so that you are aware of any difficulties that the children may experience. If children are going to record some of their sorting arrangements, then you may wish to photocopy sheets 90 and 91.

Resources needed
A set of mathematical shapes which should include cubes, cuboids, cylinders and spheres. Cones, triangular prisms and pyramids may also be included. The shapes do not have to be identical in size. Therefore two or three sets could be combined.
PE hoops can be used for the Venn diagram. Each hoop needs to have a plain, tie-on label.
Cards made from photocopiable pages 86 to 89; copies of photocopiable pages 90 and 91 for recording (optional).

What to do
Arrange the children around a table or on the carpet, with all the necessary equipment. If you have decided to work with a large group, of ten or more children, you may wish to divide them into two teams. One sorts and the other tries to guess the mystery clue of the sorting arrangement. Then they change over. This 'team' approach is particularly helpful for children who need extra support.

Explain the organisation of the game to the children. Tell them that they will be taking it in turns to arrange the shapes in the hoops or Venn diagram. Start with just one hoop. The children should place shapes in the hoop that are similar in some way. Those that are not must be placed outside the hoop. Give an example of a sorting arrangement, such as all those shapes which have a curved face inside the hoop and those with no curved faces outside the hoop. Discuss with the children what other similarities and differences they might look for: the shapes of the faces or the number of faces, the number of edges or corners, the names of the shapes and so on. You may wish to let them practise sorting for a few times. Then you are ready to play the game with the cards. It is called 'Guess the Clue'.

The pile of cards should be placed face down in the middle of the group. To start, one child takes the card from the top of the pack, secretly reads the clue on it and then arranges the shapes accordingly. The person to this child's left goes first at guessing the clue, and play moves around the group until a child has the right answer and so wins the card. If no one guesses the clue, then the child who did the sorting keeps the card, but not before the clue on it has been shown to the group so that they can check that the sorting has been done correctly. If the sorting is incorrect, the card goes to the bottom of the pile. The child to the first player's left now has a turn at taking a card and re-sorting the shapes so that another mystery clue can be guessed. Play continues in this way until everyone has had two or three goes at sorting. The children with the most cards are winners. You may wish pupils to record some of the sorting arrangements on the copies of photocopiable page 90.

SHAPE, SPACE AND MEASURES

Suggestion(s) for extension

Include cones, prisms and pyramids in the collection. Ask the children to sort the shapes using two criteria. You will therefore need two hoops. Also you must divide the pack of cards into two piles, one of cards about names and faces and the other of cards about edges and corners. Pupils choose a card from each pile. If you want them to record, they will need copies of sheet 91.

Suggestion(s) for support

Remove some of the cards so that children have only two kinds of criteria to look for, for example, faces and corners. Gradually introduce cards about edges and names as they progress. Let children work as a group, rather than individually, to identify the clue card. If the group progresses to sorting using two criteria, a tree diagram may be more helpful than the Venn.

Assessment opportunities

Observe children as they play the game. Are there some terms with which they have difficulty? Are children becoming familiar with the names of all the shapes? Do they understand why some shapes can be in the same group, such as a triangular prism and a cylinder (both solids have two faces the same, one at the top and one at the bottom) or, for example, why a cube is also a cuboid? Are some children still using names of two-dimensional shapes for three-dimensional solids? Can children describe the properties of the faces correctly? Although written work provides long-term evidence of a completed task, observing pupils during a task like this provides far more insight into their learning.

Opportunities for IT

The children could extend their initial sorting work by using a branching database (as in the first activity 'Unpacking the shopping'). This type of software works like a key, asking children a series of questions which have only a yes/no answer until it arrives at the name of the shape that the child has selected.

Questions to identify a sphere might be:
▲ Does it have square faces?
Answering no might lead to:
▲ Does it have circular faces?
Answering no might lead to:
▲ Does it have curved faces?
Answering yes might lead to:
▲ Does it have straight edges?
Answering no might lead to:
▲ You have chosen a sphere.

The initial database could be set up in advance by you, or the cards used as starting prompts for the children to create their own database. The children will probably need initial support in the use of this software, particularly in changing the statements on the cards into questions which have a yes or no answer. For example, the 'has all straight edges' card needs to be reworded as the question, 'Are all the edges straight?'

Display ideas

Have a collection of packaging on display, especially those which have more unusual shapes as they are a good starting point for work on nets when carefully opened out. A display of the children's graphical data also provides a stimulus for further discussion. An empty tree diagram with opportunities for children to sort the shapes for others to guess what criteria has been used also keeps interest going.

Reference to photocopiable sheets

Photocopiable sheets 86 to 89 should be mounted and cut up to make the clue cards needed for this activity. Photocopiable sheets 90 and 91 can be used by children to record results of the activity. They are helpful in enabling pupils to concentrate on the mathematical aspect of the task, rather than being side-tracked by laborious recording.

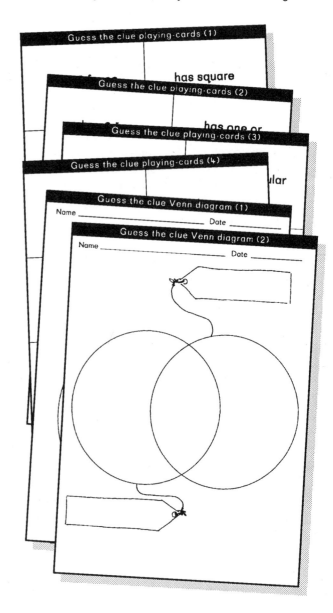

SHAPE, SPACE AND MEASURES

Two-dimensional shape

Many adults are more familiar with the names of two-dimensional shapes than with those of three-dimensional ones. Possibly this is because of the multitude of two-dimensional shapes that we can see around us: in patterns on material, wallpaper, and in drawings representing three-dimensional shapes. As adults we are usually able to create an image in our minds of three dimensions from a two-dimensional drawing, and we have an understanding of the solidness of that shape even when it is not there to see or touch. A talented artist can create a picture, say, of fruit, using shadows, changing shades of colour and perspective so skilfully that we feel we could reach out and take an apple from the painted bowl. However, this is not what young children experience.

The ability to consider three-dimensional aspects in drawing is one that develops fairly late. Initially, most children will draw flat pictures with no reference to depth. Later they will draw what they think they can see, rather than what they can actually see. They will draw a house, showing not only the front but both the left- and right-hand sides. It is much later that children consider representing only what they see. Therefore pupils need plenty of opportunities to work with flat shapes, to describe and discuss them, to use them to make patterns, to begin to understand some of their properties and to put names to them. A great advantage of working with flat shapes is the comparative ease with which children can record, and provide tangible evidence to assess.

SHAPE, SPACE
AND MEASURES

◆ SHAPES AROUND THE CLASSROOM

To recognise and describe two-dimensional shapes and patterns within a classroom environment.

†† *Whole class or groups, and individual recording.*

🕐 *30–45 minutes.*

Previous skills/knowledge needed
Children need to be experienced in listening to a story and describing shapes and patterns. They should also be able to colour within lines.

Key background information
A square and a rectangle are both quadrilaterals. Both are formed by having two pairs of parallel lines which cross at right angles. However, a square is a special kind of rectangle as it has four equal-length sides. Therefore it is a *regular* quadrilateral. Rectangles which are not squares can also be called *oblongs*.

Flat shapes are not two-dimensional because they have depth, however small. They can be used to represent two-dimensional shapes as two-dimensional shapes cannot be manipulated. Care should be taken to refer to 'flat shapes', not 'two-dimensional shapes', in these cases.

Preparation
Read *Flat Stanley* by Jeff Brown (Mammoth, 1989). Make a 'postbox' by cutting a slit in the base of a shoebox. Find a strong brown envelope that will fit through the slit. Provide the children with 2cm² paper.

Resources needed
The book *Flat Stanley*, the shoebox 'postbox' and strong brown envelope (see 'Preparation'), 2cm² paper, red and yellow crayons.

What to do
Start by reading the story *Flat Stanley* to the children. Ask the children what flat things they could put into an envelope and send through the post. Show them the postbox you have made from the shoebox, and the strong brown envelope. Now they can try out some of their ideas by placing the item in the envelope and 'posting' it through the slit. When appropriate, move the discussion on to the two-dimensional shapes to be seen around the classroom. Point some out, such as the floor and ceiling tiles, so that the children begin to get an idea of what is being asked of them. Let the children give their examples. Ask questions that will enable them to concentrate on the number of edges the shape has, or the length of the edges, whether some are longer or shorter, or

even all the same. Name the shapes, for example square floor tiles, so that the children become accustomed to attaching a mathematical name to a common everyday article. When the children are ready to record, provide them with a sheet of 2cm² paper each. Demonstrate how two squares side by side can be coloured in to form a rectangle. The children should create their own floor patterns, colouring squares red and rectangles yellow, or vice versa.

Suggestion(s) for extension
Provide the children with 2cm² paper and three colours to make their own floor patterns. The pattern should tessellate but the rectangles should be positioned in both vertical and horizontal directions. One colour only should be used for the square, the second colour for the horizontal rectangles and the third for the vertical rectangles. The squares and rectangles should be drawn and coloured without gaps, as shown in the diagram below:

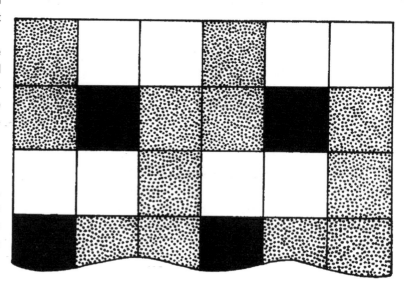

Suggestion(s) for support
Ask the children to colour in only one shape, for example rectangles. Both coloured pencils should be used, colouring each rectangle in one block of colour. The rectangles should tessellate.

Assessment opportunities
The children's coloured patterns will provide a record of their ability to identify different quadrilaterals, but will not show the range of language that individual pupils use. If you wish to assess this, you will need to work with smaller groups and perhaps use a previously prepared checklist on which the following might be included: names square correctly, names rectangle correctly, counts the number of edges, counts the number of corners, can identify the longer/shorter sides, explains the difference between a square and a rectangle. You can then easily identify pupils who are able to use a wide range of language correctly.

Opportunities for IT

The children could extend this activity by using a simple graphics package to experiment and explore the way that shapes are built from squares. It would be useful to use a package which has a background grid and a 'snap to grid' option, which means that when squares are created or moved to a new position they automatically line up with the squared background grid. This helps children to create regular shapes and patterns. The activity could be extended to include rectangles as well as squares.

This activity could be used to introduce a range of basic graphics features such as drawing squares, using a mouse to move them to new positions, filling them with a selected colour and printing the final picture.

Alternatively, specific software like My World (SEMERC) could be set up to do the same thing, with a range of different-coloured squares and rectangles arranged around the drawing area so that children could pick them up and drag them to the appropriate position.

Display ideas

Use the children's work as part of a display on two-dimensional shape. Collect pictures from magazines showing floor and tile patterns and include these, together with some material and wallpaper offcuts, in the classroom display.

MOSAICS

To recognise two-dimensional shapes within a pattern.

†† *Large group.*

🕓 *20–25 minutes.*

Previous skills/knowledge needed

Children should have had some experience of working with two-dimensional shapes.

Key background information

Two-dimensional shapes (polygons) are flat shapes which are bounded by straight lines. They have specific names related to the number of sides they have. For example, a polygon with three sides is called a *triangle* and one with five sides is called a *pentagon*. When the internal angles are the same and the edges are all the same length, the shape is known as a *regular polygon*. A regular four-sided polygon or quadrilateral is known as a *square*.

Preparation

Study the shaded-in version of photocopiable sheet 92 reproduced above right. It shows some of the different polygons to be found within the pattern of hexagons. Then photocopy sheet 92 so that you have one for each child.

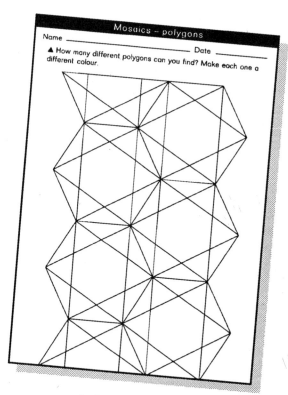

Mosaics – polygons

Name _____ Date _____

▲ How many different polygons can you find? Make each one a different colour.

Resources needed

Coloured pencils or felt-tipped pens for each child or small group, photocopies of sheet 92.

What to do

Give each child a copy of photocopiable page 92 and explain the task to them. They have to look for different kinds of polygons and colour them in, one colour per shape, so that the completed mosaic pattern has as many different shapes as possible. Demonstrate by showing the children a small shape, for example an equilateral triangle, and then help them to look for a larger example of an equilateral triangle. You could use this activity as a starting point for work on geometric patterns found in everyday life or on artistic patterns from other cultures. Children can be told the names of shapes which will include triangle, quadrilateral, pentagon and hexagon.

Suggestion(s) for extension

Ask the children to find all the shapes on photocopiable page 92.

Suggestion(s) for support

Restrict the variety of shapes that the children need to find: only triangles, or only regular shapes (equilateral triangle and hexagon), for example, or perhaps only two kinds of shapes, such as shapes with three sides and shapes with four sides.

Assessment opportunities

The amount of information you get from the children's recording on the photocopiable sheets will depend on whether you have restricted the task in any way. It may be that some

SHAPE, SPACE
AND MEASURES

children are only able to find regular shapes (be sure to provide them with experience of irregular shapes at a later date), whereas other children may look further and find a much greater range of regular and irregular shapes. Can the children name the polygons correctly?

Display ideas
Display the children's work alongside examples of geometric patterns found on wrapping paper and fabric, in Islamic art, computer art and so on.

Reference to photocopiable sheet
Photocopiable sheet 92 consists of a regular pattern of hexagons, inside which are the outlines of many regular and irregular polygons. Children should identify as many different polygons as they can, colouring each one differently. Some children may be able to draw an outline around the shapes and write the names of the polygons inside.

FOUR IN A ROW

To make simple patterns which have reflective symmetry.
†† *Large or small groups, and individuals.*
🕐 *20–30 minutes.*

Previous skills/knowledge needed
Children should be able to use scissors to cut squares in half.

Key background information needed
Dividing a square in half, from corner to corner, results in two right-angled triangles. Two of the corners of the square form one corner of each triangle. Dividing a square in four, from corner to corner, results in four right-angled triangles. The right-angled corner of each triangle is formed where the diagonals bisect.

Preparation
Make copies of photocopiable sheet 93 for those children who will need this for support. Collect sticky paper in two colours and cut it into squares. The squares will need to be 3cm × 3cm for pupils using the photocopiable sheet.

Resources needed
Sticky paper squares in two colours, and possibly some interlocking triangular shapes (such as Clixi or Polydron), scissors, paper (plain, lined or squared, as appropriate), rulers, coloured pencils, photocopies of sheet 93.

What to do
Introduce the children to the activity by talking about square shapes and triangular shapes. Ask them to point out squares and triangles around the classroom. Show them two squares of sticky paper and cut each one in half, diagonally, to make a total of four triangles. Repeat this with two of the sticky paper squares you prepared in the contrasting colour. You should now have eight triangles, four of each colour. Show the children how you could use these to make a linear repeating pattern. Let the children investigate the range of patterns they can make, using sticky paper squares in the same way as you have shown. They can record their favourite pattern by sticking the pieces on to plain paper. You may wish to provide lined paper for pupils who find it difficult to keep the shapes in line. When their linear pattern is complete, ask the children to repeat it, immediately underneath, so that it reflects the original one.

Suggestion(s) for extension
Ask the children to cut their squares into four and to investigate linear patterns made from four small triangles. Instead of using sticky paper squares, children may prefer to work on squared paper, dividing the squares with a ruler and recording their patterns with coloured pencils.

Suggestion(s) for support
Interlocking triangular shapes may be a better resource for this activity, for children who have difficulty in cutting paper.

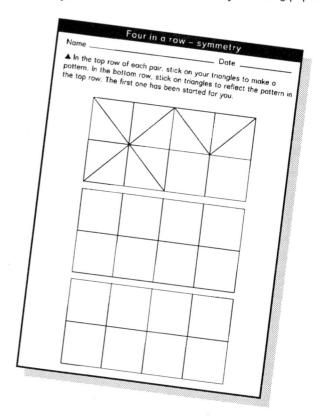

Provide children who do use the sticky shapes with photocopiable page 93, to aid them with their recording.

Assessment opportunities

Although you will have a final record of the patterns that the children complete, you will be able to assess more from watching and listening to them as they work. Do they notice that some patterns using four triangles may look like the patterns which used two triangles? Do some triangle patterns make a square pattern when they are repeated below the first? Do pupils notice other occasions of symmetry in their patterns?

Display ideas

Provide an interactive display with interlocking flat shapes that the children can be invited to make into reflecting tile patterns. The children's work on the wall can form a background to this.

Reference to photocopiable sheet

Photocopiable sheet 93 is intended for those children who require additional support with their recording. An example of reflective symmetry has been started at the top of the sheet. The children should complete this first and then try out their own reflective patterns in the empty grids below.

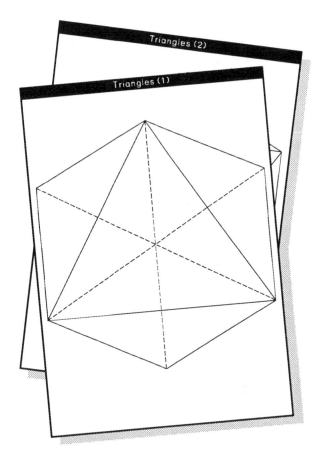

TRIANGLES

To investigate geometrical features of triangles and classify triangles according to mathematical criteria.
†† *Pairs.*
🕐 *20–30 minutes.*

Previous skills/knowledge needed

The children need to be able to cut accurately with scissors.

Key background information

Equilateral triangles have all three sides of equal length and all interior angles the same size. Isosceles triangles have two sides of equal length and two interior angles the same size. Right-angled triangles have a right angle for one of the interior angles. Scalene triangles have sides which are all of different lengths. Right-angled triangles are either isosceles or scalene.

Preparation

Make enough copies of photocopiable page 94 to give three to each pair; each copy should be a different colour. Then make one copy per pair on white paper to act as a reference for the children. Additionally, make one white and one coloured copy (a different colour to the previous three) of photocopiable page 95 for children needing extension work.

Resources needed

Copies of photocopiable pages 94 and 95 on white paper and on coloured paper (see 'Preparation'), scissors, glue, plus any triangular-shaped resources which are used in your classroom.

What to do

Provide each pair of children with one white copy of photocopiable page 94, which they may need to refer to as they work, and three different-coloured copies to cut, manipulate, glue and record. Tell them that they can cut out the shapes on the coloured copies but that they must cut only where the lines are marked. There are dotted and unbroken lines on the hexagons which may help when you give the instructions: for instance, ask one of the pair of children to cut around the edge of the hexagon and then cut it into pieces using only the solid lines; the other child, having cut out another coloured hexagon, should cut it into pieces using only the broken lines; finally, the remaining hexagon can be cut using both the solid and broken lines. This task can also be done step by step so that you can demonstrate and piece together the smaller-cut shapes to form a triangle. For example, four of the triangles (equilateral) formed when cutting on the dotted lines make a large triangle of a similar shape.

Once the children have cut their coloured hexagons into pieces, they can investigate and discuss it together, manipulating them, trying out if two (or more) together match another triangle or make a new example. By referring to their

SHAPE, SPACE AND MEASURES

white copy and manipulating the coloured pieces on top of the diagram, rather like a jigsaw, the children can look for as many different triangles as possible. For instance, some may be formed by combining two smaller triangles of one colour which match a triangle in another colour. As they find examples of triangles (which should differ in size or shape) they should record them by gluing them into place and adding a sentence to describe what they have found out. Encourage them to record using some geometrial features, such as 'This triangle is the same size as these two' (two triangles stuck together to form one) or 'This triangle has one side the same length as this one' or 'This triangle is made from three triangles. Two of its sides are the same length.'

Suggestion(s) for extension

Give the children both hexagons, that is, copies of sheets 94 and 95, and let them investigate freely to find as many triangles as possible. They may differ in size or shape, or similar triangles may have been formed by using different-shaped pieces.

Suggestion(s) for support

Start by using the hexagon on photocopiable page 94. The children should cut along the dotted lines only, to make six equilateral triangles. Let them investigate these and find which of the triangular-shaped classroom resources have the same features and are therefore also equilateral triangles. Repeat this activity, but cut the hexagon only along the solid lines to obtain three isosceles triangles and one large equilateral triangle.

Assessment opportunities

Recorded work will provide evidence for assessment. For less able pupils, or pupils who have difficulty with written recording or expressing themselves clearly, it may give only a narrow picture of their learning. You can get further information by asking them open-ended questions such as: 'What can you tell me about the sides of these different-shaped triangles? Have you tried folding your triangles? What did you find out?' More able pupils may also have found out some interesting facts to do with the angles of one triangle

matching those of another triangle, or triangles which are the 'same size' as another (an early stage relating to area).

Display ideas

Pupils' completed work can be displayed. You could extend this display and make it interactive by putting out flat shape resources nearby and inviting the children to make certain shapes from them: for example, 'How many triangles do you need to make the next size triangle?'

Reference to photocopiable sheets

Photocopiable sheets 94 and 95 contain hexagons which the children can cut into different-shaped triangles. Most children will work with photocopiable sheet 94. It is necessary to have each hexagon in a different colour in order to help children reflect on how they have composed their triangles from hexagons which have been cut in different ways.

REPEATING PATTERNS

To investigate patterns and find which shapes best cover an area.

†† *Groups of four to six children.*

⊕ *20–30 minutes.*

Previous skills/knowledge needed

The children should be familiar with printing techniques and have an awareness of what constitutes a regular pattern.

Key background information

Shapes in a regular pattern that fit together exactly, with no spaces between, are described as tessellating.

Preparation

Collect together various objects which can be used to print geometrical shapes, such as vegetables, sponge, polystyrene, corks and wood offcuts cut to shape. If you decide to use vegetables for circular prints, keep one whole for the start of the activity, but cut up the rest so that they are ready for printing. Sort the circular pieces so that you have both large and small to give to the children.

Resources needed

Tables covered with protective material such as polythene or vinyl-coated cloth, a selection of items for printing, a whole carrot or parsnip, two colours of paint (mixed to a thicker consistency than usual), newspaper for children to print their trial runs, thick quality paper on which to print patterns.

What to do

Show the children the whole carrot or parsnip and ask them what shape would result if you cut across it sideways. Make sure that they are aware that you are not making a lengthways

cut. Ask them what would happen to the shape if the vegetable were cut near the top, the middle or the bottom. (An increase or decrease in size.) Finish this discussion by cutting up the vegetable. Then provide each group of children with a selection of geometrical shapes, including both large and small 'circles', for printing.

Explain that they are going to print some patterns using no more than two shapes. Show them how they should print the shapes so that they touch each other, but without overlapping. There needs to be as little white space as possible between the shapes. Demonstrate a regular pattern using only two shapes so that they are sure of what is required. Point out where too much white space can be seen. Demonstrate again with a better example. Let them try out different shapes and print some patterns on newspaper before they print the version they think is the best on the good quality paper.

Suggestion(s) for extension
Provide the children with three or four colours of paint and pentagonal shapes to print with.

Suggestion(s) for support
Provide the children with some examples of patterns you have done earlier. Let them copy them before they try creating their own. Discuss the patterns with them.

Assessment opportunities
You will have many opportunities for assessment. Use the time when the children are trying out their designs on newspaper to observe which of them understand regular patterns. Discuss their designs as they work and when they are finished. Ask them: 'Whose pattern has covered the paper best? Why do you think there is only a small amount of the white paper showing? Is there a better shape which would not leave white spaces?'

Opportunities for IT
The children could use an art or graphics package to create their repeating patterns. The activity could be used to introduce or extend their ability to make shapes, fill them with colour and move and position them on the screen to create a repeating pattern. The children might also be introduced to the copy or replicate function, so that once they have drawn their original shape they can reproduce that shape as many times as they wish; young children often find it quite difficult, for example, to create a number of circles which all have exactly the same diameter.

Display ideas
Make an exciting display of wallpaper and wrapping paper with geometrical designs. Showing the children's work alongside these will give you another opportunity to discuss shapes which cover an area and those that leave gaps.

SOCK PATTERNS

To investigate reflective symmetry in everyday items.
†† *Large group discussion followed by individual exploration.*
🕐 *30–45 minutes.*

Previous skills/knowledge needed
The children should have had experience of matching activities and of cutting with scissors and gluing to record.

Key background information needed
Three-dimensional shapes and two-dimensional shapes can be symmetrical. Shapes can have two kinds of symmetry. One is called line or reflective symmetry and the other is called rotational symmetry. The simplest example of line (or reflective) symmetry is a shape or pattern with *one* line of symmetry. The two halves reflect each other's pattern or shape, as if in a mirror held upright on a line between them. A shape has rotational symmetry if, when rotated about a central point, a segment of the shape can be seen to match exactly the position of another segment: for example, capital letters S and H when rotated through a half-turn match the image of the original position.

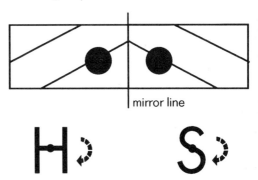

mirror line

Preparation
Collect some examples of reflective symmetry: patterned paper or fabric, pairs of gloves and shoes. Photocopy sheet 96 for each child and sheet 97 for those requiring extension work. You may wish to use photocopiable sheet 98 for further support with some children.

Resources needed
Non-breakable mirrors, capital letter templates (used for display board headings), scissors, glue, coloured pencils or crayons.

What to do
Start by showing the children some examples of reflective symmetry: patterns, shapes and pairs of items, where one half reflects the shape of the other. Show them how to hold a mirror along a central line and let them see how half of the pattern or pair plus its mirror reflection make a complete

SHAPE, SPACE AND MEASURES

picture. Encourage the children to find more examples of reflective symmetry around the classroom. Ask them to point out the line along which they would hold the mirror. Let them work with mirrors and capital letter shapes to see if they can find the line of symmetry in A, H, M, O, T, U, V, W, X, Y. Try later with letters that have a horizontal line of symmetry: B, C, D, E, H, I, K, O, X.

When you feel that the children have grasped the idea of reflective symmetry, give out photocopies of sheet 96. First the children should cut out each sock, around the cutting line. They can use the mirrors to look at the reflection of each one and check to see if they have another sock in the set that matches that reflection. Once they have found a pair of matching socks, they can glue them into their books or on to a piece of paper and colour them. At the end, the children should be left with two socks that don't match.

Suggestion(s) for extension
Ask the children to alter the two socks that don't match in some way so that they become a pair. Provide them with photocopiable sheet 97, on which they should draw in the patterns on the blank socks to make three pairs. There is room for the children to add more elements to the sock patterns if they wish.

Suggestion(s) for support
You may find that children become confused with patterns that have diagonal stripes or circles. If so, use the plain socks on photocopiable sheet 98 either to create simple patterns of your own for them to match or for children to create their own matching pairs.

Assessment opportunities
There are likely to be several opportunities for you to assess children during the early discussions. Children who have a real sense of symmetry are easy to spot. The sock pattern activities will produce evidence for assessment. Are children able to match horizontal lines? Are they able to match more complex designs which have diagonals and circular patterns? Do they have the diagonals slanting in the right direction? Are the circles the right size and correctly positioned? Do the children who used photocopiable sheet 97 find completing diagonal patterns difficult? Do they continue to use more examples of diagonals or finish their sock patterns with something much simpler?

Opportunities for IT
The children could explore the concept of symmetry using a simple graphics or art package. They can draw their first shape and add extra patterns, and then challenge other pupils to create a second shape with mirror symmetry. The copy and flip function, which turns the shape over, could be explored. The children could use this to check that they have correctly drawn the mirror image.

Some software like Tiler (Warwickshire Educational Computing Centre) automatically builds up symmetrical patterns. As children create a pattern, using square blocks on one side or quarter of the drawing area, the pattern is reproduced on the other half of the screen.

Display ideas
A dynamic wall display can be created which can include a wide range of examples of symmetry as well as the children's sock patterns. Suitable items might be gloves, unusual socks, patterned head scarves, greetings cards, wrapping paper, wallpaper, decorative boxes and pictures of buildings and of reflections in water.

Reference to photocopiable sheets
The photocopiable sheets for this activity have varying levels of difficulty. Photocopiable sheet 96 is suitable for many pupils as a starting point. Photocopiable sheet 97 can be used for children requiring extension work. Photocopiable sheet 98 could be used to draw simpler patterns for children who need further support. It could also be used by pupils working in pairs. Each child in a pair will need a copy of the photocopiable sheet, on which they should first decorate just one sock of each pair. Then they should exchange sheets and try to draw the matching socks.

SHAPE, SPACE AND MEASURES

Position and movement

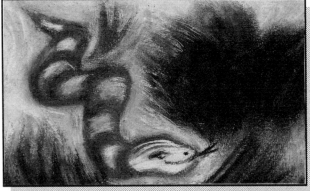

From early on, children relate to and explore the space around them, stretching out to touch a colourful mobile or dropping toys from their pram. The toddler pushing a trolley across a room soon becomes adept at steering and learns when it is necessary to steer between obstacles.

As children grow up, they become more adventurous, climbing stairs, squeezing into small spaces or hiding under the bed. Their spatial explorations lead them to develop a sense of boundaries: some real, and some imaginary, when they pretend to fly through space. Helping to put away toys or shopping enables children to learn more about positional space. Does this fit inside that? Is there enough space on the shelf for two more?

When they start school, children have another environment to explore. There are new materials and construction kits to investigate, PE equipment on which to balance, climb or jump, and a playground in which to skip and run.

Movement is dynamic and forever changing – reflecting, rotating, or in straight or curving lines – whereas position is static and concerned with the relationship between people and objects. As children play and move, they begin to use the language of position. It is important that they develop an understanding that the language used to describe position is relative. It is often this aspect that gives rise to confusion, even for adults.

It is important that children have opportunities to experience a wide range of movements and learn to use positional language accurately for communication, so that they develop a better understanding of all aspects of shape and space.

SHAPE, SPACE
AND MEASURES

HIDE AND HUNT

To follow instructions and use appropriate language to describe position and movement.

†† *Whole class/large group.*

🕑 *20 minutes.*

Previous skills/knowledge needed

Children should be accustomed to using large spaces for individual and collaborative floor work.

Key background information

A key aspect of understanding the space around us is to know and be able to use positional language to describe where we are. This is central to early learning in shape and space. It is important early on to identify terms that children do not fully understand or pairs of terms that they confuse with each other. At a later stage of their learning, children need to use these terms in sequence to form more complex directions.

Preparation

Choose a book that contains positional language. Some possible examples are *The Lighthouse Keeper's Catastrophe* by Ronda and David Armitage (Puffin, 1988) and *Rosie's Walk* by Pat Hutchins (Puffin, 1970). Read the book and identify six or eight words, such as 'inside, over, through, behind, around, across', that you wish the children to use when describing position. Decide whether you will use the school hall or the playground for the activity and then make a sketch map for yourself once you have decided where the pieces of apparatus will be.

Resources needed

A story-book that makes use of positional language (see 'Preparation'), PE apparatus (for example, cones, rods, hoops) a sketch map of the school hall or playground showing where the apparatus will be, lengths of material or old curtains (optional).

What to do

Read the story to the children and discuss the identified words describing position. Ask the children to demonstrate what is meant by them. If you are timetabled to have the hall after break you may wish to read the story beforehand, so that you have the maximum amount of time in the hall involved in the activity. Once in the hall or playground, tell the children that they are going to play a game called 'Hide and hunt'. Discuss the places where they may need to look for someone who is hiding, and what apparatus will be used in the hall (or playground). Using your sketch map as a reminder, get one group at a time to construct the hiding places. Quite simple arrangements will suffice, for example cones and rods to crawl under, several cones to hide behind, hoops between cones to creep through and so on. If you are using material or curtains as well, then these can be draped over parts of the apparatus to make it more realistic as a hiding place. Check them for safety once completed.

First let the children have a time of free exploration, searching out places where someone might hide. Use the positional language you will be focusing on for that lesson. When the children have completed their own exploration, ask each group to nominate one person to hide. Ask them to choose where to hide and to take up their positions (under, next to, beside and so on) ready for the hunt. Get each hider to tell you quietly, so that hunters cannot hear, where each will be hiding. You may wish to jot it down so that you can keep track of the words being used. Half the groups are hunters while the other half are observers. Once the hiders are in position, the remainder of their group explore the space and whisper, 'We're going on a hunt. Where will we find her?' The hiders each have a turn at giving a wrong instruction such as, 'Behind the high mountain.' The groups stealthily move to the correct positions and say, 'She's not here!' Finally it is the turn of the observers, at your cue, to chant, 'There's someone hiding... [states their position], there's someone hiding...' and so on for each person hiding. The group to whom the hider belongs moves to the correct place when told by the observers and collects their member. The groups then change over and the activity continues until all the apparatus and positional language have been experienced. During this time several children should be able to have a turn at being hunted.

SHAPE, SPACE AND MEASURES

Suggestion(s) for extension

A group of children could be given a sequence of two or three positional instructions that they have to follow in order to 'find' the hider. The greater the number of instructions, the more complex the task becomes.

Suggestion(s) for support

For children who find the language of position difficult, concentrate on one positional word but change the hider's location: for example, 'behind the mountain', 'behind the tree'.

Assessment opportunities

Ask the children to describe where a hider is located and observe the actions they use to clarify their answer. You will then be able to assess their level of competence and confidence in using positional language. Any children involved in a sequence of activities can also be assessed for their ability to follow instructions.

Display ideas

Children could be involved in making a model of a jungle made from junk materials and identifying the positions of hiding places. The display could then be used as an additional area of learning, through play activities related to position. A set of wildlife animals could be included, for children to hide and find. They should then talk about where the animals were found.

Resources needed

A collection of mazes from puzzle books, one large sheet of paper (about A2 size), a pencil and eraser, a thick felt-tipped pen and a small toy car for each pair of children, photocopies of sheets 99 and 100, a programmable toy such as Roamer or PIP, sugar paper and sticky tape.

What to do

Discuss routes around the classroom with the children. Ask one of the pairs of children to demonstrate verbal instructions: one child should direct the other from one part of the classroom to another. Before they start, remind them of the meaning of left and right. Show them how their left hand can be held

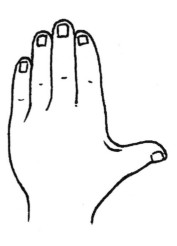

out palm downwards to create a capital 'L', with the thumb being the foot of the 'L' and the fingers held together to form its upright. Make sure that the child giving the instructions is aware that the directions given need to relate to the person following the route and not to himself.

MAZES

To use instructions about going left and right to follow a route.

†† *Pairs.*

🕐 *45 minutes.*

Previous skills/knowledge needed

Children should have experience of using a flow chart to follow sequential instructions.

Key background information

In everyday life, space is in three dimensions. Movement happens in all three planes. However, this reality is represented in two dimensions in maps, plans and drawings. Describing a route in words removes it from real life by another stage. There is no pictorial representation of the route; only the key words to describe certain points along the way.

Preparation

Collect some examples of mazes from puzzle books or design some simple ones yourself. Make copies of photocopiable sheet 99 for each pair of children.

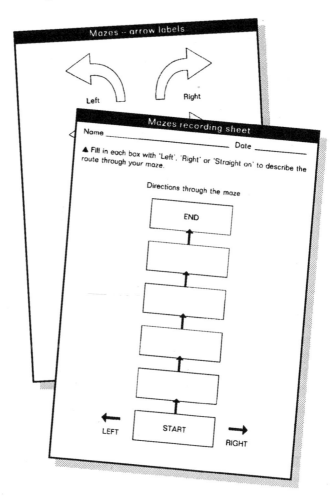

SHAPE, SPACE AND MEASURES

Discuss the maze examples with the children. Let them identify the 'through' route and the roads that go nowhere. Then ask the children to draw a 'through' road for their toy car on their large sheet of paper. They should do this in pencil. Explain that they should start at one corner or edge of the paper and end on another corner or edge. Get them to mark the start and the finish. The route must be clear and although it can twist and turn, with corners and bends, it must not loop back over itself. Ask the children to take their toy car along the route to check that it is continuous and without loops over itself.

Next ask them to choose up to five corners or bends along the route where they wish to add other roads. They will need to rub out part of their original road outline in order to draw in the extra roads. These extra roads must go nowhere, as they are cul-de-sacs, but they should make the original route more difficult to follow. They must not cross over the original route or return to it. Ask the children to check their finished maze to see if they can still follow the 'through' route with their toy car. Ask them to check that they meet five junctions along the way. If everything works, they can go over their pencil drawing with felt-tipped pen.

Now the children can record their route on photocopiable page 99. Each box on the sheet represents a junction along the route. The children should fill in 'left', 'right' or 'straight on', as appropriate. When they are ready, ask each pair of children to work with another pair. One pair tries to follow the route through the other pair's maze by following the written directions on the sheet. Are these correct? Do the children get distracted by the cul-de-sacs?

Suggestion(s) for extension

Use a programmable toy such as Roamer or PIP to plan a route and record the number of instructions it takes to get from one point to another on the route. Written instructions can be recorded, for example:

```
FORWARD 5
TURN LEFT
FORWARD 3
TURN LEFT
FORWARD 7
```

Another pair of children could try out the route to see if they can get from the start to the finish, visiting all points (junctions) along the route.

An alternative to the route could be a large grid of squares. If the squares are drawn as 30cm they will match the Roamer units. Different squares could contain different pictures and the children could plan their routes to get from one picture to another. The squares could be mapped on to an island to make the game more interesting, with rivers, bridges, mountains and so on, and the Roamer set to get from one place to another via certain features.

Suggestion(s) for support

Have a straight 'road' running through the classroom and use a programmable toy for pupils to move along the route. Have three or four places to visit on either side of the route so that the children have to decide, at those points, whether they need to turn left or right to leave the main route. After each visit, they should return to the main route and continue to the next decision-making point. When they come to draw their own maze for the toy car, get them to add one additional road at a time, up to a maximum of three. Before they record their route on photocopiable page 99, they might find it helpful to identify the junctions on their maze and place right-turn and left-turn arrows, cut out from photocopiable page 100, beside the junctions.

Assessment opportunities

As the children work, you should be able to assess their confidence and ability to use the terms left and right correctly. Are their directions correct? Can they be followed by other children?

Opportunities for IT

You may wish to use some of the many software packages which have been written to encourage children to pilot an object through a maze or course. This will help children to develop the concept of left and right turns and to plan a route through a series of obstacles. Examples include Grid IT (Widgit) and Go Go Pathways (SEMERC).

Display ideas

The finished mazes and directions could be displayed as part of a Road topic and embellished with road signs and some pictures of buildings along the route.

SHAPE, SPACE AND MEASURES

Reference to photocopiable sheets

Photocopiable sheet 99 has five empty boxes in which children record the directions through the maze they have made. It helps if the children look in the same direction as the toy car when they follow the route. If you do this activity with children who have become proficient at using left and right directions, you may wish to cover the arrows at the bottom of the page before photocopying it. The labelled arrows on photocopiable sheet 100 can be cut out as required and placed alongside the appropriate junctions. This may be helpful for children needing further support.

POSTING LETTERS

To use a regular non-standard linear measure to construct straight-line movement and repeat the action.

†† *Small groups.*

🕐 *45 minutes.*

Previous skills/knowledge needed

Children need some experience in estimating distances and using a programmable toy.

Key background information

As an object moves from one point to another, it creates an image in our minds of a line being drawn from the first point to the next. From this, we begin to formulate ideas of distance. The need to measure the distance arises if you want to repeat the movement with a fair degree of accuracy.

When something moves from close by to much further away, it does not really alter in size, though it *looks* smaller. For a young child this can be quite difficult to accept. Likewise a child may not understand that the return distance from B to A is the same as that travelled from A to B.

Preparation

Provide each child with a sheet of A4 paper on which to draw one house. These houses will be cut out, labelled and used to make a street of houses for the postman to deliver letters.

Resources needed

A programmable toy such as Roamer or PIP, the children's drawings of their houses, sticky or masking tape.

What to do

Explain to the children that they are going to cut out their drawings of houses and make a plan which will give the new postman some information about a street of houses to which he will make deliveries. All the houses are in a straight line and are the same distance apart. So, once the children know the distance between the first and the second house, they can place all the other houses the same distance apart, taping each one to the floor. (The advantage of using shapes taped to the floor is that it avoids the kind of inaccuracies which can occur with models that move around. Also the programmable toy can manoeuvre directly over the shapes, enabling the children to check their distances more easily.) They can then decide whether to number or name the houses. The postman needs to know how far it is from the first to the last house, and also how far it is back again.

If Roamer is to be used effectively, it is important that the distance between the first and second house is equivalent to the basic unit used by Roamer. This is initially set at 30cm, so that entering FORWARD 1 moves the Roamer forward 30cm. (If the houses are different distances apart, the children will find it impossible to get Roamer to stop exactly at any house.) An alternative to this is to alter the step size of the Roamer itself, so that entering FORWARD 1 moves the Roamer 10cm only. However, if the step size is too small, then the numbers involved may become too large for the children's own understanding.

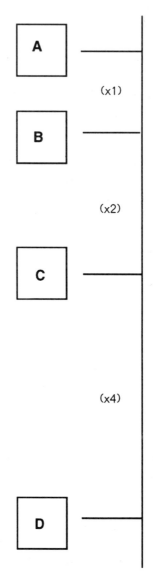

Figure 1

SHAPE, SPACE
AND MEASURES

Suggestion(s) for extension

Once the children have completed the task, ask them to place four houses in a straight line so that the space from A to B is doubled to find the position of C. The distance from B to C is then doubled to find the position of D. Can they calculate the distance for the programmable toy to travel from A to D? What is the distance from A to D and back again to A? (See figure 1 on the previous page.)

Suggestion(s) for support

Some children may find it easier to interpret distances and the movement of the programmable toy from one house to another if they are able to use a line of houses which has been prepared for them. Once they have experienced the activity this way, they may then be able to create their own street. Make sure that the distance they choose between the first and second house is different from the one in the prepared example, to give them experience of other distances to calculate.

Assessment opportunities

Assess the children's ability to use the step size of the programmable toy when working out the distance at which to place the next house. As the children calculate the total distance between houses, do they record or do they engage in mental calculation? Do they use tally marks, repeated addition or multiplication? Do they double the total to find the distance to the end of the street and back?

Display ideas

Decorating the children's drawings of houses, which can then be used as the basis of a display, will involve the children in further work on shape. They can draw on rectangular or square windows, add more rectangular chimney pots and so on. They could make the houses into symmetrically designed detached ones, or semi-detached houses (examples of reflective symmetry). The finished display of a street of houses could also be a starting point for further investigative work on routes.

ROUND THE VILLAGE GREEN

To understand and use quarter- and half-turns.
Pairs.
30–45 minutes.

Previous skills/knowledge needed

Children should have previous experience of controlling a programmable toy with simple instructions and sequences of instructions. They should also know how to use 'left' and 'right' to explain direction.

Key background information

Some children may find the concept of rotation (turning) very difficult to come to terms with. Movement in a straight line is easy to see. You can count the steps and the distance can be measured. Turning involves movement on the spot. The person or object has not moved from the original position, but simply faces in another direction. There are no steps to count and it is not appropriate to introduce degrees for measuring in early work on this kind of movement. Often movement through rotation is taught in separate, discrete stages by focusing, separately, on activities such as finding square corners, moving through a quarter-turn, turning clockwise from N to E, turning a 1/4 turn, turning 90 degrees, and turning 0.25 of a turn. For some children (and adults) it comes as quite a surprise to find that each of these separate topics is another way of talking about the same thing!

Round the village green

SHAPE, SPACE AND MEASURES

Preparation

Copy photocopiable sheet 101 and cut out the five pictures. Attach four of the pictures to the floor to form a square. It is helpful to use the programmable toy for this to ensure that the steps between each picture and the next are whole numbers. Take the last picture and place it outside the square, keeping it on the same line as two of the other landmarks so that there are now three on the same straight line, as shown in the diagram below. Mark the straight roads with chalk or paper strips, as shown.

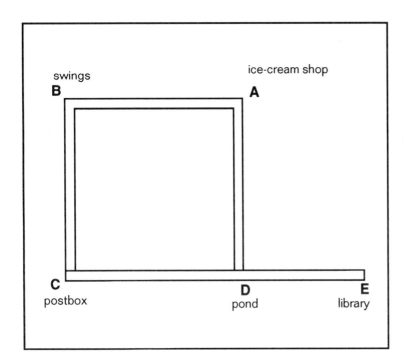

It is not possible to programme Roamer to move in half- or quarter- turns as a single command. To make the activity more accessible to children, the unit of turn can be reset so that:
▲ a full turn would be LEFT 4;
▲ a half-turn would be LEFT 2;
▲ a quarter-turn would be LEFT 1;
▲ a three-quarter-turn would be LEFT 3.

As Roamer cannot be programmed for a half-degree the unit of turn needs to be set to 23 degrees. This can be set by entering the commands:

Ç [23] sets the unit of turn to 23 degrees. (Although this makes a right angle slightly over 90 degrees, this will rarely cause any problems.) The new unit will remain active until Roamer is turned off. You will need to reset it the next time it is used for this activity.

Resources needed

A programmable toy such as Roamer or PIP with the unit of turn set to 23 degrees (see 'Preparation'), five illustrations cut out from photocopiable sheet 101, sticky tape or masking tape, chalk or paper strips.

What to do

Gather the children around the village green map that you have stuck to the floor. Explain to them that they should imagine that they live near to the swings (point B) and want to visit all the other places on the map in turn, moving along the marked roads. They have to post a letter, feed the ducks at the pond and return their books to the library. They can also buy themselves an ice-cream, either at the beginning of the journey or at the end. This allows them to decide which way round they wish to do their jobs. Tell them that they will need to find the distances between places by estimating and then trying them out with the Roamer. When they have this information they can write a sequence of directions showing how they would cover the whole journey.

Suggestion(s) for extension

Ask the children to visit the swings, the ice-cream shop, the pond and the postbox, then return to the swings, in that order in a clockwise direction. Unfortunately, they cannot use the right-turn instruction, only the left. How much of a turn does the toy have to make to be in the correct direction to continue to the next place? Now give the children only three places to visit – say, the swings, the postbox and the ice-cream shop. This means that they can cut across the village green, and so they have to work out how to turn through half a right angle.

Suggestion(s) for support

Ask the children to move from the postbox to the pond and then to the library. How much of a turn do they need to do to turn round and retrace their steps? Once they understand a half-turn, introduce a quarter-turn. Get the children to act it out for themselves by turning their bodies on the spot. What are they facing at the start? What are they facing after a half- or a quarter-turn?

Assessment opportunities

Observe the actions the children take when using the programmable toy and listen to their explanations to each other. Are they using trial-and-error methods to gauge the degree of turn? Are they gradually refining this as they reach each successive corner? Are some children using the phrases 'quarter-turn' or 'half-turn'? Are they being systematic and recording new information carefully so that they can build up a sequence of instructions later?

Display ideas

If you have enough spare room, this activity could be left in place to form an interactive display. Other children can then try out the tasks. Alternatively, you could change the task by asking children where they might end up if they started at,

for example, the chalkboard with the programmable toy facing the windows and then went FORWARD 6, TURN RIGHT, FORWARD 3, TURN LEFT, FORWARD 5. The pictures from photocopiable sheet 101 could form part of a display, and with the addition of other pictures could create an imaginary map to support work in geography.

Reference to photocopiable sheet
The pictures on photocopiable sheet 101 allow you to set this activity in the context of a village green. However, if the children have been doing work about their own school locality, it may be preferable to use resources arising from that.

FILLING SHELVES

To follow and give instructions for position.
†† *Large group.*
🕐 *30 minutes.*

Previous skills/knowledge needed
The children should be familiar with a range of vocabulary associated with three-dimensional shapes.

Key background information
In simple activities regarding position, you can tell quite easily if a child does not understand a particular term. However, when an activity involves being able to comprehend and follow a sequence of instructions, it is more difficult to know whether the child does not understand a particular positional term or whether it is the sequence of instructions that is the problem. Adults, too, encounter difficulties when a string of instructions becomes too long or complex: for example, the tall red tin that is on the top shelf next to the yellow packet which is behind the blue and green tins that are between the spaghetti and baked beans! Build up the sequences step by step, gradually increasing the level of difficulty, so that children who encounter problems can be identified early on.

Preparation
You will need access to a bookcase or a set of three shelves. If this is not possible, shelves can be constructed quite easily using some empty cardboard boxes of similar size, placed on their sides, one on top of the other. The bases of the boxes form the backs of the shelves. It is a good idea to tape the finished assembly tightly around the outside. Wide, masking tape is useful for this.

Collect tins and packets of various shapes and sizes and cover them with three or four different-patterned types of wrapping paper, so that they cannot be recognised by their original contents. As you wrap the containers, make sure that no two containers are identical. Photocopy sheets 102 and 103 for those who require it.

Resources needed
A set of shelves (see 'Preparation'), a collection of tins and packets covered with wrapping paper of various designs, copies of photocopiable sheets 102 and 103, scissors, Blu-Tack, glue.

What to do
Place a selection of the covered tins and packets on the shelves. As you position each item, describe where you are putting it, to give the children an idea of what the task is about. Ask the children, in turn, to place another item on a shelf: for example, 'Emma, take the tall, striped packet and place it on the middle shelf between the cylinders.' Be careful not to give away more clues than you need about colour and design or children will use these instead of the positional words to enable them to place the objects. Emma would need to understand 'middle', 'between' and 'cylinders' to find the correct position. Once all the items have been put on the shelves, let the children take turns at giving a sequence of clues about the position of an item that they want the rest of the group to take off. If the first guess is correct, the article is removed. If not, it should remain on the shelf.

This activity can continue over quite a long period of time, using any spare time available before play or lunch break, for as long as the children's interest is maintained and learning is taking place. Bringing in new rules to make the task more complex develops the pupils' ability to sort and classify the information they are giving or receiving.

Suggestion(s) for extension
Increase the number of shelves to four or five. Encourage the children to use phrases such as 'to the right of...', 'to the left of...', 'the second shelf from the top...' and so on. With a small group, try making them sit so that their backs are turned towards the shelves while the instructions are given. They then have to remember the instructions before they can apply them, on turning round to face the shelves.

SHAPE, SPACE AND MEASURES

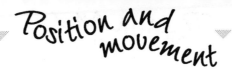
Use photocopiable sheets 102 and 103 and work in pairs. First the children need to cut out the items from sheet 103. Then Partner A should describe to Partner B where to place items on the shelves on sheet 102. So that the activity can be repeated, give the children Blu-Tack. They can then position and remove the items several times.

Suggestion(s) for support
Reduce the number of articles to be placed on the shelves. If the children cannot cope with three shelves, use only two and add a third one later.

Assessment opportunities
Focus on specific children during the activity. Are they better at following instructions or giving them? Do they use a restricted or a wide range of positional vocabulary when giving instructions? Do they appear hesitant when following particular phrases, such as 'in between' or 'to the left/right of'? Can the pupils using photocopiable pages 102 and 103 record complex instructions? For example, can Partner A record two or three instructions and read them aloud to Partner B? And can Partner B listen to these two or three instructions before finally sticking the pictures into place? This could provide tangible evidence of a language-based activity. The partner's written instructions would need to be attached to the completed sheet.

Display ideas
The set of shelves could continue to be used as part of a mathematical interactive display, with examples of children's recording on the photocopiable sheets forming a background. Later, more pictures and containers could be added, to make a classroom shop.

Reference to photocopiable sheets
Photocopiable sheets 102 and 103 provide pictures of shelves and objects to place on them. If these are used to provide evidence of a language-based activity, as described in 'Suggestion(s) for extension', the pictures of the items will need to be stuck down with glue for a permanent record.

CIRCLES AND SQUARES
To explore and recognise rotating shapes.
†† *Large group followed by individual work.*
⏲ *30 minutes.*

Previous skills/knowledge needed
Children need to have experienced rotation in practical situations.

Key background information
The completion of photocopiable page 104 is a stage removed from a practical activity. Pupils need to understand the act of rotation in a certain direction and be able to create an image of it in their minds before they can record it in concrete form. It is only then that children are in a position to check their work. To visualise, predict, record and finally check is a complex process.

Preparation
Make a collection of items that rotate, such as a toy helicopter, a windmill (the type often bought at the seaside), a wheel, a clock with hands, a round tin or box with a separate lid. Also find an example of rotation being used to create a pattern, possibly on fabric or wallpaper. Make enough copies of photocopiable sheet 104 to give one to each child.

Resources needed
Items that can be used to demonstrate and predict rotation (see 'Preparation'), copies of photocopiable page 104 and coloured pencils.

What to do
Set out the collection of resources so that all the children in the group can see them clearly. Discuss the movement of different objects as you rotate them. Mark one of the blades on the helicopter, or one of the spokes on the wheel, so that pupils can see how far you have rotated it. Provide lots of

SHAPE, SPACE
AND MEASURES

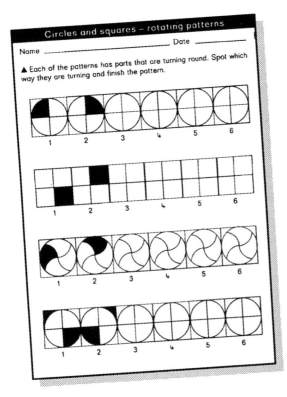

Suggestion(s) for support

There are several approaches to try for those children who find rotation difficult.

▲ Give them only the first two patterns on photocopiable page 104 to complete.

▲ Cut off examples 3–6 of each pattern, which are unmarked.

▲ Take each pattern in turn and colour the appropriate segment(s) as in the first example of the pattern they are investigating. The coloured segment can now be rotated visibly from position 1 to position 2 as in the diagram on the photocopiable sheet. The children should then be aware of the turning movement and be able to work out whether it was a quarter-turn or half-turn and so on.

▲ Let them cut a pattern on half a potato and print repeating patterns which rotate. The pattern will need to be quite simple, such as a zigzag line, so that the children can see the position changes when rotated a quarter-turn, as shown in the diagram:

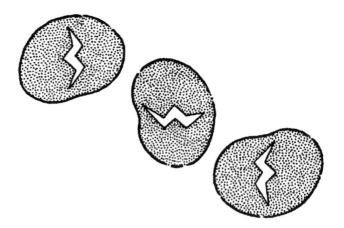

examples of quarter-turns and half-turns. Rotate in clockwise and anticlockwise directions. When you feel they are ready, show the children the starting position of an item that you are going to rotate. Then hold it behind your back and rotate it, for example by a quarter-turn. Show the children the item again. Can they tell you how much you have rotated it? This requires them to hold an image in their mind and then to compare it with what they see when you show them the new position.

Let the children also have opportunities to rotate the articles on display and to look at an example of rotational pattern to aid their understanding. Look at the first example on photocopiable page 104. Explain to the children that the shaded section is like the blade on the helicopter and it has turned from the first position in section one to the second position in section two. How far has it rotated? Is it a quarter-turn or a half-turn? Next ask them where it should be shaded in section three if it does the same amount of turn again? If necessary, complete the first line of examples with the children so that you are sure they understand what to do. Explain to them that some patterns may go in the opposite direction and remind them that this is called going in an anticlockwise direction. Then they should be ready to embark on completing the patterns on photocopiable page 104.

Suggestion(s) for extension

Ask the children to create some of their own patterns that rotate. They may wish to make a simple template that they can move around a point to help them. Can they create a simple pattern of elements that are identical when drawn, but appear to rotate once colour is added?

Assessment opportunities

There will be opportunities during the discussion period to assess whether some children can verbalise the notion of rotation. Their recording on sheet 104 should give a clear indication of their understanding of rotation.

Display ideas

A display of objects that turn would create interest, and some of the children's recording could be shown alongside it. This could be the starting point for artwork on repeating, reflective and rotational patterns.

Reference to photocopiable sheet

Photocopiable sheet 104 should not be used before the children have had plenty of opportunity to discuss rotation, manipulate rotating items and act out the movement for themselves. Some children have difficulty in visualising rotational movement. They need plenty of practical experience and a concrete example to rotate, to support them as they record.

Length

There are several stages which children need to experience when learning about measurement. The earliest stage does not involve actual measuring but does require making direct comparisons. Two children can be compared side by side to ascertain who is taller. From comparing two, they can progress to comparing three, so encountering the use of 'tall', 'taller', 'tallest'. This stage of comparing is of considerable importance and should not be rushed if children are to understand the language used and ultimately the notion of difference, which requires knowing, 'How much longer?' or 'How much shorter?'

Later children need to learn to use some form of arbitrary measurement, like a straw. They count how many times they have to lay it from one end to the other. Comparing the numbers needed for two items allows them to know whether one item *is* longer than the other. Young children find indirect comparison more complex than earlier measuring stages. Again it is a stage which must not be hurried. Children will need a variety of practical, investigative situations in which to become involved through doing, talking and recording.

There comes a point when children have to appreciate the need for a standard unit of measurement if we are to continue making comparisons with some degree of accuracy. If a child and an adult measure the same desk with hand spans, they get very different results. Once children embark on the final stage of using standard units, they may well become involved in lengthy calculations to make comparisons. However, while they become aware of the need to choose the right measuring tool and unit of measure, they should not lose sight of the approximate nature of measurement or of the value of being able to make a good estimate.

SHAPE, SPACE
AND MEASURES

BIG AND BIGGER

To use comparative language associated with linear measurement.

†† *Whole class followed by smaller groups.*

🕐 *30–45 minutes.*

Previous skills/knowledge needed
Children should be used to working with Plasticine and making models.

Key background information
Length is measured by counting the number of units that cover a distance from the start to the finish. This is different from counting quantities of discrete items, such as the number of sweets in a packet. Length is a continuous quantity which, by nature, can never be exact. Therefore we can only ever measure to a certain degree of accuracy. There are several stages of development that children need to experience. Direct to indirect comparison, using non-standard to standard units, estimation and measurement, followed by a gradual move towards greater accuracy.

Preparation
Find a story-book suitable for the age group, which makes reference to size, allowing comparisons to be made as animals, objects or people get bigger or smaller. Some examples are *The Bad-Tempered Ladybird* by Eric Carle (Puffin, 1982), *Jim and the Beanstalk* by Raymond Briggs (Hamish Hamilton, 1985) or *The Shrinking of Treehorn* by Florence Parry Heide (Puffin, 1984). There are also many stories about giants which could provide the starting point. Collect items for measuring linked to the story. You will need two of each, one doll-sized and one adult-sized. Also find a small number of different-sized soft toys to compare and discuss. Only photocopy sheets 105 and 106 for those children who can comprehend recording at such an early stage of development.

Resources needed
The chosen story-book (see 'Preparation'), soft toys of varying sizes, doll-sized items from the home corner and adult-sized items to make comparisons, Plasticine or junk materials for model-making, copies of photocopiable sheets 105 and 106 (if appropriate), glue for some pupils.

What to do
Read the story aloud, pausing at appropriate places to ask the children about the sizes of the animals or objects involved. For example, in *The Bad-Tempered Ladybird*, how much bigger than the ladybird might the wasp or the stag beetle be? When the story is finished, use the collection of soft toys to extend the discussion as to which toy is taller or longer than another. Set out the toys for all the children to

see and choose one that is going to be 'measured'. Let two or three children at a time guess which toys are bigger, (that is, taller or longer) than the one you have picked out. This gives them some early experience in estimation. Let the children place one of the toys that they think is bigger next to the one you have selected so that they can make a direct comparison. The act of placing them side by side to compare height or length is important. Many children are unaware that they need to line up the objects they are comparing at one end. As long as the children are not sensitive about their height, choose pairs to compare with each other. Who is taller? Who is shorter? It is important not to hurry this early work.

Divide the class into four groups. Two groups will concentrate on height and two on length. If you are using giants as your starting point, the ideas are endless. For example, children could consider the height of the giant's hat, boots or cup, and the length of his socks, scarf or bed. Continue discussing bigger or smaller as you look at the doll-sized items from the home corner and compare them with adult-sized items. When the children are ready to make their own examples from Plasticine or junk, have one group making tall items, another group, short items, the third, long items and the last, short (in length) items. There will be many opportunities for using the words 'short' and 'shorter', 'long' and 'longer' and 'tall' and 'taller' while making the items, and

SHAPE, SPACE
AND MEASURES

later there will be plenty of scope for groups to make direct comparisons of the completed objects. At a later date, children can swap groups so that they can compare height instead of length and vice versa.

Suggestion(s) for extension

Pupils who are ready for recording can use photocopiable sheets 105 and 106. Later they can move on to tasks that require them to compare three or more items. These introduce them to superlatives, such as 'longest', 'tallest', 'widest' and 'shortest'.

Suggestion(s) for support

Some children may need to consider only one dimension at a time. They will probably find heights easier to compare than lengths, as, for heights, the items will be standing either on the floor or on the table. To compare lengths, they need to line up the items carefully alongside each other. Do not move on to comparing length until you are sure that the children understand 'tall' and 'taller', and 'short' and 'shorter'.

Assessment opportunities

Most of the assessment will come from watching and listening to the children. In particular, you will want to ascertain who uses the appropriate language confidently and who finds difficulty. Question the children to extend their powers of observation and use of language. For example: 'Who can see a sock that is even longer? Is there a hat that is shorter than both of them? Can you find a scarf that could go between those two?' The photocopiable sheets will also provide an opportunity to assess written work.

Opportunities for IT

Children might use specific software like the Goldilocks activities screens on My World (SEMERC) to explore the concept of big and bigger. It will also give them opportunities to create pictures by moving objects around the screen.

Display ideas

Whatever theme you are using should provide a really good display. The story-book will be part of it, as well as the soft toys, the items from the home corner and the adult-sized items. There will also be the Plasticine and junk models which should be labelled appropriately. Make the display interactive by placing a different item on a piece of coloured sugar paper each day and adding a question such as 'Can you find something taller (shorter, longer) than this?'

Reference to photocopiable sheets

You will need to consider carefully when to use photocopiable sheets 105 and 106. They should not be used instead of the practical activities, nor for children who find difficulty moving on to more abstract work. Some children will be able to visualise and comprehend the differences in size, whereas other children may need to cut out the pictures and compare them side by side before sticking them into their maths book, and then they can complete the written statement. There will also be children who have not yet reached this stage of development. They should not be required to record.

LONGER AND LONGER

To compare the lengths of objects by measuring with a non-standard measure and counting the number of repeats.

†† *Small groups and pairs.*

🕒 *20 minutes per set of objects.*

Previous skills/knowledge needed

Children need to have done plenty of practical work using direct (that is, side-by-side) comparison to consider the lengths of two or three objects. Linear measurement should involve children comparing length ('Which pencil is longer?'), height ('Who is taller, Rachel or Malik?') and width ('Which door is wider – the classroom or hall door?').

Key background information needed

To communicate with others about lengths and heights and comparative sizes, we need to have a commonly agreed unit of measure. This may be something quite arbitrary, such as a straw. Nonetheless, having such a standard unit enables us to compare the measurements of things that cannot be compared directly, side by side. Thus two doorways, for example, can be measured and compared to see which is the taller.

Preparation

If you have recently done the previous activity 'Big and bigger', you may wish to use objects from your collection and the items that the children made. If not, then you will need to make a new collection of interesting items for the children to measure. They could be linked to a cross-curricular topic or a geographical topic involving measuring within the school grounds. Using colours can be helpful to your organisation where, for example, red items are small, yellow and blue items are in-between sizes, and green items are the largest. Decide how you are going to organise the groups involved in this activity. Are you going to have a round of objects to be measured, so that all groups have the chance to measure everything during the course of a week? Or are you going to have one group measuring short objects and another group

SHAPE, SPACE
AND MEASURES

measuring longer ones and so on? Make sufficient photocopies of sheet 107 (at least one for each pair of children), and sheet 108 for each child needing extension work.

Resources needed

A collection of objects to be measured for their length or height; some tools to use as arbitrary measures, for instance lollipop sticks, pipe-cleaners, short pieces of ribbon, plastic straws, felt-tipped pens, paper-clips, empty audio-cassette boxes, structural apparatus rods; flip chart or similar and a thick marker pen; copies of photocopiable sheets 107 and 108.

What to do

Children will need to work in pairs within a small group. Explain to them that they are going to use a tool to measure some objects for length or height, and record the measurements on sheet 107. Demonstrate how to measure with a tool. Make sure the children know where to begin and end. The children in each pair can take it in turns to measure and record. If it takes 'a bit more' of their measuring tool, but not another whole one, then they can record this as well. Show them the words on the bottom of the worksheet, and provide them with the correct spelling of each tool so that they are not hindered from their measuring and recording task by spelling problems. Let each pair measure at least three items. Make sure that the pairs in a group are not given the same tool with which to measure. When each pair has finished, they can measure the objects again, using another tool, if you feel they need more experience. When all the groups have experienced measuring short and long items and you have enough data for children to exchange information, then you can move into stage two of the activity. For this you may wish to gather the children together on the carpet. You will need to have to hand the collection of objects which have been measured.

Start by reading out an example from a child's worksheet: for example, 'The red bus measures 7 paper-clips and a bit more.' Ask them: 'Has anyone else got anything that is measured with paper-clips? Is it shorter or longer?' Record the information on the flip chart for all to see, and check it by placing the objects side by side and comparing them directly. Let the children take turns to ask for information from each other, as you have just done. Towards the end of this period, ask the children to compare two items that have been measured using two different tools. Make sure that the shorter item has a greater number of repeats than the larger. Finally, make some block graphs from the data. One graph could be about a particular number: all the objects included on it are the same number long, but *different* tools have been used to measure them. Another graph could be about objects which were all measured with the *same* measuring tool.

Suggestion(s) for extension

When the children have measured one item, tell them to estimate the length of the other objects and record their estimates, before they measure and record the actual lengths. A copy of photocopiable sheet 108 will help them with this. You will need to explain to them that it is difficult for everyone to estimate; they will get better at it, the more they do it. Make it feel like a game where they are trying to improve against their own performance. You could even devise a way of them awarding points to themselves if they guess within 5 of the actual measurement. They can then try to improve on their own performance by estimating within 3 or 2 of the actual measurement.

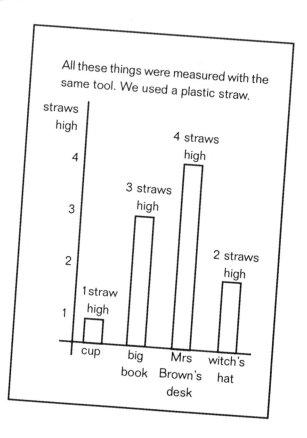

All these things are the same number long. They are all 7.

car	7 paper-clips long
bus	7 lollipop sticks long
carrot	7 pegboard pegs long
doll's scarf	7 ribbons long

How many long?

All these things were measured with the same tool. We used a plastic straw.

straws high — cup: 1 straw high; big book: 3 straws high; Mrs Brown's desk: 4 straws high; witch's hat: 2 straws high

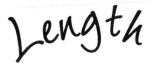

Suggestion(s) for support

Many children have difficulty with repeated measurement, particularly when they cannot keep their eyes on the place to which the last measurement reached. This is very apparent when children measure using hand spans. Firstly they do not extend their hands fully enough. Also they find placing one hand next to the other very difficult. It is. Try it yourself!

Some children find that the concentration needed to measure gets in the way of their counting and they lose count. Give these children enough of their measuring tools for them to lay them end to end alongside the article being measured. This allows them to measure and to check their counting at the same time.

Assessment opportunities

You will want to observe children as they work, to check that they are in fact measuring properly. They should be starting and ending at the correct place, repeating without overlapping or leaving gaps, and counting the repeats accurately. Through listening to the language they use, you should be able to identify children who are progressing with measurement and are able to compare their counts and make deductions about the lengths (or heights) of different objects: for example, 'The lorry is longer than the bus. It's 5 more than the bus.' Try to elicit such information by questioning the children about what they have found out. The written work should also provide assessment opportunities.

Opportunities for IT

The children could use graphing software to make pictograms or block graphs of their measuring. Different graphs could be drawn, for example the same objects measured with different tools or different objects measured with the same tools. These can be printed out and used as a part of the class discussions and display.

The children could also use Roamer or PIP to give them practice at estimating length. If the space is available, children could set up two objects different distances apart and try to send the Roamer between them. How many goes does it take before they refine their original estimate to a correct one?

Display ideas

Use the graphs for part of your display. Alongside them place two or three of the items which have been measured, with a line of lollipop sticks or paper-clips to show their length. Find some pictures as examples of long, longer and longest.

Make the area interactive by displaying a new item to be measured and recorded each day. Provide a unit of measure that the class has not used before. This will give further opportunities for estimation.

Reference to photocopiable sheets

Photocopiable sheet 107 is a worksheet for the children to fill in. In the top section they should record which tool they

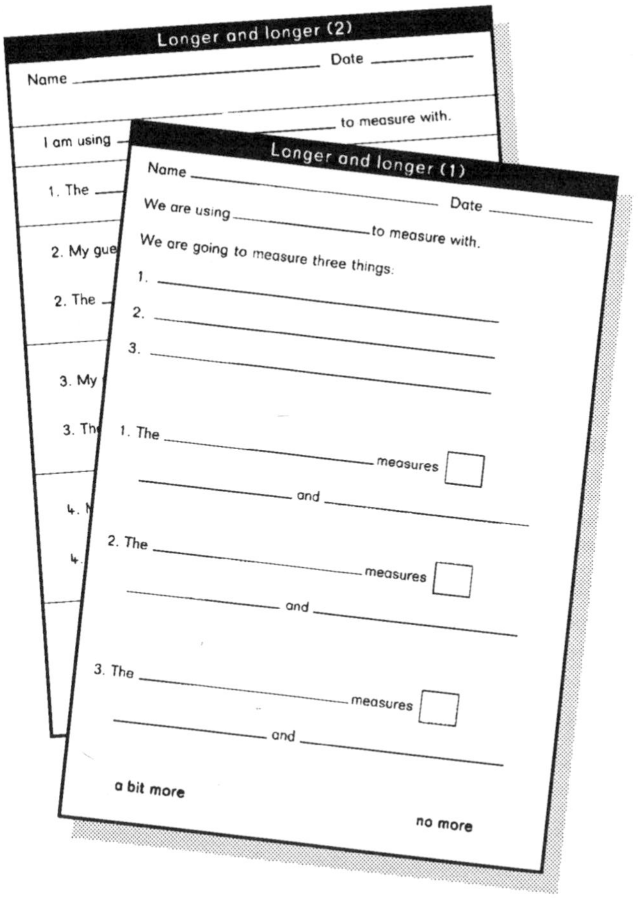

are going to measure with and which items are to be measured. As they measure each item, they can record the result in the section below. Sheet 108 is a worksheet for those children involved in the estimating and measuring task suggested as extension work. It will only be used by children who have reached this stage in their learning.

WHOPPERS!

To understand the need for standard units.

Large group/pairs.

10–15 minutes per pair.

Previous skills/knowledge needed

Children should have done practical work in measurement using body measures, such as hand spans, and other arbitrary measuring tools. They should have had experience of measuring using both direct and indirect comparison.

Key background information

Early stages of children's learning to measure, using direct comparison and non-standard units, are essential steps towards their understanding the need for an agreed standard unit. When objects cannot be placed side by side, measuring them using personal body measures and arbitrary measuring tools does not allow really accurate comparison.

Length

Preparation

Decide on the context for this large-scale measuring activity. You may be able to link it to a class topic, or you may prefer to work around an idea from a story-book, such as *The Bad-Tempered Ladybird* by Eric Carle (Puffin, 1982) or *The Selfish Giant* by Oscar Wilde (Puffin, 1982). For example, the children could be involved in measuring a whale or a sleeping giant.

Use paint or thick felt-tipped pens to draw the object which is to be measured on to a roll of lining paper. Make sure that you have a large enough place in your classroom or corridor to display this later, but do not put it up just yet. Cut long strips, 2cm wide, from 2cm² paper. You need one for each child.

Resources needed

Possibly a story-book, as described in 'Preparation', a large drawing of the character/object to be measured (using paint or thick felt-tipped pens), long 2cm-wide strips of 2cm² paper, scrap paper and pencils, coloured pencils or crayons, glue, length of rope or bamboo cane to use as arbitrary measure, interlinking plastic cubes for children requiring support.

What to do

If you are using a story to provide the context for measuring, read it to the children, or simply remind them of it if it is very familiar. Tell them that they are going to measure the character or object you have drawn. They can work in pairs, and you will ask one pair at a time to come and see, for example, 'the whale'.

Tell each child of the pair to estimate the length in strides and write their guess on a piece of scrap paper. Next let them both have a turn at measuring the whale in strides. They should record both their answers on their pieces of paper. Now get each child to colour a strip of 2cm² paper, colouring the same number of squares as the number of strides he or she took when measuring. While they are involved in this part of the task, another pair of children can set to work estimating and measuring the whale.

When all the children involved in this activity have completed recording the number of strides on their paper strips, these can be stuck on to the whale in the form of a bar chart.

You will need to draw a base line so that the strips can be lined up accurately. Once they are all in place, the vertical axis can be drawn and suitable intervals marked on it, so that children can retrieve particular data from the graph. Now might be the time to display the finished work, if there is space in your classroom, so that you are ready for the large group review.

This part is very important. Discussion needs to focus first on why there was a difference between the estimates and the actual measurements in strides and then, in particular, on why so many different lengths in strides are recorded on the graph. It is most important that the children understand that the length which was measured did not change (that is, the whale did not get longer or shorter), but their strides differed in length. It is a good idea to demonstrate this by having a child and yourself measure the whale again, so that it becomes obvious that your strides are longer than the child's. Ask the children for their ideas on what could be done to make all their measurements the same. You may need to intervene and suggest using the same measuring tool. Let the children try out this idea, using an arbitrary measure such as a length of skipping rope or a bamboo cane, and compare their results. They can use the term 'and a bit more', if needed.

Suggestion(s) for extension

More able pupils can collect data from other children to add to their own. Six to eight measurements should be enough. Get them to draw their own bar charts and label the axes. This could be a good opportunity to present data in the form of a pictogram. Footprints could be drawn, each one representing two strides.

Suggestion(s) for support

Some children may need help with their counting, if they have difficulty counting in time to their strides. It may be preferable for some children to work in a small group to record their data graphically. Structural apparatus is very useful to demonstrate the link between block and bar charts. Each child in the small group should choose one colour from some interlinking plastic cubes. They need to count out the same number of cubes as the number of strides they took when measuring 'the whale'. If you have a plastic grid on which the cubes can be built vertically, it clearly shows how the 'graph' builds a block at a time. Also the resulting column of coloured blocks can be compared to a friend's column (in another colour) which may be taller, or shorter, or even the same size as your own. The single-coloured columns look similar to a bar chart, especially if they cannot be counted as separate blocks, as when viewed from a distance.

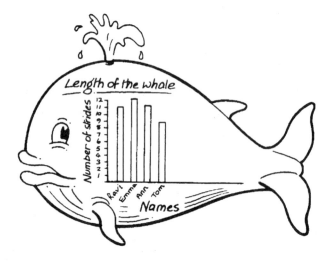

SHAPE, SPACE AND MEASURES

Assessment opportunities

As children discuss the outcomes of the practical work, you can gauge their stage of development. Can they explain why stride measurements varied? Which children are having difficulty coming to terms with the notion of the length being unchanged but the numbers of strides being different? These children do not yet understand conservation of a physical quantity. They will need further practical experiences before they develop the concept of conservation of length. Which children have developed the concept of conservation? How do you know? What did they say? Which children can explain why it is better to use a measuring tool?

Opportunities for IT

Children could use graphing software to record and display the number of strides taken to measure the whale. Some software allows pictograms to be drawn, while other software records information as block or bar charts. Graphs could be drawn showing the length of the whale using different arbitrary measuring devices. The graphs could be used to focus discussion on the need for a standard unit of length.

Display ideas

Once all the children have finished measuring and recording graphically, the object can be displayed along a wall, either in the classroom or in the corridor. It can be used for children to refine their measuring skills. Have a selection of non-standard measuring tools nearby. Using these will give children important practice at starting to take measurement from the correct point and placing the repeats accurately end to end.

TRAINS

To refine estimating skills and use standard units.

†† *Pairs and groups.*

🕐 *10–15 minutes per pair, when measuring.*

Previous skills/knowledge needed

Children should have had practical experience in estimating length and using a standard-length tool as an arbitrary measure. They need to have had opportunities to make comparisons with other groups' data.

Key background information

Children ultimately need to appreciate that the quantity to be measured remains unchanged (conserved), regardless of the measuring tools being used, and this requires plenty of practical experience. When they begin to use standard units, don't abandon the practice of getting them to offer estimates before they carry out the actual measuring. This requires them to think about which unit of measurement would be appropriate.

Preparation

Collect some pictures of trains. They could include steam trains, if you wish to make a link to a historical topic; or 'Le Shuttle' and modern Inter-City trains for a topic on transport. Cut pieces of sugar or lining paper to the size you want the children's train engine and carriages to be. You may want the engine to be twice the size of a carriage. Also cut out some circles for wheels and strips for carriage couplings. Photocopy sheet 109 – either one for each child or one for each pair.

Resources needed

Pictures of trains for reference, engine- and carriage-sized pieces of paper, circles and strips for wheels and couplings, paint, thick felt-tipped pens, wax crayons, copies of photocopiable page 109, metre sticks and trundle wheels.

What to do

First, the children involved in this task need to prepare the engine and individual train carriages. Your collection of pictures should provide a stimulus. All the carriages need to be the same size. Children should draw on doors, windows and other features that they may think of. However, wheels do not need to be drawn as the cut-out circles can be added later, when the train picture is displayed. You may wish the train engine to be twice the length of a carriage and to have two children drawing it. Once the engine and three or four carriages have been completed, measuring can begin. Find a space to line the pictures up, one behind the other. You may wish to attach (by stapling) a short strip of paper behind the engine and one behind each carriage, as they are completed, to link the carriages together.

Children can now work in pairs. Ask them to measure the length of the train in strides and record their data on photocopiable page 109. Now get them to measure their own stride with a metre stick. Can one of the children make a stride nearly a metre long? Can the other make strides only half a metre long? Can they each measure the train again, one doing nearly-a-metre strides and the other doing half-metre strides? Does one of them take approximately twice as many strides as the other? Are their results this time different from when they first measured the train by strides? Now ask them to estimate the length of the train in metres and record their estimate. Finally, they should measure the length of the train using a metre stick and record that result. The next pair of children can use a trundle wheel, instead of a metre stick, at this final stage of the activity. It is quite a complex tool for children to use, so it is essential that you demonstrate and teach the skill.

As more pictures are completed, they can be added to lengthen the train, and so the next pairs to do the measuring come up with different data. This helps keep the children's interest going, and also overcomes the age-old problem of the first ones to finish telling other children 'the answer'.

When all the children have finished, have a large group review of what they have found out. How near were their estimates? Were the measurements of a train 'x' carriages long, taken with a trundle wheel and a metre stick, the same or different? About how many carriages do you need to measure 2 or 3 or 4 metres?

Finally, take another opportunity for all the children to be involved in estimating and measuring, as you get them to consider the space where you are going to display the train. First ask them to estimate the length of the space and record their answers. Do they think there is sufficient space for the train? Will there be space left over? Next they can measure the space with both the trundle wheel and the metre stick and compare the results with their estimates. This is also an opportunity to discuss whether the trundle wheel is better than the metre stick for measuring. Trundle wheels are better for long distances and curved lines, but are difficult to use in tight corners and awkward places.

Suggestion(s) for extension

Get the children to record their measurements to the nearest centimetre, instead of 'a bit more'. When they have finished work on the train, ask them to estimate and measure a range of distances around the school. This could be linked with geographical fieldwork in the school grounds. Children could estimate and measure the distance between two trees or two playground benches, or the length of the path from the mobile classroom to the nearest or furthest school entrance. They could also estimate a distance from where they are standing to another point (without striding out the distance). Get them to estimate and then measure the length of a straight path, or a path that turns a corner and is partly out of sight. They should use both metre sticks and trundle wheels and discuss which is better for the job. Ask them to record their work diagrammatically or in a graph.

Suggestion(s) for support

Some children may find measuring with a trundle wheel difficult because they are unable to keep track of the clicks. If this is so, let them start by using a metre stick. If they still lose track of the number of repeats, let them have enough metre sticks to lay them end to end over the whole length of

the train. If you do not have enough metre sticks, cut some lengths of card or stiff paper to use with them.

Assessment opportunities

Assess the pupils' ability to estimate. If they find it difficult, is it because of lack of experience, or is the distance to estimate too great? Assess the language they use when measuring. Are they using the phrase 'and a bit more' or are some children beginning to read the scale on the metre stick? Have they understood that the metre stick and the trundle wheel measure the same distance? Are they able to explain why one tool may be better than another in different situations?

Display ideas

The finished train should in itself provide an eye-catching display with some of the train pictures and the children's recording alongside. The train could also provide a resource for further mathematical work, perhaps on number, for example two wheels on each carriage for counting in twos, three people to a carriage for counting in threes, numbering the carriages for cardinal number and so on. The display could be used for mental arithmetic work in spare moments before break or lunch. For example, you could practise ordinal number and addition by asking: 'How many people are there altogether in the third, fourth and sixth carriages?'

Reference to photocopiable sheet

Photocopiable sheet 109 should be used as the children work on the task. They can use one sheet each or work on one per pair. There is a section to be completed for each stage of the activity.

SHAPE, SPACE AND MEASURES

Mass

In our everyday language we speak about weighing an object, or knowing the weight of an object, but the correct term is *mass*, which we measure in kilograms and grams (or pounds and ounces). An object's mass is the amount of material it contains, and therefore it does not change. For example, a piece of lead pipe is made from a certain amount of lead. We can ascertain the amount by placing the pipe on one side of a balance and putting weights on the other side. When the two sides balance, the number of kilograms and grams equals the mass of the pipe. If we were able to repeat this exercise on the moon, the same lead pipe and the same kilogram and gram weights would still balance each other. This is because the gravity on the moon would act on both sides of the balance, just as the earth's gravity acts on both sides. The mass of the lead pipe remains unchanged.

By contrast, if the whole experiment was repeated using kitchen scales, we would find that the weight of the lead pipe on the moon was less than its weight on earth. That is because kitchen scales record the pull of gravity acting upon the object being measured. The gravitational pull of the moon is about one-sixth of the earth's and so, although the amount of lead is unchanged, it would weigh about one-sixth of what it weighed on earth.

Even though young children do not understand gravitational pull and weightlessness, they are aware of it from watching television programmes about astronauts apparently able to float in space. Therefore, this complex concept should be considered with great care when teaching children, so that they do not become confused at a later stage in their learning.

SHAPE, SPACE
AND MEASURES

HEAVIER OR LIGHTER?

To use language, including comparatives, associated with measuring mass.

†† *Small groups.*

🕐 *20–30 minutes.*

Previous skills/knowledge needed

Children should be used to taking turns, observing activities and listening to other children's explanations.

Key background information

It is very easy for young children to confuse the mass of an object with its size. They may well think that large objects must be heavier than small ones. In the early stages it is important to choose resources with care, so that unnecessary confusion does not arise. Initially, there should be very clear differences in the masses of the objects that you ask children to consider; and the heavier things should also be the larger ones.

Preparation

Collect a range of everyday articles of different sizes and masses, and some identical plastic carrier bags. If you have done the activity 'Unpacking the shopping' (see page 14), you may find that you can reuse many of the items from that. You will need two examples of three of the items in the collection, for the purpose of balancing. Make sure that the larger items have more mass than the smaller ones. Alternatively, you may prefer to make the packages for this activity by filling empty containers of varying sizes with enough sand to give them clearly different masses, and wrapping them in colourful paper. The following containers are useful as they have lids: small and large cottage cheese tubs, large margarine tubs and ice-cream containers. Photocopy sheet 110 so that you have sufficient arrows to order all the containers and cut them out. You may wish to colour and then laminate the arrows, as they will be well used during many measuring activities.

Resources needed

Articles of different sizes and masses (see 'Preparation'), some plastic carrier bags, arrows made from photocopiable sheet 110, pan balances or bucket balances.

What to do

Begin by allowing the children to handle the packages. Let them tell you about them. If the packages are covered with wrapping paper, the children may well tell you about the patterns and colours, but at some point someone is bound to mention that one of the packages feels heavy. This provides a natural starting point for the investigation of which package is heavier or lighter than another. Make sure that each child in the group handles and balances all the articles

at every stage of the activity and that different children go first when a new pair of packages is considered. Give them plenty of time to describe what they notice and encourage them to communicate it to others in the group.

First choose two items, one much heavier than another. Let the children take turns at holding one in each hand to assess which is the heavy one. Large articles may be easier for children to handle if they are placed in plastic carrier bags. When all the children have had a turn, see if they can agree which package is heavy. Any child who is unsure should have another go. Once they are agreed, let them check by placing the two packages on to a pan balance. They will discover that the lower pan contains the heavy object. Finally, place the correct arrow, 'is heavy', alongside the article, so that a sentence can be constructed from what the children see: for example, 'The spotty package is heavy.' Continue in this way, each time choosing two packages for the children to compare, between which the difference in mass is less than before. As the difference decreases, some children may find it more difficult to assess which object is heavy.

Introduce 'is light' when appropriate and go through the whole process again. When the children have experienced heavy and light, introduce 'is heavier than' followed by 'is lighter than'. Only compare two objects at a time, placing the correct arrow between them to create a visual sentence. Ask the children to read the sentence aloud. You may find the arrow 'is lighter than' creates confusion as it points to the heavier article. If so, do not use it but, once they have completed 'is heavier than', ask the children which package is lighter. You may wish to tackle this activity in smaller chunks over a period of days.

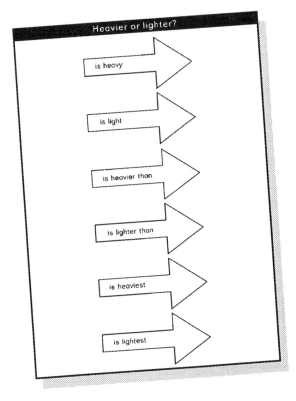

Mass

Suggestion(s) for extension

Pupils who appear confident and have understood the activities can progress to comparing the masses of three packages and, later, four or five. They will need a balance to check. They should use the arrows 'is heavier than' and 'is lighter than' at each stage. They might make a written record as follows:

The spotty package is heavier than the blue.

The blue is heavier than the red.

It would also be appropriate to introduce 'is heaviest' at this stage, and to get the children to record with pictures and writing if you feel they are ready.

Suggestion(s) for support

Keep the task purely practical, with verbal feedback, if there are children who become confused when using the arrows. Leave that part of the activity until a later date. If children have difficulty assessing which package is heavier than another, as the difference in mass decreases, then let them only handle articles between which the difference is significant.

Assessment opportunities

Most of the assessment will come from observing and listening to the children as they work. Are they using the correct language and with confidence? Are they handling the packages with care to assess their relative masses or are they looking for clues from other children's actions? Can they manage the more formal approach of the arrows? Can they order three items and use the correct language?

Display ideas

Collect pictures and posters from magazines and friendly greengrocers or supermarkets, and use them to form the background to a class shop where children have opportunities to balance interesting items. Can they make fruit and vegetables from clay or Plasticine and have a greengrocer's shop? Or could the packages from the activity be used in a class post office? Collect used boxes, padded envelopes and brown paper so that the children can wrap up the articles and then weigh them before posting.

Reference to photocopiable sheet

Photocopiable sheet 110 has arrows with parts of sentences printed on them. Using them is not an essential part of the activity and you may wish to reserve the sentence-building work which they encourage for use only with pupils who are ready to begin recording in this way.

 TUBBY TEDDIES

To compare the mass of objects using non-standard units and a simple measuring instrument.

†† *Whole class and groups.*

🕐 *30–45 minutes per group.*

Previous skills/knowledge needed

Children need to have experienced direct comparison of two objects which differ in mass, to have practised ordering three objects, and to have had opportunities to check their predictions with a balance.

Key background information

Objects which differ significantly in mass are easy to compare, but difficulties arise when items are nearly similar. It is then that a balance is needed to check if one object 'is the same as' or 'heavier than' another. It is at this point that children can be introduced to the idea of using quantitative values for mass, so that objects can be balanced against a number of units.

SHAPE, SPACE AND MEASURES

Tubby teddies recording sheet

Name _____ Date _____

My _____ is heavier than _____ _____

My _____ is lighter than _____ _____

My _____ is the same as _____

My _____ weighs the same as ☐ _____

My _____ weighs the same as ☐

Preparation

Ask the children to bring in a favourite doll or toy animal from home. You may wish to try to concentrate on teddy bears, as most homes have one and they are a great source of interest. Taking body measurements of toys spares any embarrassment which some children might feel if their own height or weight were used as the subject of the lesson. Collect objects which are irregular in size, to use as non-standard units: for example, acorns, conkers, pine cones, medium-sized pebbles or variously sized cotton reels. Make enough photocopies of sheet 111 to give one to each child.

Resources needed

A collection of dolls, toy animals or teddy bears, sets of irregular-sized non-standard units and a pan balance or bucket balance for each group, photocopies of sheet 111, flip chart or similar.

What to do

Divide the children into groups and give each group one kind of non-standard unit to use with their scales. Then gather all the children together to start. Encourage them to talk about their teddy bears before you introduce the idea of weighing them. This may arise naturally if there is a particularly fat teddy which the children predict as being 'heavy'. Ask some of the children to compare their teddies, which are clearly different in mass, by holding one in each hand to see which is heavier or lighter. Follow this with asking children to compare teddies which have similar masses, so that you can suggest checking their predictions with the balance scales. Use this opportunity to demonstrate how the scales

should be used and how the two sides balance when two items have the same mass. Reinforce this by asking some children to demonstrate with pairs of teddies. Find two teddies which exactly balance each other so that the terms 'the same as' and 'balances' can be used.

Let the children work in their groups to find which teddies balance each other. When appropriate, ask the children to try balancing each teddy with the non-standard measures you have provided for their group. They can record the information on sheet 111. Then let each group try balancing their teddy bears with the other non-standard units, and record those results too. This will give the children practice in weighing, to achieve balance, as well as providing them with a range of data.

When the practical work is completed, gather the class together again to discuss what the children found out, and record some of the information on the flip chart. (Keep it, as you may find it useful to refer to again at a later date, when you begin work on standard units.) Ask the children how much the heaviest/lightest teddy weighed in each group and record it. Ask them which is the heaviest/lightest teddy in the class. Ask them if the teddy bear which balanced 23 conkers would balance the one which balanced 23 pine cones. Continue in this way, allowing opportunities for the children to recheck information or data that they find puzzling. This task will lead some children to begin to question the value of using irregular non-standard measures.

Suggestion(s) for extension

Be prepared for any children who may question the value of using non-standard units, which are themselves irregular in size. Get them to balance each other's teddy bears again using the same units, to find out if there are discrepancies. Ask them for suggestions for how they might overcome this problem. They may ask to use units that they can see are regular in size, for example similar-sized cotton reels. Let them balance the bears again, using these regular units, and have another group or pair of children check the results to see if they are consistent.

Suggestion(s) for support

Some children have difficulty getting the scales to balance. To correct the balance, they may add units to the side which contains the bear instead of taking units away from the other side. Help these pupils by starting again, with the teddy in one side and adding one unit at a time to the other. If it is difficult to achieve an exact balance, try giving the children other units with a smaller mass each, such as acorns.

Assessment opportunities

Observe how the children use the balance. Are they using it correctly? Are they achieving a good balance and counting the units accurately? Listen to the vocabulary they use. Are they describing how the bears balance with words that reflect how the balance works? Do they use 'balances', 'equals', 'the same', or 'nearly the same', as they talk to each other in the group? Are some children taking particular care to choose units of a similar size? Ask them why they are doing this.

Opportunities for IT

The teddies topic could be used as a basis for creating a class database about the children's teddies. A database could be created by you after discussion with the children about those aspects of the teddies which are measurable or different from each other. The class could then decide on the most interesting things to record for each teddy. An example would be:

Height	32cm	(1 and a half straws)
Mass	230g	(23 conkers)
Colour	light brown	
Age	6 years	
Sounds	growl	yes/no
Eye colour	brown	

The activity could use either standard or non-standard units depending on the stage reached in the children's understanding and use of measuring units. The children could edit and amend data in the future as they become more proficient at measuring in standard units.

The database could be used as a basis for searching and sorting information about the teddies, asking questions such as:

▲ Which is the oldest teddy?
   Could be found by sorting on age and printing the results;
▲ Which teddies make sounds?
   Could be found by searching on sounds including 'yes' and printing the results.

Display ideas

If you are doing a topic on 'Ourselves', the work on 'Tubby teddies' could form an extension, with many opportunities for measurement, handling data (or creating a computer database) and interrogating the data. For example, information on height, weight, age, colour of fur, whether or not they have articulated limbs, glass-like eyes, or a growl, could be collected and recorded in Venn, Carroll or tree diagrams, block graphs, bar charts and pictograms. The children's mathematical recording, plus written work and pictures about their bears, should provide plenty of ideas for display.

Reference to photocopiable sheet

Before photocopying sheet 111, you should fill in some of the blank spaces on it. If you have decided to use teddy bears for the lesson, for example, write 'teddy' in the first and last space of the top line. You may prefer to leave all the spaces blank and explain to the children what should be written in them. This is necessary, in fact, if various animal toys are being used. The children would then complete the sentence on the sheet, for example: My *elephant* is heavier than *Jessica's rabbit*. The last two sentences on the sheet have a box for the number and a space for the name of the unit being used.

MYSTERY PARCELS

To understand the need for using a standard unit when measuring mass.

†† *Small groups/large group.*

⏰ *15–20 minutes.*

Previous skills/knowledge needed

Children need to have had experience of balancing objects with irregular-sized non-standard units, using a pan balance or bucket balance. They should understand 'heavier than', 'lighter than' and 'the same as'.

Key background information

Using irregular-sized units introduces pupils to the fact that mass can be communicated as a quantity, but it does not allow them to make comparisons with any accuracy. To communicate and compare measurements with a reasonable degree of accuracy, a regular standard unit is required.

Mass

Preparation
Prepare four parcels of varying masses, each covered in different-coloured paper so that they are clearly identifiable. Collect four different types of objects to use as regular-sized non-standard units: for example, marbles, large pasta shells, cotton reels, place-value rods and plastic interlocking cubes. Make photocopies of sheet 112, one for each child.

Resources needed
Pan balance or bucket balance for each group and four sets of regular-sized non-standard units, four coloured parcels of different masses, flip chart or similar, photocopies of sheet 112.

What to do
Explain to the group that each child has to weigh all four parcels. For each parcel, they should use a different unit, and then record their result on the sheet. Demonstrate how they should fill in one of the examples. It may be appropriate to give them the spellings for the units. If you prefer to discuss the outcome with a large group, then you will need each group to complete this part of the task before continuing. When you are ready for discussion, tell the children to bring their worksheets with them. Ask them which parcel is the heaviest and record their answers on the flip chart. You should have several answers, as the children are likely to respond by giving you the parcel which required the greatest number of units to balance it. For example, individuals choosing their heaviest parcel may provide the information such as:

▲ The red parcel weighs 15 rods (child 1).
▲ The blue parcel weighs 23 cotton reels (child 2).
▲ The green parcel weighs 18 cubes (child 3).
▲ The red parcel weighs 20 marbles (child 4).

Ask the children which is the lightest, the second heaviest and so on. Each time record their answers. By this point, some children may have realised there is a problem because they have used different units from each other. Allow time for the children to reflect on the problem and pose some of their own solutions to it. By using careful questioning you may be able to help those pupils who are still unsure of what the problem is and arrive at a solution. Let them weigh the parcels again using only one unit so they can compare their second set of results with the first.

Suggestion(s) for extension
Ask the children how they could find out which is the heaviest or lightest of their parcels. Perhaps they could record in writing, or with diagrams, what they think the problem is or how they could solve it.

Suggestion(s) for support
Some children may find the feedback of a wide range of information from a large group rather confusing. You may wish to restrict these pupils to only three parcels and three

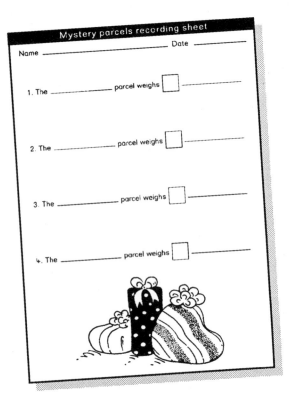

units and keep the discussion just within their own group. This will give them all an opportunity to contribute.

Assessment opportunities
Listen to the children's explanations during the discussion period. Which children are able to see there is a problem when comparing different units? Who can provide an explanation? Who is able to suggest a solution to the problem? Has anyone been able to record the problem and/or a solution to it in writing? Have they outlined the need for everyone to use the same measuring unit?

Display ideas
Make an interactive display with the parcels and a different range of regular-sized non-standard units. Use it as an opportunity for children to estimate the mass of each parcel. Produce slips of paper on which they can record how many of a unit they think will be needed to balance one of the parcels. Collect their predictions in an empty tissue box.

Name: _____
I think the_____ parcel will need _____
to balance the pan balance.

At the end of a given period of time, the parcels can be weighed and the slips of paper checked to find out which children have made a good estimate. Most children will find this good fun, rather like a competition.

Reference to photocopiable sheet

The children will need photocopiable sheet 112 to record on while they work. In each sentence, the first blank is for a word (for example, the name of a colour) that identifies the parcel in some way; the box is for the number of units; and the final blank is for the type of unit used (for example, marbles).

WHAT A MUDDLE!

To begin using standard units of mass and calibrated scales.

†† *Pairs.*

🕐 *10–15 minutes per step of the activity.*

Previous skills/knowledge needed

Children should have handled objects to compare their mass and used simple balances. They should have reached an understanding of the need to use standard units.

Key background information

Many young children mistakenly believe that size and mass are linked. They often think that the larger an object is, the heavier it must be. It is important for them to have experiences which will help to restructure this logical misconception into new learning. This activity provides such an experience.

Preparation

Six parcels need to be prepared and labelled. It is important that you follow the guidelines for both the size and mass. If you possibly can, start with twelve similar-sized containers, such as cuboid-shaped margarine tubs, as this will make the preparation considerably easier. In addition, you will need plenty of dry sand (or similar) to fill the tubs. Parcels A, D, and E will require one tub each. Parcel B will need two tubs. Parcel F will need four tubs and parcel C will need the last three tubs. Put sand in the tubs so that the finished parcels will weigh the following amounts: A = 100g, B = 600g, C = 850g, D = 150g, E = 250g, F = 400g. For parcels which include more than one tub, it is better to distribute the sand evenly between them. Bind the tub lids on with masking tape, and bind the tubs together, for parcels needing two or more. Then wrap each parcel in brown paper. When all the parcels

are wrapped, tie some string around them in two directions so that they look ready for posting. Label them with the letters A to F, as outlined above. As long as the letters are clear, there is no need for them to be too large. They could be placed where a stamp might eventually go. Get six tie-on labels and write a different person's name on each one, as follows: Mr Brown, Mr Green, Mrs Red, Mrs Silver, Mr White and Mrs Yellow. These will be for parcels A, B, C, D, E and F respectively; but do not attach the labels to the parcels. Make photocopies of sheets 113 to 116, one for each child.

Resources needed

Six prepared parcels and six tie-on labels with names as described, pan balances or bucket balances, metric weights and calibrated scales (50g intervals are sufficient) which are capable of weighing up to 2.5 kilograms, photocopies of sheets 113 to 116.

What to do

It is important that the activities in this lesson are completed in the specified order. Set up to four pairs of children working at intervals. They should all start from step (1).

Step 1: Put a balance, parcels A, B and C, and their labels on a table. Explain to the children that the parcels were wrapped up for posting, but that the secretary was called away on another job before she had had time to tie on the labels. Now the parcels are in a muddle and no one knows to whom each one should be sent. However, you have some clues which you are sure the children will be able to sort out for you. These three clues appear on worksheet 113. The children will need to look at the clues and order the parcels, using the pan balance without the weights. Once they have identified where the labels belong, get them to record their answers on the worksheet, and then give that worksheet in. They can then move on to step (2).

Step 2: This is the same as step (1), except that the children should have parcels A, D and E and their labels; and should record their answers on sheet 114, on which three more clues appear.

Step 3: This is the same again, but this time the children should have parcels B, C and F and their labels; and sheet 115 for the clues and for recording their answers.

Step 4: When the pairs of children have finished steps (1) to (3), let them have their recording sheets back and also give

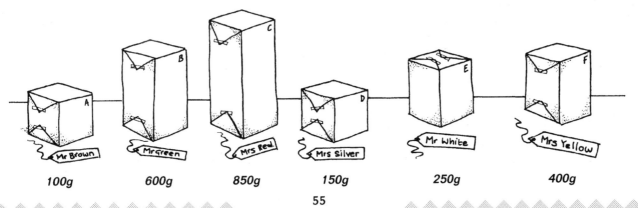

A — 100g · B — 600g · C — 850g · D — 150g · E — 250g · F — 400g

SHAPE, SPACE AND MEASURES

out copies of sheet 116. The children can now attach the labels to all six parcels. They should also weigh each parcel, using metric weights, and record their results. Finally, they can try to find two or more parcels which have a combined weight equalling a given amount. Some children may well be able to do this by addition, but should be encouraged to check by weighing the parcels together.

Suggestion(s) for extension

At step (4) give the children calibrated kitchen scales to use instead of the balance.

Suggestion(s) for support

Give the children only two parcels to order: at step (1) B and C; at step (2) A and D; at step (3) C and F. Get them to guess first, compare by handling, check with a balance, and finally find the parcels' mass with metric weights. (Do not use the photocopiable sheets with these pupils.)

Assessment opportunities

You will be able to assess a great deal from the written evidence, but you will not be able to see how the children deal with the tasks practically. Watch them to see if they order the parcels logically or if they have to repeatedly handle or weigh them. Are some children surprised by smaller parcels being heavier than larger ones? Do the children use the balance correctly? Do they add weights in a haphazard fashion or do they set about it systematically? Are they able to count and record the weights correctly? To find which parcels combine to make certain weights, do the children add their recorded answers, investigate using the scales, or use the scales only for the purpose of checking? Do the children using calibrated scales read the parcels' weights correctly? Do they understand that this is another way of finding the same information?

Opportunities for IT

Once the children have weighed the parcels with metric weights, they can record the weight of each parcel using graphing software. This will provide a bar chart of the six parcels. They can use this to work out further questions on the combined weights of parcels. For example:
▲ Which two parcels together weigh one kilogram?
▲ Which parcel weighs four times as much as parcel A?
▲ Which two parcels are closest together in weight?
   The children could also explore the sort options so that the graph is redrawn for them from heaviest parcel to lightest parcel.

Display ideas

The activities could form part of a topic about 'People who help us' or part of the work going on in the classroom post office. Related pictures, posters and post office forms (created by the children) could all add to the interest.

Reference to photocopiable sheets

Photocopiable sheets 113 to 116 contain the information which the children will require for steps (1) to (4). They are designed so that the children can fill in the blanks with their answers. This facilitates their recording so that time is not spent laboriously writing rather than concentrating on the practical task. These photocopiable pages are not suitable for pupils requiring support and working with only two parcels at a time.

SHAPE, SPACE
AND MEASURES

Capacity

Many people find capacity and volume difficult to estimate and are constantly surprised to find that a container holds a great deal more than anticipated. This is usually because we have not had sufficient experience of handling the article or quantity in question. Therefore we have no familiar mental image to judge by. How many of us remember the introduction of metric quantities of food, packaged in sizes which were unfamiliar? Suddenly, our ability to pour approximately half a pint of milk changed overnight as we tried to pour half a pint from a litre carton. It is important that we provide children with plenty of practical experience of capacity so that they can form their own mental images to recall and judge by in new and unfamiliar situations.

Gauging capacity and volume requires us to make a complex three-dimensional judgement and liquids seem to be particularly difficult to judge! The spilt cup of tea always goes much further than we expected! A solid shape is more manageable. We can manipulate our mental image of it, cutting, moving or counting the number of times it might occupy a particular space. Young children need to be involved in activities which help to build concepts about both capacity and volume, and much of their work will revolve around the associated language.

Capacity is the amount of space inside a hollow container and gives rise to the use of words such as 'full', 'empty', 'more' and 'less'. Gradually children will encounter more specific measurement with units of a litre and half-litre. Volume is the amount of space occupied by a solid shape and, by and large, is described in the same language as capacity.

SHAPE, SPACE
AND MEASURES

WHICH HOLDS MORE?

To use comparative language when measuring the capacity of two or more containers.

† *Pairs.*

🕐 *15 minutes.*

Previous skills/knowledge needed

Children need to have had experience of filling containers with sand and water and emptying them. They should be able to use 'full', 'nearly full', 'half-full' (approximately), 'nearly empty', 'empty', in the correct situation.

Key background information

Young children often have difficulty with the concept of capacity, especially when pouring liquid from a full but smaller container into a larger one. It is common for them to think that, because the larger container still has space for more liquid, the smaller container holds more because it was full to the brim.

Preparation

Decide whether to use sand or water for this task. Collect six containers. Two should have the same capacity but be different from each other in height. The other four make a set and you should mark them clearly A, B, C and D. One (A) is needed to set the 'standard'. B should hold less than A; C should hold more than A; and D should hold the same amount as A. Using sticky tape, fix a strip of paper or masking tape down the outside of vessels B, C and D. Prepare three labels on folded card so that they will stand up. These labels should be as follows: 'holds less than A', 'holds more than A', 'holds the same as A'.

Resources needed

Six containers and three labels (see 'Preparation'), dry sand or water, strips of paper or masking tape, washing-up bowl.

What to do

Work with one pair of children at a time, making sure that both are involved in the tasks and one is not just a passive observer. Using the two containers which have the same capacity, ask one of the children to fill one of them to the top, and intervene so that they can use previously learned language, such as 'nearly full'. When the container is full, ask whether the children think that the other container will hold more, less, or the same? Then get the second child to pour the contents very carefully from the first container into the second. (Have both containers inside a plastic washing-up bowl so that any spilt sand or water can be collected up and put into the appropriate container.) Again, ask the children whether the second container holds more than, less than or the same as the first. Get the first child to pour the contents back into the first container, and repeat the exercise again until you are sure that the children have understood the task. Then you can move on to the next activity using containers A, B, C and D, and the prepared labels.

First get one of the children to fill container A. Then ask about each of the containers B, C and D in turn. Each time ask the children if they think that the vessel in question will hold the same as A, less than A, or more than A. Get them to place the labels next to the containers as they predict their relative capacities. Now get the children to pour the contents from A into either B, C or D and mark on the strip of paper where the contents came to. (This is not possible on container B, which holds less than A.) Now they can refill A and repeat the exercise by filling one of the two remaining vessels. Finally, they refill A again and transfer the contents to the last empty vessel.

Suggestion(s) for extension

Provide the children with a large variety of containers which they should sort into sets, placing them inside one of three hoops. Let them investigate to find sets of containers which 'hold more than A', 'hold the same as A', and 'hold less than A'. They could record the outcome in pictures or writing.

Suggestion(s) for support

Any children who are having difficulty with predicting capacities need more practical experience. If you have used sand for the activity, let them repeat it with water, lentils, salt or rice. Each time they use a different resource it will look like a new task, as well as providing the extra experience and support needed.

Assessment opportunities

Observe the children and question them as they do the tasks. Are they using the correct language to make comparisons? As they get more experience, pouring from one vessel to another, are they beginning to get an 'eye' for capacity? Are there children who have difficulty understanding 'holds more than' when the container it applies to is not full?

Display ideas

The extension activity would provide not only a good starting point for a display but also a useful resource for other children to investigate and check. Any unusual containers that children bring in to school could be added. The class should first make some predictions of which set each new container might go in and check these out.

COUNTING CUPS

To compare the capacity of containers by measuring with non-standard units and counting the number required.

†† *Small groups.*

🕐 *15–20 minutes.*

Previous skills/knowledge needed

Pupils need to be able to count, fluently, the number of times that a smaller container is refilled in order to fill a larger one.

Key background information

Quantities measured are rarely exact. Therefore pupils will need to be able to talk about and record their work using language that describes approximate outcomes. Phrases such as 'and a little bit', 'nearly', 'about' and 'half' will enable them to describe what happens most clearly.

Preparation

Collect six to eight plastic bottles of varying shapes, heights and capacities, but with two or three of them having the same capacity. The children are going to find out how many eggcupfuls each bottle will hold. Check that the bottles do not require the children to count to a number beyond their experience. Mark each bottle with a different-coloured label or piece of sticky tape so that they are easy to identify, and note down how many eggcupfuls each bottle will hold. If you wish to use the arrow labels on photocopiable sheet 117 you may need two copies of the sheet depending on the number of bottles being used for the task.

Resources needed

Six to eight plastic bottles (selected and labelled as described in 'Preparation'), a funnel, an eggcup and a large washing-up bowl, sand, salt or lentils, squares of paper on which to record, pencil, sticky tape (optional) and arrows made from photocopiable page 117 (optional).

What to do

Start by showing the children the collection of bottles and their coloured marks. Explain to them that they are going to take it in turns, using the eggcup, to fill each bottle with sand (or salt or lentils). Show them how to do it by placing one of the bottles inside the bowl (to catch any spilt sand) and filling it up using the eggcup and funnel. Start counting as you do this, so that the children can count with you. Record the number of eggcupfuls needed to fill the bottle on a piece of

Capacity

paper. Empty the bottle and either stand it on the piece of paper or get one of the children to stick the piece of paper to the outside of the bottle. The children can then complete the task in the same way, filling each of the other bottles in turn and recording the number of eggcupfuls for each. Once the bottles have been filled and the amounts recorded, ask the children to put them in order, either from the least number of eggcupfuls to the most, or vice versa. You may find the labels made from photocopiable page 117 useful for this part of the task.

Suggestion(s) for extension

Two or three of the bottles, although different in shape, will be found to hold the same amount. If the children are allowed to use the eggcup to fill only one of the bottles, how can they prove that the others hold the same amount too? This will enable you to assess their understanding of conservation. They should suggest tipping the sand from one bottle to the next. The sand should fill each one to its top, thus proving that their capacities are the same.

Suggestion(s) for support

Reduce the number of containers to four, each with a different capacity. You may find that you also need to replace the eggcup with a larger vessel, such as a teacup or mug.

Assessment opportunities

Observe the children as they fill the containers. Are they filling them to the brim and keeping an accurate count? Have they used appropriate language when less than a whole

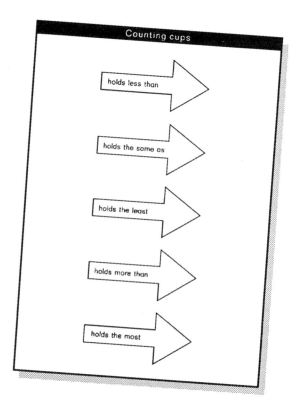

eggcupful is required to finish filling the container? Have they ordered the bottles correctly? Were they able to use the arrows correctly? How did they overcome the problem of ordering the containers that held the same amount? Which children understood conservation? Can they describe how some containers which appear to be very different in size and shape can still have the same capacity?

Opportunities for IT

The children could use simple graphing or pictogram software to record the capacity of the different containers. The results can be sorted to put the different containers into order. If different groups use different substances to measure with (sand, salt, sugar, water) the results can be compared to show that the capacity of a given container is the same whatever the substance used to measure it.

Display ideas

The results from the children's work could be used to make a pictorial block graph, with pictures of eggcups representing the numbers required to fill each container. Discuss with the children what they should do when a half-full eggcup is also needed.

Reference to photocopiable sheet

Photocopiable sheet 117 contains arrows with parts of sentences printed on them. Children need to have the arrows to place and move around as they reflect on their task. If the arrows are laminated to extend their lifetime, they will prove useful for many activities involving ordering containers according to their capacity.

SHAPE, SPACE AND MEASURES

TEDDY BEARS' PICNIC

To use simple instruments for measuring capacity and volume and understand the need for a standard unit.

†† *Two groups of four children.*

🕐 *25–30 minutes.*

Previous skills/knowledge needed

Pupils need to have had earlier experiences of filling containers and counting the number of non-standard units required to fill them to the brim.

Key background information

Capacity is to do with the amount of space inside a hollow container. It can be measured by using liquids and other materials which have a pouring quality, such as sand, salt and lentils. Volume is to do with the amount of space occupied by a solid shape, for example the number of cubes needed to fill an empty box. In both cases a quantity has to be counted in order to communicate the information.

Preparation

Collect the following picnic equipment: a teapot, an empty litre bottle (one which previously held a fruit cordial would be ideal), a half-litre jug and an empty sugar box. You will also need two different sets of four small containers plus some cubes, to use as non-standard units. The following ideas may be helpful:

▲ Set A – eggcup, teacup, small basin, small jug, plus 2cm interlocking plastic cubes or wooden cubes;

▲ Set B – 35mm film container, spice jar, yoghurt pot, small plastic bottle, plus 2cm interlocking plastic cubes or wooden cubes.

Make sufficient photocopies of sheet 118.

Resources needed

Equipment for the picnic (see 'Preparation'), two sets of small containers plus 2cm plastic or wooden cubes, lentils, water and funnel, photocopies of sheet 118.

What to do

You may wish to link this lesson with some storytelling, for example using the fairy tale *Goldilocks and the Three Bears* or the song *The Teddy Bears' Picnic,* and ask the children to bring in their teddy bears to set the scene. Start by explaining to the children that they are going to help the bears to get ready for a picnic, and to make sure that they take the correct amounts with them. The bears want to take enough for everyone but do not want any left over to have to carry home again.

The first group of four children should start with the containers and cubes making up set A. Each child should choose one of the small containers (to use as the non-standard unit) and a piece of picnic equipment. The child who takes the sugar box will also have the cubes. Tell the children to use their small container to fill their item of picnic equipment with lentils, counting how many containerfuls they need. They can work in pairs, as long as both children get the opportunity to measure practically. Except for the child with the sugar box (who should repeat the activity using the cubes), the children should next count the number of containerfuls of water they need to fill their piece of picnic

SHAPE, SPACE
AND MEASURES

cubes as they remove them. Later, get them to refill the box again, this time, counting as they go. At each stage they will need to record the information.

Assessment opportunities

Have the children measured as accurately as possible? Did their second set of measures (using water) match the first? How do the children react when they find that the sugar box, when using cubes, has the same results for both groups? Can they explain why? Can any children pose a solution to the problem?

Display ideas

If you have done the 'Tubby teddies' activity (see page 51) and based a display on that, this task could also be part of it. The children now have another opportunity to extend their knowledge of the different ways in which to record data. Use the picnic equipment as an interactive display for estimating quantities. Provide some additional small containers to be used as non-standard measures.

Reference to photocopiable sheet

Photocopiable sheet 118 is an aid for recording measurements in the course of the practical task. Children will need to write in the number required and the name of the non-standard measure they are using. It should not be seen as the only possible method of recording the results. However, the sheet does allow children to see a structure that can help them to organise their information and assist later discussions. The data could also be presented graphically for a more visual display.

equipment. The group can record all their results on photocopiable sheet 118.

When the first group has finished, a second group of children should repeat the activity, using set B containers, and record their information, as before. Once both groups have finished, bring them together to share their information. Let them discuss their work. Give them an opportunity to suggest why there are differences in all but one of their results (the cubes into the sugar box should be the same in both cases). Ask them what would happen if they used only the smallest container from each set for measuring, they used only one container and so on. It is important that your questioning enables pupils to reflect on the problems of having a range of results which, except for the cubes in the sugar box, cannot be compared.

Suggestion(s) for extension

Ask the children to devise their own method of recording the information which they will need to communicate clearly with another group. As a group, they could use pieces of card, folded so they will stand up, to display their results. Each card would be used for their recorded information and could be placed in front of the appropriate container. This activity could also provide an opportunity for children to record their results graphically as a block or bar chart.

Suggestion(s) for support

It may help to have pairs, rather than fours, working on the task. Let the two children work together to fill the teapot, jug and bottle using one of the small containers. Then tell the children to fill them again using another small container, then another and finally the last of the four small containers. Get them to fill the sugar box with the cubes. They can count the

Teddy bears' picnic

Children's names _____ Date _____

1. The teapot contains:
   ☐ _____ of lentils and
   ☐ _____ of water.

2. The squash bottle contains:
   ☐ _____ of lentils and
   ☐ _____ of water.

3. The jug contains:
   ☐ _____ of lentils and
   ☐ _____ of water.

4. The sugar box contains:
   ☐ _____ of lentils and
   ☐ _____ of cubes.

SHAPE, SPACE AND MEASURES

Capacity

GUESS AND TEST!

To refine estimating skills and use standard units.

†† *Rotating groups.*

🕐 *45–50 minutes.*

Previous skills/knowledge needed

Pupils need to have had experience of estimating in non-standard measures. They should understand litres as a measure of capacity and cubes as a way of measuring volume.

Key background information

Capacity and volume are both difficult to estimate. It is hard to get a 'mental picture' of them to manipulate. Some people find that it is easier to judge volume because they can manipulate 'solid' images of a series of blocks, stacking and counting them. It is essential that children have plenty of opportunities to estimate, to manipulate images and, finally, to measure.

Preparation

Decide how many groups you will divide the class into. You will need to collect that number of sets of equipment. Each set consists of three or four containers, as varied as possible in height, shape and capacity (mark each one with a letter or colour to make it easy to identify) and an empty box with the right dimensions to take 2cm cubes with as little wasted space as possible. You will also need 2cm wooden or plastic cubes; some dry material for measuring capacity (for example, sand, dried peas, lentils, birdseed or rabbit food); a litre measuring jug or bottle, a funnel, and paper and pencils. You may wish to make the boxes yourself, from cardboard, so that the volume of each is 24 cubic centimetres. The internal measurements will need to be slightly larger than shown to ensure that the boxes accommodate the cubes with ease. The measurements of the boxes (length × breadth × height) are as follows:

1) 24 × 1 × 1
2) 12 × 2 × 1
3) 8 × 3 × 1
4) 4 × 3 × 2

Resources needed

Several sets of equipment (see 'Preparation'), each on a separate table.

What to do

Start with the whole class together. Get them to recap on any work they have done previously on measuring the capacity of containers. If necessary, remind them how they measured different containers using a litre measure. Fill a litre bottle with water and pour it into a litre bowl so that they have an image of a litre to help them when estimating. Explain that they are going to work in groups and move from one table to another. On each table they will find different containers and different materials to use for measuring capacity. Send each group to a table to start. You will give them five minutes there to estimate (guess) the capacity of each of the containers in litres and the number of cubes to fit in their box. They can work collaboratively, and will need to write down their estimates. At the end of the five minutes each group must move on to another table and repeat the activity. When each group has visited each table, everyone will come back to the carpet area to make a table together of all their estimates on the flip chart.

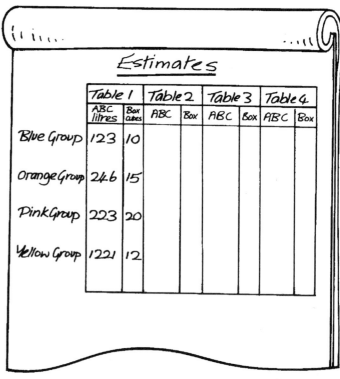

Estimates

	Table 1 ABC litres	Table 1 Box cubes	Table 2 ABC	Table 2 Box	Table 3 ABC	Table 3 Box	Table 4 ABC	Table 4 Box
Blue Group	123	10						
Orange Group	246	15						
Pink Group	223	20						
Yellow Group	1221	12						

Next the group should go back to the tables where they started, but this time measure the capacity of the containers, using the litre jug, funnel and measuring material. They will thus find out (test) how near their estimates were to the actual measurements. This time they can fit the cubes into their box. Again they will need to record their results. As before, the groups should repeat this activity at each table, and finally come back to the carpet area so that all the capacities can be recorded and everyone can discuss the results.

Suggestion(s) for extension

Provide the children with different containers and get them to estimate how many half-litres each contains. Then they should check their estimates by actual measuring. Also, see if the children can make different-shaped cuboids with plastic interlocking cubes. Each cuboid they make must contain 36 cubes.

Suggestion(s) for support

It may be too soon for some pupils to estimate with litres. Let them measure the capacities of eight containers and sort them into three sets:
▲ holds more than a litre;
▲ holds a litre;
▲ holds less than a litre.

Assessment opportunities

Try to observe some of the children as they begin to estimate. Are they making wild guesses or are they making judgements by 'eye'? Are the children collaborating? Are they observing or listening to others, in order to learn several techniques for estimating? Are they using the litre measure with care and counting accurately? Are the groups becoming more able to estimate as they move from table to table? Are children filling the boxes by using all the space available and counting accurately?

Display ideas

Use the activity as a starting point for an interactive display. Change the containers regularly and get the children to estimate, sometimes in litres and sometimes in half-litres. Let them put their estimates on to pieces of paper with their name, and post them into a class postbox. Review them when appropriate. Get the children to measure the capacity of the containers so that they can find out if their ability to estimate is improving.

Time

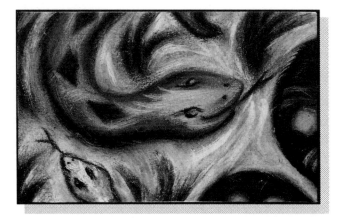

Time is measured using a non-metric system. Children's previous experience using metric units cannot help them when they come to learn the standard measures for time. In order to measure,time, children have to understand how two hands move around the clock-face. One whole revolution of the minute-hand measures the passing of one hour, but the hour-hand, moving only one-twelfth of the way round the dial, has also measured the passing of an hour. The hour-hand's movement marks sixty minutes, but the minute-hand's marks only five minutes. How strange that movement from one number to the next can equal sixty or five!

In the early stages of learning to measure, children compare and order objects. But time cannot be measured by direct comparison in the same way. Instead, it becomes necessary to compare two activities which are taking place at the same time in order to find out who, or which task, takes less or more time. When children measure length or mass, they can check their measurements. With time, this is not possible because time has moved on!

Early on, children's number work is often supported through the use of number lines. They are taught to read from left to right, to begin at one or zero, to count on and then... they encounter the clock-face. Suddenly the number twelve becomes the starting or ending point and it is necessary to start from one place, read around a dial to another, while also noting the position of the hour-hand. It is not surprising that most teachers (and parents) find teaching children to tell the time a challenge. It is important to develop the concept of time gradually, so that pupils become aware of the passage of time as well as learning to read the time from a clock-face.

SHAPE, SPACE
AND MEASURES

FAST FUN!

To compare and order events using language associated with time.

✝✝ *Four pairs.*

🕐 *5 minutes per task.*

Previous skills/knowledge needed

Pupils need to have done plenty of preparatory work on matching and ordering events: for example, matching events associated with a particular time of the day or week, and ordering activities which follow routines and days of the week.

Key background information

A clock is a measuring instrument and the rotation of its hands is one of many visible signs of the passage of time. Others include the changing seasons, night following day, and the ageing process of living things. Young children are usually more interested in the passage of time, anticipating the next exciting event, than they are in measuring time. They need to know that the passage of time can be measured by reading a dial on a clock. We cannot use direct comparison to measure time. However, two events which take place at the same time can be compared to see which takes the shorter or longer time. This is a complex concept and needs to be taught in gradual stages, constantly reinforced with activities and language work.

Preparation

Make eight stand-up labels. Four should have 'faster' written on them and the remaining four, 'slower'. Collect the resources required for the activities.

Resources needed

Large wooden beads and two laces, interlocking plastic cubes, pegs and two pegboards, dried peas, two spoons, two identical empty containers which can be filled to their brims with the dried peas, four 'faster' and four 'slower' stand-up labels.

What to do

Gather together the eight children and explain the four tasks to them:

▲ to thread beads on a lace until either a required number have been threaded or the lace is full;

▲ to use interlocking plastic cubes to build two towers 10 cubes high;

▲ to place a required number of pegs into a pegboard;

▲ to use a spoon to scoop up dried peas and fill a container with them to the brim.

Each pair of pupils is to be given the materials for one of these tasks. Then each of the two children must work as quickly as possible to see who can finish the task faster. Once the pairs of children have their resources, start them

all together. The first one to finish in each pair can place the appropriate label in front of their completed task. You may wish to record who finishes faster from each pair before they exchange resources and try another activity. Discussion should centre around the time taken. Who is faster and who is slower?

Suggestion(s) for extension

Ask the children which activities they think are faster and which slower to complete. Tell them to work in threes on a task they consider fast. As each child finishes, get them to record as follows: first to complete – 'fastest', second to complete – 'faster', third to complete – 'fast'. Tell them to do another task which they consider slow and record, 'slow', 'slower', 'slowest'.

The children could then work in fours, each child having a different resource as outlined, and seeing which out of the four tasks is the fastest and slowest. The results can be ordered.

Suggestion(s) for support

You may find some children need to start by having a different task from their partner, so that they can record which task is fast and which task is slow to do.

Assessment opportunities

Assessment will need to centre around the children's use of language. Do they extend their vocabulary to include 'quicker', 'shorter' or 'longer'? Do they order slow activities correctly? How do they overcome the problem of ordering four activities?

Display ideas

Have a display about things that move slowly or quickly, and activities that are faster or slower to do.

SHAPE, SPACE AND MEASURES

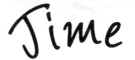

Time

HOW LONG DOES IT TAKE?

To use arbitrary units when measuring time and understand the need for a standard unit.

✝✝ *Rotating groups.*

🕐 *10 minutes per task.*

Previous skills/knowledge needed
Pupils will need to be able to count beyond 20.

Key background information
Measuring the duration of an event by counting shows that the passage of time can be given a numerical label. This can help pupils to understand the quantitative aspect of time. Similarly, a digital clock 'counts' the time. This is just one of the many stages children need to pass through before they embark on 'telling' the time.

Preparation
Decide whether you are going to base this on activities in the classroom, or to introduce it as part of a PE lesson, and collect the appropriate resources. Suggestions for activities are:

▲ filling a tin with marbles, one at a time;
▲ writing their name 10 times;
▲ building a tower with bricks;
▲ threading beads on a lace;
▲ skipping twenty times;
▲ walking along benches;
▲ hopping across the hall on one leg.

A pendulum can be made by tying a small weight to some string and suspending it in an open doorway. The hanging string should measure 1 metre. A water clock can be made from any simple plastic carton, such as a 568ml cream carton. Pierce a very small hole in the base with a sewing needle and then cover the hole, inside, with Plasticine. Fill the carton with water and gently pierce the Plasticine up through the base with an extremely fine needle so that a regular drip of water is produced. If the water runs through too quickly, it is easy to stem the flow by pressing down on the Plasticine with the unsharpened end of a pencil.

Resources needed
Equipment for activities, for example marbles, bricks, beads, laces, tin, skipping-rope, PE equipment; timing equipment – ball, drum, water clock, xylophone, egg-timer, metronome, pendulum (see 'Preparation'); flip chart; digital stopwatch (for extension work).

What to do
Explain to the children that they are going to move in their groups from one activity to the next. At each one, one member of the group will complete the task while the others watch and count how long it takes. They must use the same method for counting each time and record the number for each activity. Each group should choose a different method of counting from the following:

▲ handclaps;
▲ regular beats on a drum;
▲ bouncing a ball;
▲ drips from a water clock;
▲ beats on a xylophone;
▲ egg-timer turns;
▲ metronome;
▲ swings of a pendulum.

Make sure that one group uses a method which produces regular counts, for example a metronome. When all the tasks have been completed, bring the groups together and discuss the results. It helps to record their information in table form on a flip chart, so that they can see that the first task took 15 claps, 20 drips, 8 drum beats and so on.

Discussion needs to focus on which group was the quickest or slowest at a particular task. How do they know?

How long does it take?				
Name of task	Group 1 (claps)	Group 2 (drips)	Group 3 (drum beats)	Group 4 (pendulum swings)
Write name 10 times	15	20	8	10
Build a tower – 15 bricks	21	22	18	19
Thread 15 beads				
Skip 20 times				

Can they repeat a task and check their results? Let them demonstrate to the whole class how they clapped, or beat the drum or counted the water drips, so that they can begin to see the problems of using arbitrary measures.

Suggestion(s) for extension
Children could be asked to see how many beads they can thread, or how often they can write their name, in a certain

SHAPE, SPACE AND MEASURES

Time

time. For example: 'How many beads can you thread in ten handclaps?' They should guess first, record their guess and then do the task and record the outcome. Were they quicker or slower than their guess?

Alternatively, children could work in pairs, each participating in two activities and watching and recording for the other. Can they record how many claps it takes to fill the tin with marbles, and how many claps it takes to build the brick tower? Which task does each child complete more quickly/slowly? Are they both quicker at the same task? Let them repeat the tasks, timing them with a digital stopwatch.

Suggestion(s) for support

Some children have difficulty counting beyond ten. Give them an egg-timer as their counting tool. If it takes 30 to 60 seconds to empty, they are not likely to have to turn it over more than five or six times.

Assessment opportunities

During the discussion period look for the children who begin to see a problem with using different methods for counting and recording. Does any child suggest that they should all use the same method? Who notices that sometimes a group claps faster than on another occasion? Has anyone noticed that the metronome beats at regular intervals?

Display ideas

The children could make a large chart with all the data they have collected from the activities. Use two of the activities and a metronome to provide some investigative work for children to do in their spare moments. Which task are they quicker at?

photocopiable page 120 for children who require extra support, and prepare extra game cards from sheets 121 and 122 for children needing extension work. For all cards, the photocopied sheets can be mounted on card and then laminated for durability before being cut out.

Resources needed

A classroom clock with the minute-hand removed, a set of 24 o'clock cards, a story that makes references to time, for example *The Bad-tempered Ladybird* by Eric Carle (Puffin, 1982) or the extract from *Alice's Adventures in Wonderland* by Lewis Carroll (Puffin, 1994) when the White Rabbit is late.

What to do

Start by reading your chosen story to the children, drawing particular attention to the time elements by demonstrating them on a clock-face. Follow this by playing the game 'Am I on time?' The 24 o'clock cards should be placed in a pile, face down, in the middle of the group. One child should start by moving the hour-hand on the clock to point to a number, for example, 2. She should state the time and ask the question as follows: 'It's two o'clock. Am I on time?' The child to this first one's left takes a card from the top of the pile and reads what it says to provide the answer: for example, 'No, you're not on time because it's five o'clock.'

The clock is passed to the child with the card, who moves the hand to show five o'clock, places the card back at the bottom of the pile, and asks: 'It's five o'clock. Am I on time?' The child on his left picks up the next card and so on. Should a card and the time on the clock agree, the child with the clock scores a point, because she *is* on time. The clock is then passed to the child to the left, who moves the hand to a new time and asks, 'It's... o'clock. Am I on time?' as usual. Play can continue until everyone in the group has had three turns, or for as long as interest is maintained. It is important, when the time has been correct, that the next child moves

AM I ON TIME?

To begin using standard units of time.

†† *Large group.*

🕐 *20–25 minutes.*

Previous skills/knowledge needed

Pupils should understand taking turns to participate in a game.

Key background information

The hour-hand moves one-twelfth of a full revolution during the course of an hour and this movement is usually too small for young children to notice. They need to be made aware of this gradual movement from an early stage so that they begin to understand that the hour-hand can provide information about half- and quarter-hours, as well as the o'clock times.

Preparation

Make two copies of photocopiable page 119 and use them to make a set of 24 o'clock cards. Make sufficient copies of

SHAPE, SPACE
AND MEASURES

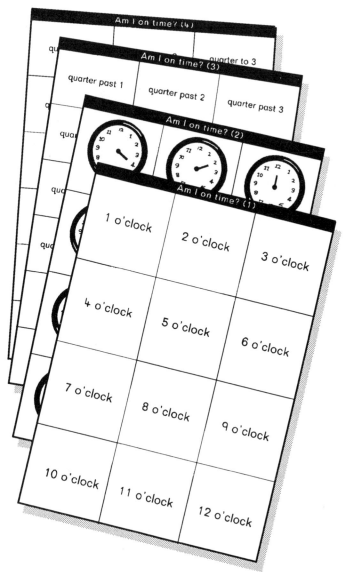

the hand to a new position and states the time, demonstrating where to position the hand.

Picking up a card from the pile is a reading and matching activity. Positioning of the hour-hand gives you further information to form assessment judgements.

Suggestion(s) for extension

See if the children can play the game by saying whether they are too late or too early for an appointment instead of 'on time'. This work can lead on to practising 'quarter past', 'quarter to' and 'half past'. Photocopiable sheets 121 and 122 can be used to make extra game cards for children who are confident with the o'clock times. Make sure that the children understand halves and quarters when applied to linear measurement. They should then be able to apply it to the distance between numbers on the clock, seeing, for example, that the hand has travelled a quarter of the way past 2, or has another quarter of the distance to travel to get to 3.

Suggestion(s) for support

Use the cards made from photocopiable sheet 120 so that the children have a picture of the time as well as the written

time to match to the clock time. When they no longer need the support of the picture, let them play the game using the o'clock cards.

Assessment opportunities

Most of the assessment will come from observing the children playing the game. Are they placing the hour-hand accurately? Are there any pupils who use 'too early' or 'too late' without being prompted? Does any child make a reference to where the minute-hand might be if one was present? These are all clues to their stage in understanding.

Display ideas

See if you can make a collection of old clocks and watches as a starting point for a shop window. Any resources that can be used for measuring time can also be added: water clocks, sundials, candle clocks, a metronome or a pendulum. Put out the o'clock cards from the game so that children can take a card and set all the clock-faces to show the time on the card. The clocks will all tell the same time, as in a real jeweller's shop window.

Reference to photocopiable sheets

Photocopiable sheet 119 should be copied twice to make a set of 24 cards for use in the game 'Am I on time?' Photocopiable sheets 120, 121 and 122 can be used to make more game cards. Photocopiable sheet 120 may be helpful for those children requiring picture clues, whereas photocopiable sheets 121 and 122 can be used to extend those children who are confidently using the o'clock times. With such children, you may prefer to start by using only the 'half past' and 'quarter past' times, leaving 'quarter to' times until a later occasion.

RACE AGAINST TIME

To refine the use of standard units of time.
†† *Small groups or pairs.*
🕐 *20 minutes.*

Previous skills/knowledge needed

Pupils should know the o'clock times and be aware of the moving position of the hour-hand. They should know which side of the clock-face deals with 'past' and which with 'to' times.

Key background information

'Past' and 'to' times need to be introduced very gradually to avoid lasting problems. Some pupils find counting forwards or backwards from 12 very confusing, although some may have coped quite well with quarter- and half-hours. The symmetrical positioning of numbers on the clock-face is helpful. The position of the minute-hand pointing to 2 is an

SHAPE, SPACE AND MEASURES

exact reflection of the position of the minute-hand pointing to 10. In both positions, it means ten minutes. The difference is whether they are past or to.

Preparation

Make three large dice. Two need to be cubes and one needs to be a dodecahedron (12 regular pentagons for the faces). The dice need to be large enough to have a label on each face. The dodecahedron dice is the 'hour dice', and its faces should be numbered 1 to 12. One cube-shaped dice is for 'minutes past'. Label its faces: 5 minutes past, 10 minutes past, quarter past, 20 minutes past, 25 minutes past, half past. The other is for 'minutes to'. Label its faces: half past, 25 minutes to, 20 minutes to, quarter to, 10 minutes to, 5 minutes to.

Dice can be made using mathematical nets and strong card or from plastic interlocking polygons (such as Clixi or Polydron). Make sufficient photocopies of sheet 123, one for each child.

Resources needed

Two cube-shaped dice and one dodecahedron dice with their faces labelled (see 'Preparation'), photocopies of sheet 123, pencils or felt-tipped pens.

What to do

Explain to the children how to play the game. Give them each a copy of sheet 123. To begin, they will need the dodecahedron dice, which shows hours, and the 'minutes past' dice. Roll the 'hour' dice first. The child with the highest

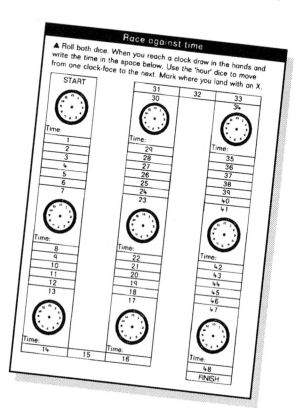

number starts the game. Play proceeds by each child in turn rolling both dice together and using the information to draw in the hands and write the time below the clock-faces on the sheet. The 'hour' dice is used to move around the game sheet. Boxes that are landed on should be marked with an 'X'. No clocks should be passed even if a higher number than required is thrown. The first to complete all the clocks is the winner. When the children are confident using the 'minutes past' dice, exchange it for the 'minutes to' dice.

Suggestion(s) for extension

Give the children all three dice to play the game. They will need to alternate the dice for the minutes, so that the first clock is a 'past' time and the next is a 'to' time and so on.

Suggestion(s) for support

Let the children concentrate only on 'minutes past'. Later introduce the 'minutes to' dice and finally let them use both a 'minutes' and the 'hour' dice. Do not rush these three steps.

Assessment opportunities

The completed record sheets will provide evidence of the children's ability to use standard units of time, including minutes. However, a short period of observation will alert you to any problems. It is important to be aware of these early on, so that the game can be adjusted to accommodate a pupil's stage of learning. There is no reason why a child cannot use a different minutes dice from the others in the group if she is having difficulties.

Display ideas

If you have a collection of clocks and watches in the classroom let the children choose one of the clocks to draw. Ask them to draw in both hands and write the time below, as they did in the game. Use the completed drawings as a background to the class clock display. Can the children use their clock drawings to tell a story where time is an important factor?

Reference to photocopiable sheet

Photocopiable page 123 is the game sheet as well as the record sheet for each child, as play proceeds.

SHAPE, SPACE AND MEASURES

Assessment

The activities contained within this section are designed to provide additional support for teachers when assessing pupils' understanding in Shape, Space and Measures. While there have been assessment opportunities outlined for all the activities in the previous chapters, the following tasks may assist teachers who require further evidence of children's learning and understanding. The tasks may also be useful to assess the knowledge and understanding of particular pupils formatively in order to plan a suitable programme of work. This is particularly helpful when awaiting the records of a child who has transferred from another school midway through the year.

The activities have been designed to assess more than one learning objective at a time and guidance is offered on what to look for and on how to interpret the outcomes. However, it is important to remember that three-dimensional work is only one component of the National Curriculum section on Shape, Space and Measures. Therefore to talk about achievement in levels is only appropriate when all the component parts are under scrutiny. It is only then that a level which best describes a pupil's performance can be applied to the attainment target of Shape, Space and Measures.

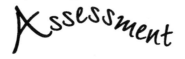
SORTING 3-D SHAPES

To describe properties of 3-D shapes using everyday language. To describe shapes using mathematical names. To recognise and describe mathematical properties including the numbers of edges and corners. To classify shapes according to mathematical criteria. To recognise reflective symmetry in simple cases.

†† *Groups of two to four children or individuals.*

🕐 *15–20 minutes for each activity.*

Key background information

Children can, if you wish, do both of these activities practically, with oral responses and with no requirement for written recording. Activities can be done individually, particularly with less able children who may need support with reading. They may also be conducted with up to four children using either the pupils' or teachers' recording sheets, or both, but because there are varying levels of achievement within this activity, assessing and recording becomes more difficult to manage. Initially, it may be better to work with only two pupils so that the experience helps you to refine your management strategies.

Children do not have to know the mathematical names of the solid shapes to be assessed at Level 1. However, they are required to know the names of solids (1) to (4) (see 'Resources needed') and to be able to describe solids according to mathematical properties to achieve Level 2. Children should be able to recognise reflective symmetry in simple cases. This may require further questioning on your part to be sure that children do understand this concept. They should be able to use mathematical names and classify solid shapes according to a range of mathematical properties, including symmetry at Level 3.

Preparation

You will need access to a large Carroll diagram and offcuts of card for children to make some of their own labels. A Carroll diagram may be made simply by drawing it on a large piece of sugar paper or card. The axes can be labelled using the criteria on photocopiable sheet 126 and kept in place with Blu-Tack. If pupils are going to record their work, then you will need to photocopy one example of sheet 124 and several of 125 for each child. Photocopy sheet 126 twice and cut along the lines to make the criteria labels (there are some empty spaces for any additional ideas). You may wish to photocopy page 127 which is an optional sheet to aid teachers when recording outcomes of pupils' assessment.

Resources needed

Photocopiable sheets 124, 125, 126, and 127 if required, a Carroll diagram, pencils, labels for the children to record on, a selection of solid shapes which should include the following: (1) cube, (2) cuboid, (3) sphere, (4) cylinder, (5) cone, (6) square pyramid, (7) triangular prism.

Try to have at least two examples of each shape but differing in size, for example two cuboids – one tall and thin, the other short and fat.

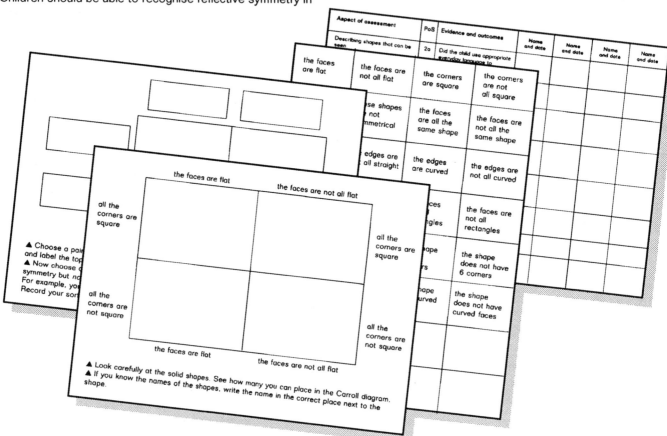

SHAPE, SPACE AND MEASURES

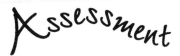

Assessment

What to do

First set out the Carroll diagram and label the axes in the same way as on photocopiable sheet 124. Place the collection of solid shapes around the edge of the diagram. Remind the children how to sort using the diagram. Explain to the children that they will take turns in choosing a solid shape, describing it, naming it if possible, and finally placing it in the correct segment of the diagram without any help from others. Tell them that when all the shapes have been sorted you will ask them some questions.

Outcome of sorting on the Carroll diagram when using sheet 124:

cube, cuboid
square pyramid, triangular prism
sphere, cylinder, cone.

When the solid shapes have been sorted, ask the children if all the shapes have been placed correctly. If they identify an incorrectly placed shape ask them where it should go and why. Ask them:

▲ What is the same about all the shapes sorted on the left-hand side of the diagram?

▲ What is different between the two sets on the left-hand side?

▲ What is the same about all the shapes on the lower half of the diagram?

▲ What is different between the two sets on the lower half of the diagram?

▲ Can they think of a reason why there is an empty segment?

The children can record on sheet 124 if required.

For the second activity children may record on photocopiable sheet 125. They will need sufficient copies to do several sorting arrangements. Set out the Carroll diagram and label one axis using criteria from photocopiable sheet 126 about faces, and label the other axis using criteria about edges or corners to provide the children with an example of what they need to do. Empty labels can be used either for the teacher or the child to add other mathematical properties for sorting the shapes. Make sure that during the activity

children have an opportunity to demonstrate their understanding of the symmetry of solid shapes by questioning them further.

Reference to photocopiable sheets

Photocopiable sheets 124 and 125 are for children's recording. Sheet 126 comprises a set of criteria with which to label the axes of the Carroll diagrams. The photocopiable teachers' recording sheet 127 provides some guidance on what to look for and how to interpret the outcomes when assessing individual children.

SHAPES AND PATTERNS

To describe properties of 2-D shapes using everyday language. To describe 2-D shapes using mathematical names. To recognise and describe geometrical features of shapes including the number of sides and corners. To classify shapes according to mathematical criteria. To recognise reflective symmetry in simple cases. To recognise right angles.

†† *Pairs or individuals.*

🕐 *15–20 minutes for each activity.*

Key background information

Pupils can be assessed on both activities through oral or written responses. However, more information is likely to be elicited orally. Both activities encompass some factual knowledge regarding the names and properties of shapes, and because of this the assessment of an individual child's knowledge needs careful management to ensure that his responses are unaided by his peers. Children achieving Level 1 do not have to know the mathematical names of all the shapes in the pattern. However, they should be able to distinguish five distinct shapes (square, rectangle, circle, pentagon and hexagon) and be able to describe the shapes in terms of *some* of their features, for example straight or

SHAPE, SPACE AND MEASURES

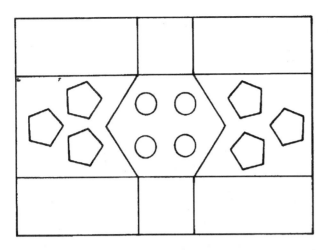

curved sides, or how many corners it has. Children achieving Level 2 should know the mathematical names of common shapes and be able to describe them in terms of their mathematical properties. The second activity, sheet 129, uses an investigative approach and provides opportunities for pupils to explore the properties of different types of triangles. They are not required to know their names, but the demands of the activity are in line with Level 3 where pupils can compare two-dimensional shapes and classify them in various ways using geometrical features, which may include reflective symmetry.

Preparation

Photocopy sheet 128 for each child and 129 for those likely to achieve Level 3. Children may find the triangles easier to manipulate if they are enlarged further when photocopying sheet 129. It may be necessary to cut out the triangles first for those children who cannot cut accurately. You may wish to photocopy page 130 which is an optional sheet to aid teachers when recording outcomes of pupil's assessment.

Resources needed

Photocopiable sheets 128 and 129 for each child, and 130 if required, pencils, mirrors, rulers, square corners, scissors.

What to do

First decide whether the children will do the activity orally or in writing. If you wish them to work alone and record their work, you will need to explain the details of the activity first, as outlined below. All children being assessed will need a copy of sheet 128.

Start by discussing the pattern on sheet 128. Ask the children to point out (or write down) the different shapes they can see within the pattern. Can they name each shape? Help can be given with spelling if they wish to record the information. Next ask the children to pick three of the shapes in the pattern and describe them using some of the following properties:

▲ Circle – has one edge, has a curved edge, or has no straight edges, is symmetrical;
▲ Square – 4 straight edges, sides are all the same length,

has 4 corners (or 4 vertices), has square corners, is symmetrical;
▲ Rectangle – 4 straight edges, 2 long sides and 2 short sides, opposite sides/edges are the same length, has 4 square corners, is symmetrical;
▲ Pentagon – a shape with 5 sides, this pentagon has 2 square corners, all the edges are straight, is symmetrical;
▲ Hexagon – a shape with 6 sides, all the edges are straight, is symmetrical.

When children describe a shape as being symmetrical, they need to point out the lines of symmetry. Finally, ask the children if there is anything special about the pattern. Direct teacher intervention should be avoided but you will need to try and elicit whether or not pupils are aware of the symmetry of the pattern. Can they demonstrate it either by folding, using a mirror or drawing one or two lines of symmetry? At Level 3 they should be able to recognise and classify using reflective symmetry as a property.

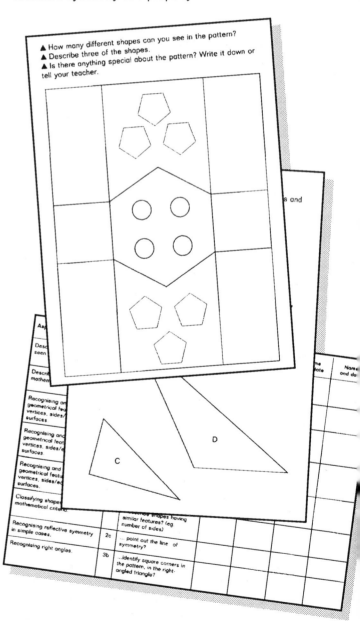

SHAPE, SPACE AND MEASURES

Children using sheet 129 will need to cut out the shapes. If they are not able to cut accurately they will need to be prepared beforehand. Explain to the children that there is only one question to answer but they then need to find out as much as they can about the four shapes and write down what they have found out. They can use any of the resources (mirrors, ruler, square corners) to help them.

The following information is for teachers and is *not* a requirement for pupils to know the mathematical names of the triangles: A = equilateral, B = isosceles, C = right-angled triangle (which is also scalene), D = scalene triangle (also obtuse-angled triangle).

Pupils should know that all the shapes are triangles and that triangles have three sides. They should be able to find out some of the following information: whether any of the triangles have sides the same length, if different triangles have sides of a similar length, if any have a square corner, whether any are symmetrical or can be folded so that the two halves match.

Reference to photocopiable sheets

Photocopiable sheets 128 and 129 are essential to the activities. There are written questions for pupils on both sheets to provide them with guidance as they work. The photocopiable teachers' recording sheet 130 provides some guidance on what to look for and how to interpret the outcomes when assessing individual children.

◆ POSITION, MOVEMENT AND SYMMETRY

To locate positions. To recognise reflective symmetry. To recognise quarter- and half-turns. To use language related to movement.

†† *Groups of up to three children and individuals.*

🕐 *15–20 minutes for group activity. 5 minutes for individual activity.*

Key background information

Simple tasks about position and movement (a dynamic process) are inevitably somewhat restricted in the range of language used and the understanding which can be assessed. It is important, therefore, to take account of evidence from previous work in mathematics and other curricular experiences to form your judgements about levels of achievement. The first activity on sheet 131 on position needs to be done individually. However the instructions can be read to pupils who require more support. The second and third tasks involving movement and symmetry require clear instructions and careful observation of pupils' responses and actions. Children should be able to understand simple positional instructions to achieve Level 1 and be able to recognise straight and simple turning movements at Level 2. At Level 3 this should include the movement of simple reflective symmetry.

Preparation

Photocopy sheets 131 and 132 for each child, and one copy of 133 for the group. Cut out the letters on page 133 along the lines.

Resources needed

Photocopiable sheets 131, 132 and 133, single-sided mirrors, rulers, red, orange, yellow, blue, green and black coloured pencils.

What to do

Provide each child with a copy of photocopiable sheet 131 and the required coloured pencils. Fluent readers can start the activity straightaway but you may feel it is helpful to read the instructions aloud first. Children who require support can have the instructions read to them step by step. It is important that the adult helper does not intervene if a child has problems understanding the positional language. However, if children have chosen the wrong coloured pencil, it is perfectly reasonable to point out their mistake.

Up to three children can be assessed together for the second and third activity. They will each need sheet 132 and a mirror to check for symmetry. Ask the children to look at

SHAPE, SPACE AND MEASURES

the shapes on photocopiable sheet 132. Using language that pupils are used to, ask them if they can point out a shape which is symmetrical. (They should not have any trouble recognising symmetry in the first example.) Next, demonstrate how to use the mirror to check that the first shape is symmetrical. Keep the page the correct way up (at all times) and place the mirror in a north/south orientation. The positioning of the page is important because other examples require the children to move the mirror a quarter-turn to check the symmetry of the shape. Ask them to check the remaining examples, making sure the page is kept the correct way up. When appropriate, ask the children what they have found out. You will need to ask them what they did with the mirror if the children are not forthcoming with this information. If they say they turned the mirror, ask them how much. Lastly, ask them what happens when they give the mirrors a half-turn. You may wish to note down if children can carry out this instruction.

The children can move on to the third activity involving the capital letters. It is important to have them all at the same side of the table when working so that each child has the same view of the letters and their relative positions. Spread out the set of capital letters on the desk and ask each child in turn to pick out letters which are symmetrical. Ask them to tell you about their letters. The children can use a mirror

and rotate or fold the letters if they find this helpful. This activity can continue for as long as you feel it is necessary to get the required evidence. As children work, ask them to explain what they need to do to check that a letter is symmetrical. This should elicit language linked to both movement and symmetry. Hopefully some children will notice that letters H, I, O and X have two lines of symmetry, and also that H, I, O, X, N, S and Z only require a half-turn to appear the correct way up, unlike all other letters.

Reference to photocopiable sheets
Photocopiable sheet 131 is to be coloured in and can provide permanent evidence. If you wish, sheet 132 can have the lines of symmetry drawn in by the children at the end of their investigation. Photocopiable sheet 133 provides a set of capital letters to be cut out (first being enlarged if necessary).

The middle one is yellow. The one on the right is green and the one on the left is red.
▲ Colour the circles first.
▲ Now colour all the bottom squares red.
Colour the square above the middle circle blue.
Colour the square below the green circle black.
Colour all the top squares orange.

LENGTH, MASS AND CAPACITY

To use the language associated with measures. To compare directly and indirectly. To measure with non-standard or standard units. To choose and use measuring instruments and read scales.

✝✝ *Small group of up to three children, working individually.*

🕐 *10–30 minutes depending on a child's ability.*

Key background information
The activity is practical and has an investigative approach. It should enable teachers to be able to assess a pupil's skills, knowledge and understanding of measurement and also many

of the elements contained in the Attainment Target 'Using and Applying'. Written evidence does not have to be recorded in a formal way, but if you also wish to assess some pupils' ability to communicate (PoS 3c) then they will need to present their information and results clearly using their own approach. The table on photocopiable sheet 134 may be helpful for other children, or they may prefer to write their information on pieces of paper placed next to the relevant containers, as in a display. At Level 1 children should be able to measure and order the containers by direct comparison of height, mass and capacity, filling one container and pouring the contents into the next to see whether it contains the same as or more than.

At Level 2 children should be measuring using non-standard and standard units. For example, they may compare capacity or mass using marbles as non-standard units and use centimetres for their linear measurements. At Level 3 they should be able to measure and use mainly standard metric units for this task.

Preparation

Photocopy sheet 134 for each child, cutting off the table and its instructions for those children devising their own methods of recording. Make a collection of three containers for each child. The containers should be different shapes and have different capacities so that there is the potential for children to demonstrate a wide range of their knowledge. A cuboid, cylinder and, if possible, a cube-shaped container would make a good collection. Label the containers A, B. and C to assist children when recording. Put all the measuring equipment and materials on a separate table alongside where the children will be working so that they can select the resources they require as they work.

Resources needed

Photocopiable sheet 134, writing materials and the following equipment: rulers, tape-measures, pan scales, a set of weights up to and including 1kg, kitchen scales, a calibrated measuring cylinder/jug, spoons, plastic cup and an eggcup. They will need a range of non-standard units to use for length, capacity and mass: for example, straws, string, lollipop sticks, conkers, dried peas, bottle tops, marbles, shells, Multilink or similar, lentils, sand, rice or small pasta.

What to do

Provide each child with photocopiable sheet 134 and their own set of containers. Explain to them that you wish them to find out as much as possible about their containers by measuring them in a variety of ways. Tell them that they will need to write down what they find out. If some children find this approach too open-ended it may help to break the activity down into smaller tasks to take place over a longer period of time. For example, it could be broken down into three tasks by asking the following questions:

▲ What can you find out from measuring how tall and how wide the three containers are?
▲ What can you find out by weighing them?
▲ What can you find out about how much they contain?

You will need to observe how the children begin their work and from time to time during the activity. Are they able to identify what they need to do and to select the appropriate materials? Are they able to find their own ways of overcoming any difficulties? Do they use the measuring equipment correctly? Do they check their results, particularly if they appear to be unexpected?

When the children have finished they will need to have an opportunity to discuss their results with you. By using an open-ended approach when questioning them they will be able to demonstrate their understanding and provide further evidence of their achievement. Some of the questions which follow may be of help.

▲ Can you tell me which is the biggest/smallest container? How do you know?
▲ If this is the tallest does it hold the most? Tell me how you know.
▲ Which one weighs the least when empty? Does this mean it holds the least as well?
▲ Why did you choose to weigh with Multilink and not conkers?

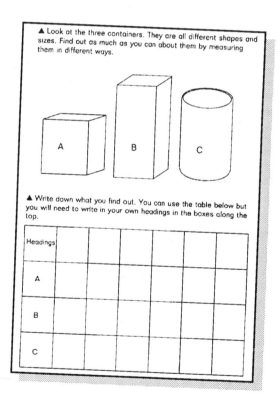

Reference to photocopiable sheet

Photocopiable sheet 134 provides the context of the activity and a simple method of recording, in the form of a table, for children who require it. They will need to write in their own headings on the table.

SHAPE, SPACE
AND MEASURES

TIME

To read and interpret standard units of time in hours and half-hours. To read and interpret standard units of time in quarter-hours and minutes. To read and measure the passage of time.

†† *Individuals.*

🕐 *10 minutes for each activity.*

Key background information

The activities are only appropriate for pupils who are using standard units of time. The measurement of time from a dial clock-face is complex and some pupils progress through the stages very slowly. To take account of this, photocopiable sheets 135, 136 and 137 increase in difficulty so that children can be withdrawn from the task once they reach a ceiling in their own level of understanding. The activities could also be done practically, using a geared classroom clock. You will need to ensure that the hands on the clock can be accurately positioned and also that the children are made aware of the need to correctly position the clock hands, particularly the hour-hand, when recording. Photocopiable sheet 138 deals with measuring the passage of time and also increases in difficulty.

The demands of the activities are in line with the requirements for Levels 2 and 3.

Preparation

Photocopy the appropriate sheets depending on the degree of difficulty (135, 136, 137 and 138) for each child unless the task is to be done orally using a clock-face.

Resources needed

Photocopiable sheets 135, 136, 137, 138, writing materials, geared classroom clock, clock-faces for pupils to use while recording.

What to do

Start by explaining the task on the first photocopiable sheet to the children. Explain the importance of the positioning of the clock hands and the movement of the hour-hand as it travels from one hour to the next. Demonstrate this movement using a geared clock and give the children a few examples of the hour-hand's position for both an o'clock and half-past time as a reminder. When ready, provide each child with a copy of the first sheet to complete. Once the children are ready to move on to the next photocopiable sheets demonstrate the positions of the hands again, as defined by the tasks, before they embark on their recording. Finally, for sheet 138, explain to the children that they need to look at both times on the clock-faces to find how much time has passed before they can record it.

Reference to photocopiable sheets

The photocopiable sheets cover the following stages of difficulty: 135 – hour and half-hour times, 136 – quarter past and quarter to the hour, 137 – 5, 10, 20, 25 minutes past and to the hour, 138 – the passage of time in minutes, and hours and minutes.

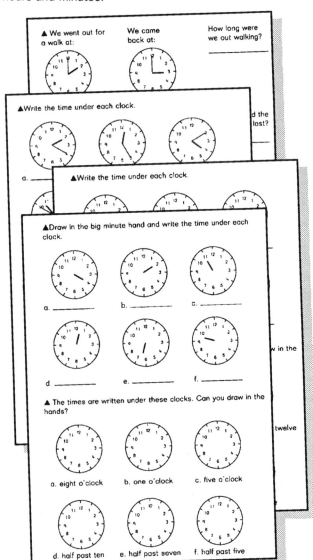

**SHAPE, SPACE
AND MEASURES**

Photocopiables

The pages in this section can be photocopied for use in the classroom or school which has purchased this book, and do not need to be declared in any return in respect of any photocopying licence.

They comprise a varied selection of both pupil and teacher resources, including pupil worksheets, resource material and record sheets to be completed by the teacher or children. Most of the photocopiable pages are related to individual activities in the book; the name of the activity is indicated at the top of the sheet, together with a page reference indicating where the lesson plan for that activity can be found.

Individual pages are discussed in detail within each lesson plan, accompanied by ideas for adaptation where appropriate – of course, each sheet can be adapted to suit your own needs and those of your class. (For example, cards which have been left blank are for your own use.) Sheets can also be coloured, laminated, mounted on to card, enlarged and so on where appropriate.

Pupil worksheets and record sheets have spaces provided for children's names and for noting the date on which each sheet was used. This means that, if so required, they can be included easily within any pupil assessment portfolio.

Photocopiable sheets 124 to 138 are to be used for the purposes of summative assessment and accompany the activities in the Assessment chapter.

SHAPE, SPACE
AND MEASURES

Buildings, see page 16

Buildings – 3-D shapes (1)

▲ Copy a building using your building blocks.

**SHAPE, SPACE
AND MEASURES**

Buildings, see page 16

Buildings – 3-D shapes (2)

▲ Copy a building using your building blocks.

SHAPE, SPACE AND MEASURES

Buildings, see page 16

Buildings – Venn diagram

Name _____ Date _____

SHAPE NAMES

cuboid

cone

cube

cylinder

pyramid

sphere

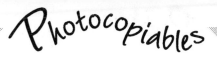

Buildings, see page 16

Buildings – Carroll diagram

Name _____ Date _____

SHAPE NAMES

cone   cuboid

                                                      cube

                        cylinder

pyramid   sphere

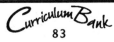
SHAPE, SPACE AND MEASURES

Sorting solids, see page 19

Sorting solids – items

▲ Cut round the pictures using the dotted lines.

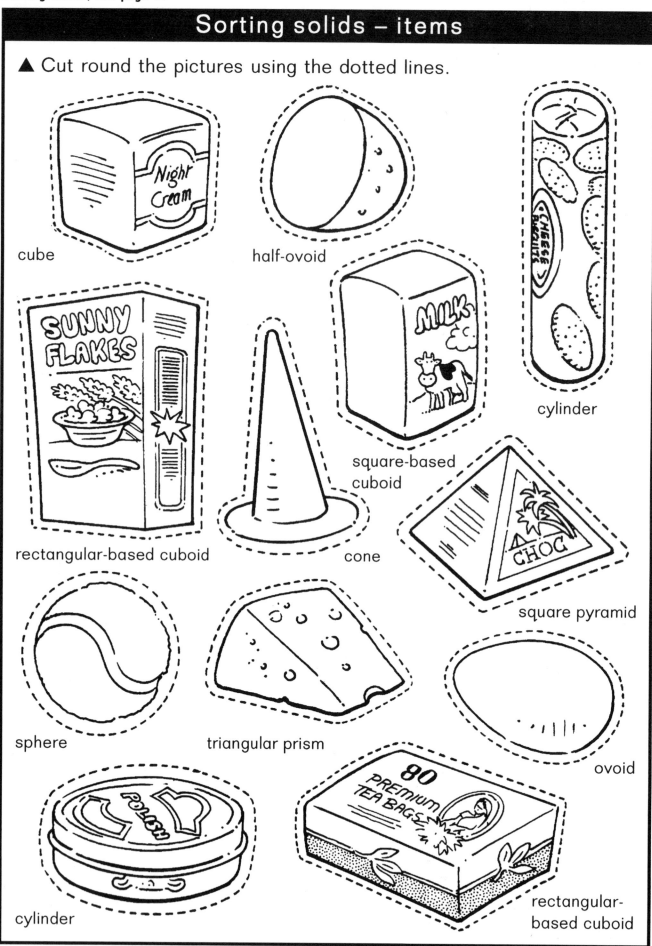

cube

half-ovoid

cylinder

rectangular-based cuboid

square-based cuboid

cone

square pyramid

sphere

triangular prism

ovoid

cylinder

rectangular-based cuboid

SHAPE, SPACE AND MEASURES

Sorting solids, see page 19

Sorting solids – shapes

▲ Cut round the pictures using the dotted lines.

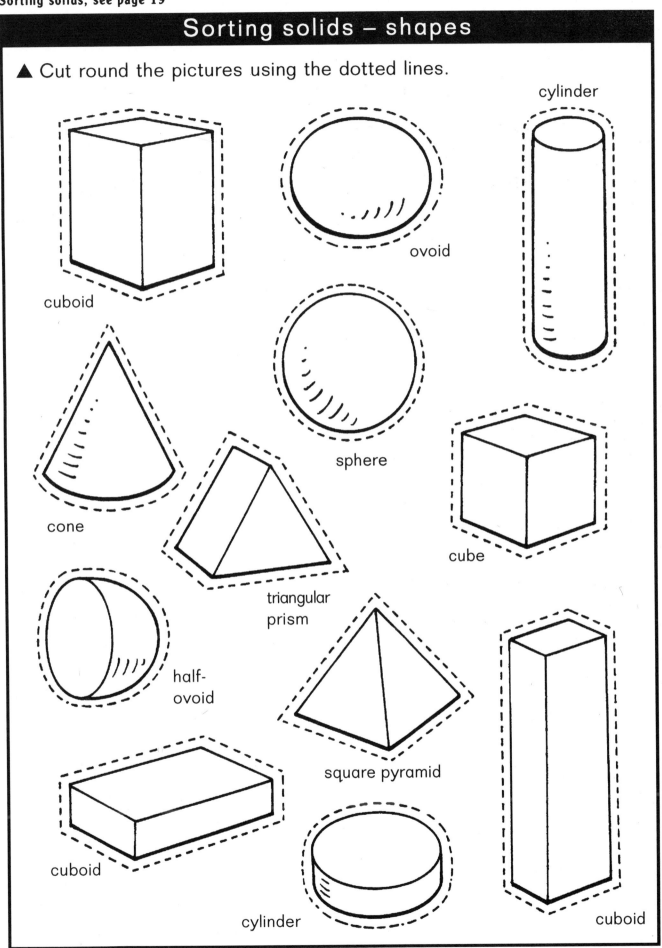

cylinder

ovoid

cuboid

sphere

cone

cube

triangular prism

half-ovoid

square pyramid

cuboid

cylinder

cuboid

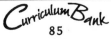

SHAPE, SPACE AND MEASURES

Guess the clue, see page 21

Guess the clue playing-cards (1)

has 2 faces the same	has square faces
all the faces are the same shape	has 4 corners
has square corners	has all straight edges
is a cone	is a prism

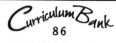

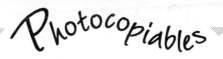
Guess the clue playing-cards (2)	
has 3 faces the same	has one or more circular faces
has a curved face	has 5 corners
has no square corners	is a half-sphere
is a cylinder	is a pyramid

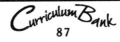

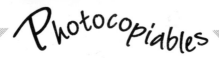
Guess the clue playing-cards (3)

has 4 faces the same	has rectangular faces
has both curved and flat faces	has 6 corners
has 6 straight edges	has no straight edges
is a cube	is a sphere

Guess the clue, see page 21

Guess the clue playing-cards (4)

has 6 faces the same	has triangular faces
has flat faces	has 8 corners
has 8 straight edges	has 12 straight edges
is a cuboid	

SHAPE, SPACE AND MEASURES

Guess the clue, see page 21

Guess the clue Venn diagram (1)

Name _____ Date _____

**SHAPE, SPACE
AND MEASURES**

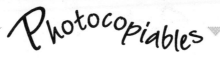

Guess the clue, see page 21

Guess the clue Venn diagram (2)

Name _____ Date _____

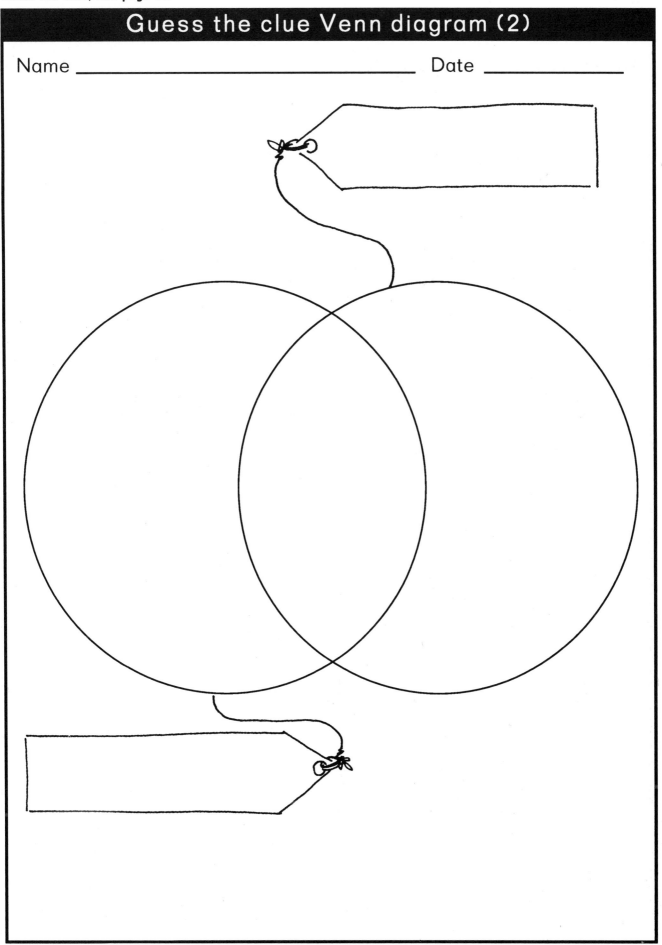

SHAPE, SPACE
AND MEASURES

Mosaics, see page 25

Mosaics – polygons

Name ——————————————————— Date ———————

▲ How many different polygons can you find? Make each one a different colour.

**SHAPE, SPACE
AND MEASURES**

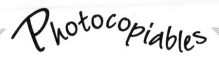

Four in a row, see page 26

Four in a row – symmetry

Name _____ Date _____

▲ In the top row of each pair, stick on your triangles to make a
pattern. In the bottom row, stick on triangles to reflect the pattern in
the top row. The first one has been started for you.

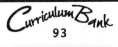
SHAPE, SPACE
AND MEASURES

Triangles, see page 27

Triangles (1)

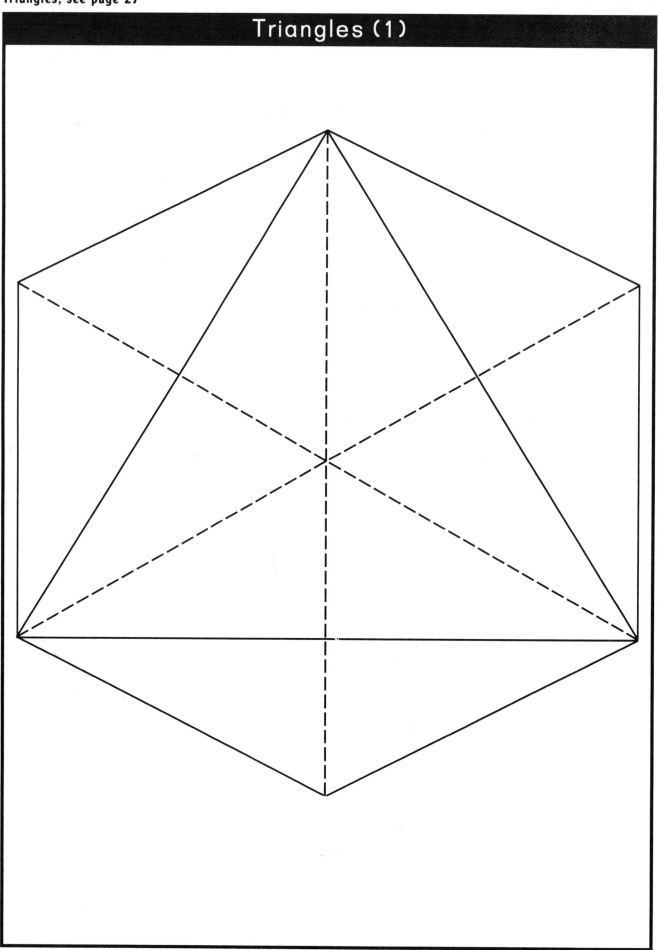

SHAPE, SPACE
AND MEASURES

Triangles, see page 27

Triangles (2)

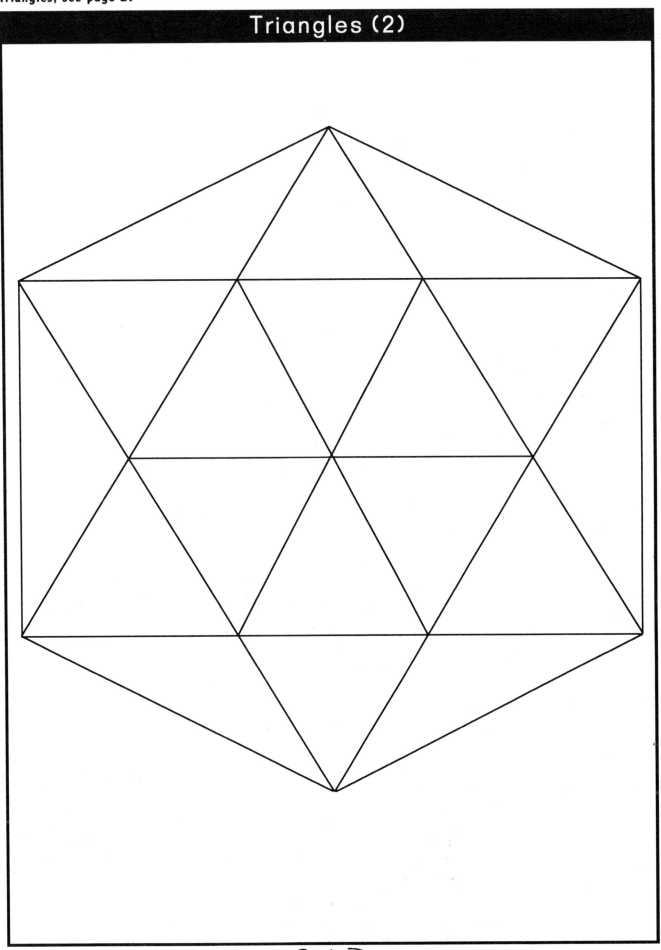

**SHAPE, SPACE
AND MEASURES**

Sock patterns, see page 29

Sock patterns – sort the socks

▲ Mrs Soap's washing has become all mixed up. Help her to sort her socks into matching pairs.

SHAPE, SPACE
AND MEASURES

Sock patterns, see page 29

Sock patterns – match the socks

▲ Make your sock patterns match.

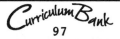

SHAPE, SPACE
AND MEASURES

Sock patterns, see page 29

Make a sock pattern

▲ Make the patterns on each pair of socks match.

98

**SHAPE, SPACE
AND MEASURES**

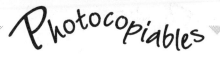

Mazes, see page 33

Mazes recording sheet

Name _____ Date _____

▲ Fill in each box with 'Left', 'Right' or 'Straight on' to describe the route through your maze.

Directions through the maze

END

↑

↑

↑

↑

↑

← **LEFT**   START   **RIGHT** →

SHAPE, SPACE AND MEASURES

Mazes, see page 33

Mazes – arrow labels

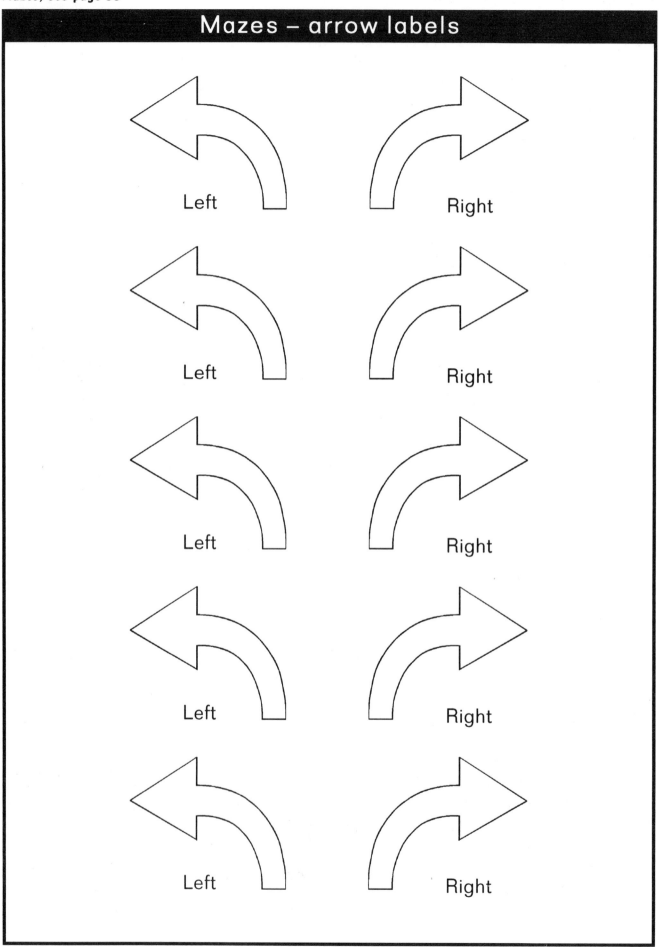

Left   Right

Left   Right

Left   Right

Left   Right

Left   Right

SHAPE, SPACE
AND MEASURES

Round the village green, see page 36

Round the village green

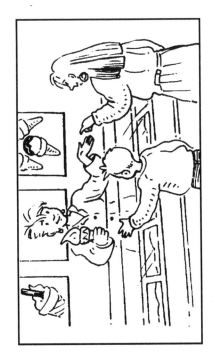

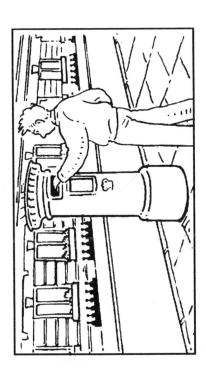

SHAPE, SPACE
AND MEASURES

Filling shelves, see page 38

Filling shelves (1)

SHAPE, SPACE
AND MEASURES

Filling shelves, see page 38

Filling shelves (2)

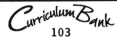
SHAPE, SPACE AND MEASURES

Circles and squares, see page 39

Circles and squares – rotating patterns

Name _____ Date _____

▲ Each of the patterns has parts that are turning round. Spot which way they are turning and finish the pattern.

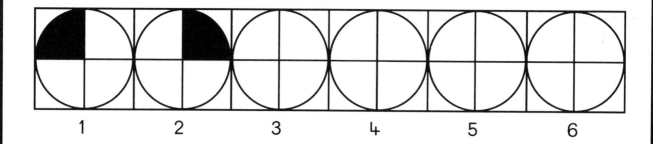

1   2   3   4   5   6

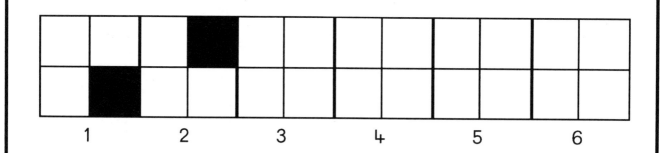

1   2   3   4   5   6

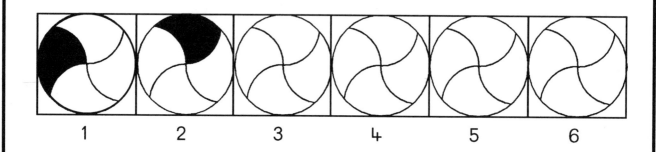

1   2   3   4   5   6

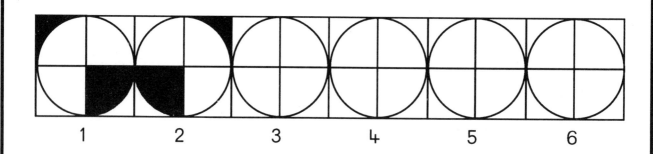

1   2   3   4   5   6

SHAPE, SPACE AND MEASURES

Big and bigger, see page 42

Big and bigger (1)

Name _____ Date _____

This ladder is

This house is

This tree is

This flagpole is

This flagpole is

This tree is

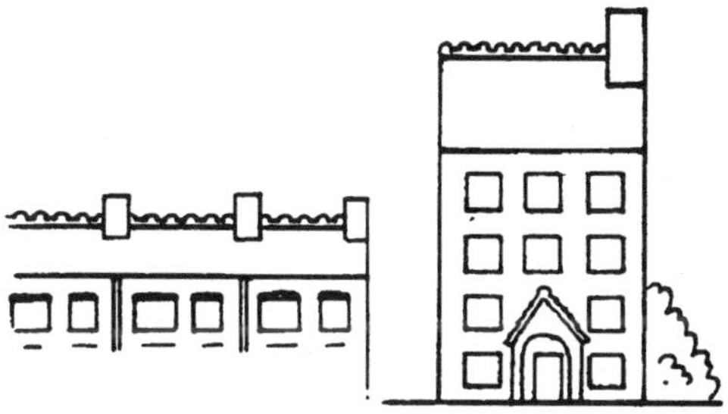

This house is

This ladder is

tall

taller

SHAPE, SPACE
AND MEASURES

Photocopiables

Big and bigger, see page 42

Big and bigger (2)

Name _____ Date _____

This snake is	This scarf is
This pencil is	This boat is
This boat is	This pencil is
This scarf is	This snake is

long   longer

SHAPE, SPACE
AND MEASURES

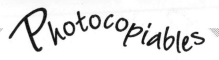

Longer and longer (1)

Name _____ Date _____

We are using _____ to measure with.

We are going to measure three things:

1. _____

2. _____

3. _____

1. The _____ measures ☐

_____ and _____

2. The _____ measures ☐

_____ and _____

3. The _____ measures ☐

_____ and _____

a bit more   **no more**

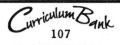

**SHAPE, SPACE
AND MEASURES**

Longer and longer, see page 43

Longer and longer (2)

Name _____ Date _____

I am using _____ to measure with.

1. The _____ measures ☐ _____

2. My guess is that _____ is _____

2. The _____ measures ☐ _____

3. My guess is that _____ is _____

3. The _____ measures ☐ _____

4. My guess is that _____ is _____

4. The _____ measures ☐ _____

5. My guess is that _____ is _____

5. The _____ measures ☐ _____

SHAPE, SPACE AND MEASURES

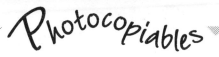
Trains recording sheet

Name _____ Date _____

1. The train has an engine and ☐ carriages.

2. We measured the train again. It was ☐ nearly-a-metre

strides and ☐ half-metre strides.

3. When we estimated the length of the train in metres, we

guessed it was ☐ metres.

4. We measured the train with a _____.

It was ☐ metres long and _____.

metre stick   trundle wheel   no more   a bit

Heavier or lighter?, see page 50

Heavier or lighter?

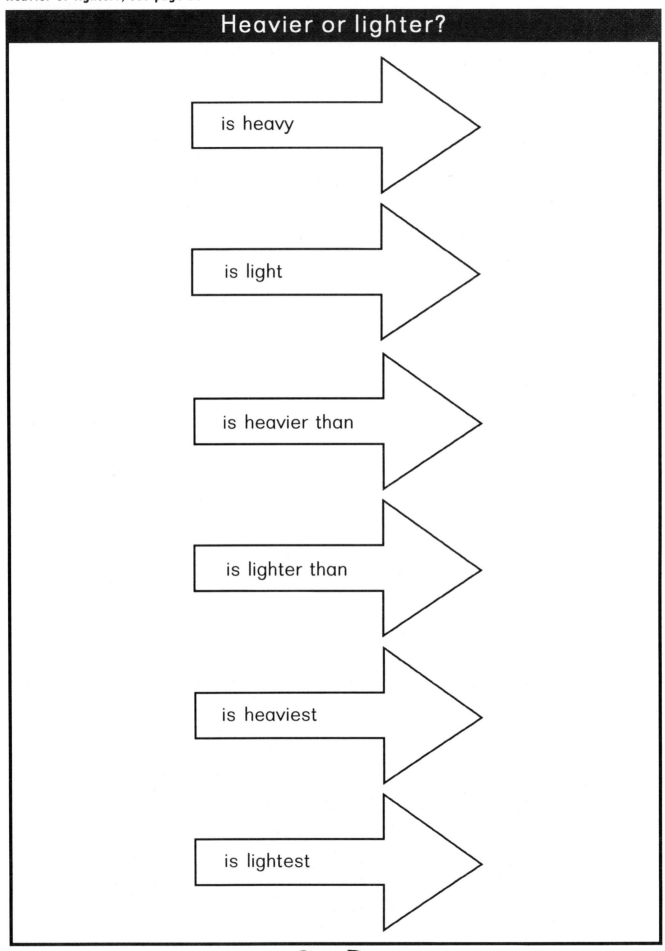

is heavy

is light

is heavier than

is lighter than

is heaviest

is lightest

SHAPE, SPACE AND MEASURES

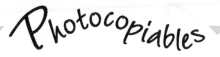

Tubby teddies, see page 51

Tubby teddies recording sheet

Name _____ Date _____

My _____ is heavier than _____ _____

My _____ is lighter than _____ _____

My _____ is the same as _____ _____

My _____ weighs the same as ☐ _____

My _____ weighs the same as ☐ _____

SHAPE, SPACE
AND MEASURES

Mystery parcels, see page 53

Mystery parcels recording sheet

Name _____ Date _____

1. The _____ parcel weighs ☐ _____

2. The _____ parcel weighs ☐ _____

3. The _____ parcel weighs ☐ _____

4. The _____ parcel weighs ☐ _____

SHAPE, SPACE
AND MEASURES

What a muddle!, see page 55

What a muddle! (1)

Name _____ Date _____

▲ You need parcels A, B and C and three name labels.

The parcel belonging to Mr Green is lighter than the parcel belonging to Mrs Red.

The parcel belonging to Mrs Red is heavier than the parcel belonging to Mr Brown.

The parcel belonging to Mr Brown is lighter than the parcel belonging to Mr Green.

Parcel A belongs to _____

Parcel B belongs to _____

Parcel C belongs to _____

SHAPE, SPACE AND MEASURES

What a muddle!, see page 55

What a muddle! (2)

Name _____ Date _____

▲ You need parcels A, D and E and three name labels.

The parcel belonging to Mr Brown is lighter than the parcel belonging to Mr White.

The parcel belonging to Mr White is heavier than the parcel belonging to Mrs Silver.

The parcel belonging to Mrs Silver is heavier than the parcel belonging to Mr Brown.

Parcel A belongs to _____

Parcel D belongs to _____

Parcel E belongs to _____

SHAPE, SPACE AND MEASURES

What a muddle!, see page 55

What a muddle! (3)

Name _____ Date _____

▲ You need parcels B, C and F and three name labels.

The parcel belonging to Mr Green is lighter than the parcel belonging to Mrs Red.

The parcel belonging to Mrs Red is heavier than the parcel belonging to Mrs Yellow.

The parcel belonging to Mrs Yellow is lighter than the parcel belonging to Mr Green.

Parcel B belongs to _____

Parcel C belongs to _____

Parcel F belongs to _____

SHAPE, SPACE AND MEASURES

What a muddle! (4)

Name _____ Date _____

▲ You will need all the parcels and your completed worksheets so that you can tie the labels on correctly.
Use the scales and the weights to find the mass of the parcels. Write them down.

A = _____ g   B = _____ g

C = _____ g   D = _____ g

E = _____ g   F = _____ g

Now:
Find 3 parcels which together weigh 500g.

Parcels: _____ _____ _____

Find 3 parcels which together weigh 1kg.

Parcels: _____ _____ _____

Find 2 parcels which together weigh 1kg.

Parcels: _____ _____

Find 2 parcels which together weigh less than 500g.

Parcels: _____ _____

Find 2 parcels which together weigh more than 1kg.

Parcels: _____ _____

Find 4 parcels which together weigh 2kg.

Parcels: ____ ____ ____ ____

What do all the parcels together weigh?

All weigh: _____

SHAPE, SPACE AND MEASURES

Counting cups, see page 59

Counting cups

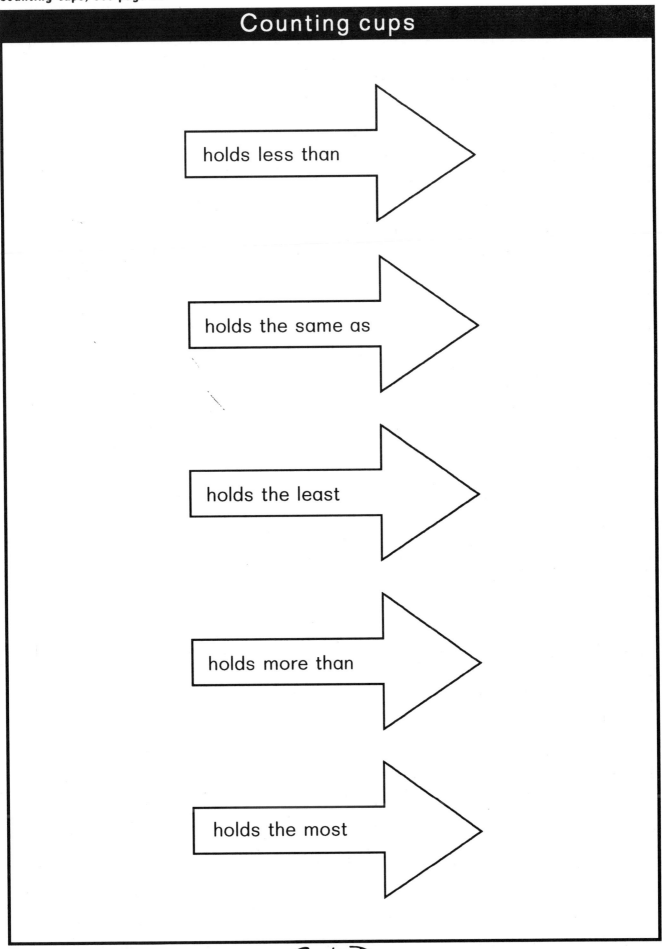

holds less than

holds the same as

holds the least

holds more than

holds the most

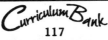
**SHAPE, SPACE
AND MEASURES**

Teddy bears' picnic, see page 61

Teddy bears' picnic

Children's names _____ Date _____

_____

1. The teapot contains:

☐ _____ of lentils and

☐ _____ of water.

2. The squash bottle contains:

☐ _____ of lentils and

☐ _____ of water.

3. The jug contains:

☐ _____ of lentils and

☐ _____ of water.

4. The sugar box contains:

☐ _____ of lentils and

☐ _____ of cubes.

SHAPE, SPACE AND MEASURES

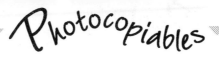

Am I on time?, see page 68

Am I on time? (1)

1 o'clock	2 o'clock	3 o'clock
4 o'clock	5 o'clock	6 o'clock
7 o'clock	8 o'clock	9 o'clock
10 o'clock	11 o'clock	12 o'clock

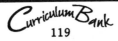
SHAPE, SPACE
AND MEASURES

Am I on time?, see page 68

Am I on time? (2)

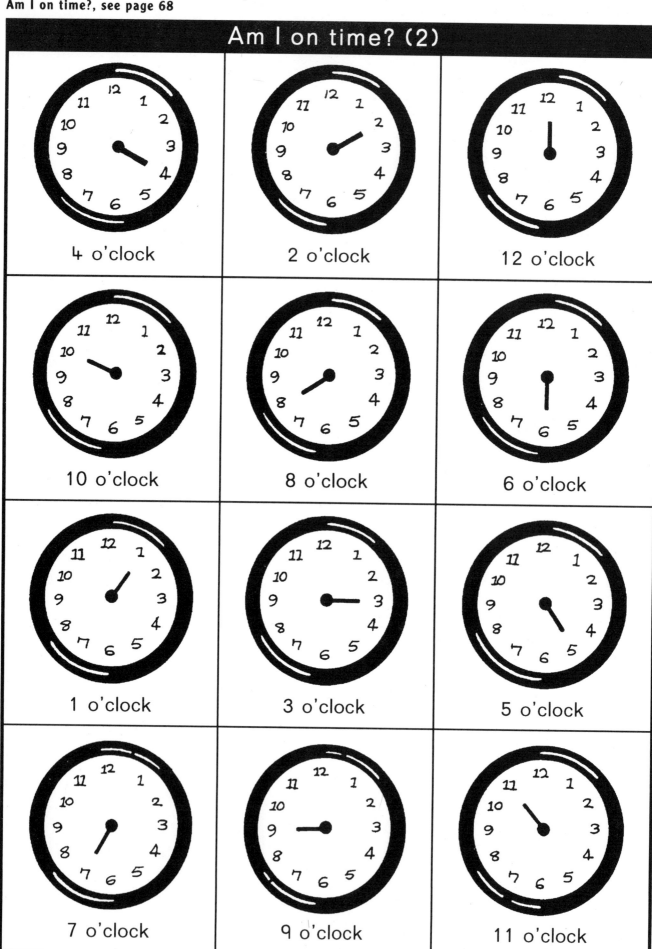

4 o'clock

2 o'clock

12 o'clock

10 o'clock

8 o'clock

6 o'clock

1 o'clock

3 o'clock

5 o'clock

7 o'clock

9 o'clock

11 o'clock

SHAPE, SPACE
AND MEASURES

Am I on time? (3)

quarter past 1	quarter past 2	quarter past 3
quarter past 4	quarter past 5	quarter past 6
quarter past 7	quarter past 8	quarter past 9
quarter past 10	quarter past 11	quarter past 12
half past 1	half past 2	half past 3
half past 4	half past 5	half past 6

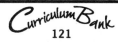

SHAPE, SPACE
AND MEASURES

Am I on time?, see page 68

Am I on time? (4)

quarter to 1	quarter to 2	quarter to 3
quarter to 4	quarter to 5	quarter to 6
quarter to 7	quarter to 8	quarter to 9
quarter to 10	quarter to 11	quarter to 12
half past 7	half past 8	half past 9
half past 10	half past 11	half past 12

SHAPE, SPACE
AND MEASURES

Race against time

▲ Roll both dice. When you reach a clock draw in the hands and write the time in the space below. Use the 'hour' dice to move from one clock-face to the next. Mark where you land with an X.

START		31	32	33
		30		34
Time:		Time:		Time:
1		29		35
2		28		36
3		27		37
4		26		38
5		25		39
6		24		40
7		23		41
Time:		Time:		Time:
8		22		42
9		21		43
10		20		44
11		19		45
12		18		46
13		17		47
Time:		Time:		Time:
14	15	16		48
				FINISH

SHAPE, SPACE
AND MEASURES

Sorting 3-D shapes, see page 72

1

all the corners are square

all the corners are not square

the faces are not all flat

the faces are not all flat

the faces are flat

the faces are flat

all the corners are square

all the corners are not square

▲ Look carefully at the solid shapes. See how many you can place in the Carroll diagram.
▲ If you know the names of the shapes, write the name in the correct place next to the shape.

SHAPE, SPACE
AND MEASURES

Sorting 3-D shapes, see page 72

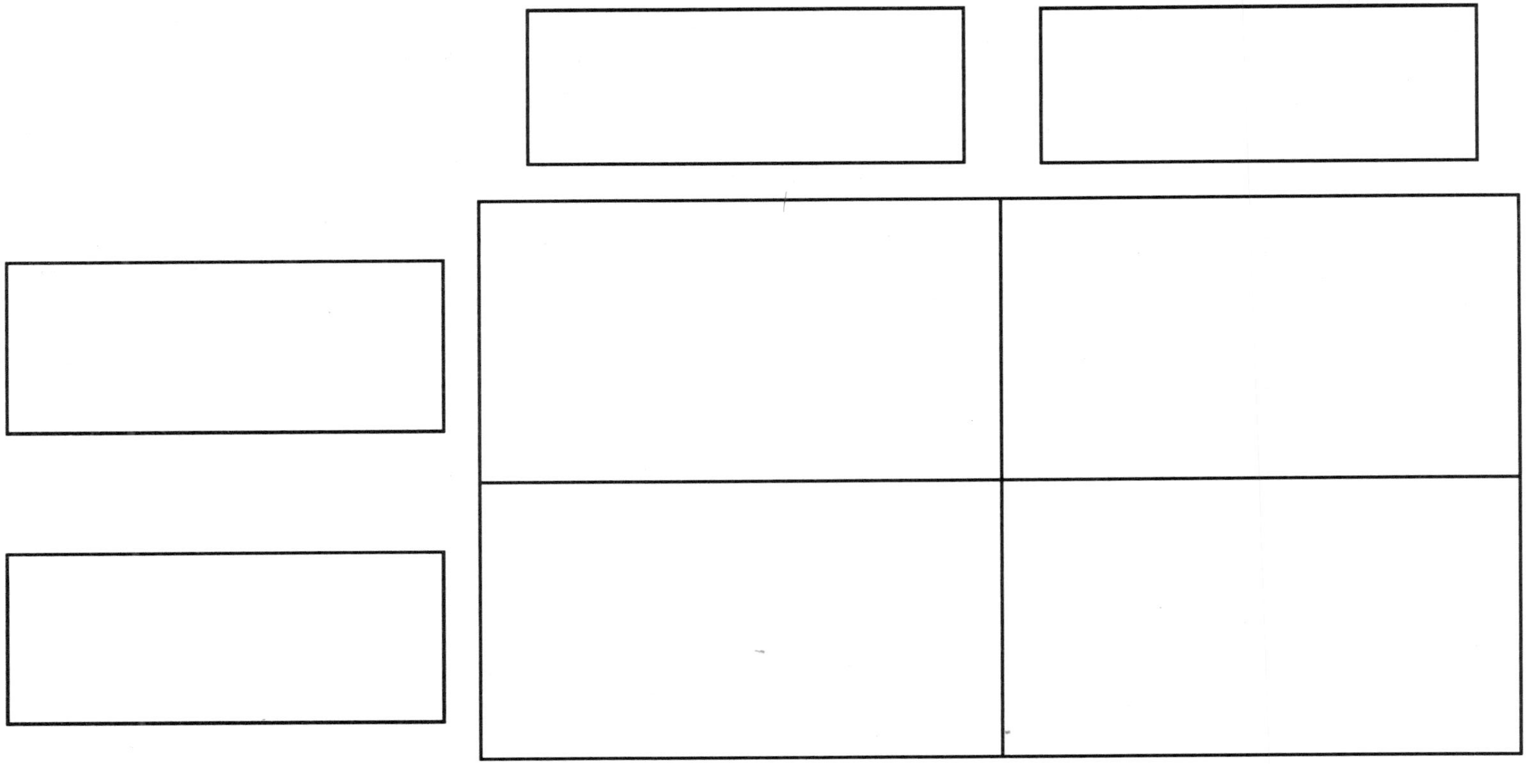

▲ Choose a pair of labels, for example 'the faces are all flat/the faces are not all flat', and label the top of the diagram.

▲ Now choose another pair of labels. They can be about edges or corners or symmetry but *not* about faces. Use the pair to label the left-hand side of the diagram. For example, you could choose: 'the edges are straight/the edges are not all straight'. Record your sorting in the diagram.

Sorting 3-D shapes, see page 72

3

the faces are flat	the faces are not all flat	the corners are square	the corners are not all square
these shapes are symmetrical	these shapes are not symmetrical	the faces are all the same shape	the faces are not all the same shape
the edges are straight	the edges are not all straight	the edges are curved	the edges are not all curved
the faces are all squares	the faces are not all squares	the faces are all rectangles	the faces are not all rectangles
the shape has 8 corners	the shape does not have 8 corners	the shape has 6 corners	the shape does not have 6 corners
the shape has 6 edges	the shape does not have 6 edges	the shape has curved faces	the shape does not have curved faces

SHAPE, SPACE AND MEASURES

Sorting 3-D shapes, see page 72

Aspect of assessment	PoS	Evidence and outcomes	Name and date	Name and date	Name and date	Name and date
Describing shapes that can be seen.	2a	Did the child use appropriate everyday language to describe the shapes?				
Describing shapes using mathematical names.	2a	...use the correct mathematical names for some/all the shapes?				
Recognising and using geometrical features including vertices, sides/edges and surfaces.	2c	...count the number of edges correctly?				
Recognising and using geometrical features including vertices, sides/edges and surfaces.	2c	...count the number of corners correctly?				
Recognising and using geometrical features including vertices, sides/edges and surfaces.	2c	...count the number of faces correctly?				
Classifying shapes according to mathematical criteria.	2b	...sort the collection correctly when the criteria were provided?				
Classifying shapes according to mathematical criteria.	2b	...sort correctly when choosing their own criteria?				
Recognising reflective symmetry in simple cases.	2c	...sort correctly? Were they able to point out the lines of symmetry?				

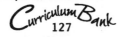
SHAPE, SPACE
AND MEASURES

▲ How many different shapes can you see in the pattern?
▲ Describe three of the shapes.
▲ Is there anything special about the pattern? Write it down or tell your teacher.

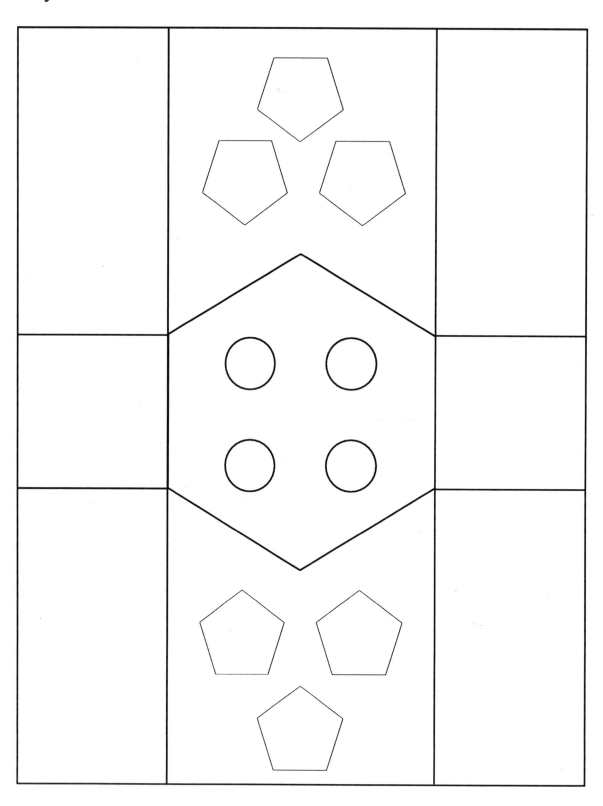

SHAPE, SPACE AND MEASURES

Shapes and patterns, see page 73

2

▲ What are these shapes called?
▲ Now find out as much as you can about all the shapes and write it down.

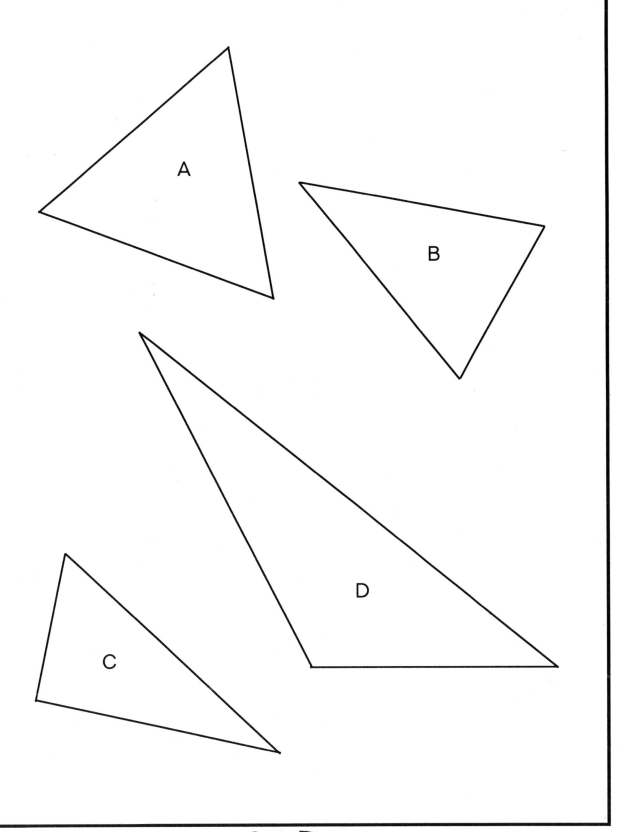

SHAPE, SPACE
AND MEASURES

3 Shapes and patterns, see page 73

Aspect of assessment	PoS	Evidence and outcomes	Name and date	Name and date	Name and date	Name and date
Describing shapes that can be seen.	2a	Did the child use appropriate everyday language to describe the shapes?				
Describing shapes using mathematical names.	2a	...use the correct mathematical names for some/all the shapes?				
Recognising and using geometrical features including vertices, sides/edges and surfaces.	2c	...count the number of sides correctly?				
Recognising and using geometrical features including vertices, sides/edges and surfaces.	2c	...count the number of corners correctly?				
Recognising and using geometrical features including vertices, sides/edges and surfaces.	2c	...describe curved and straight edges?				
Classifying shapes according to mathematical criteria.	2b	...describe shapes having similar features? (eg. number of sides)				
Recognising reflective symmetry in simple cases.	2c	...point out the lines of symmetry?				
Recognising right angles.	3b	...identify square corners in the pattern, in the right-angled triangle?				

1

▲ Colour the circles first.
The middle one is yellow. The one on the right is green and the one on the left is red.
▲ Now colour all the bottom squares red.
Colour the square above the middle circle blue.
Colour the square below the green circle black.
Colour all the top squares orange.

SHAPE, SPACE
AND MEASURES

CurriculumBank

1

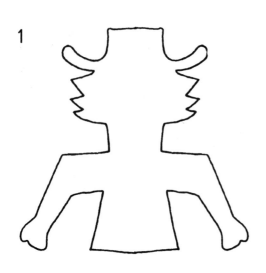

2

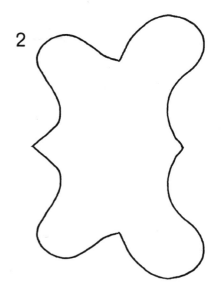

3

4

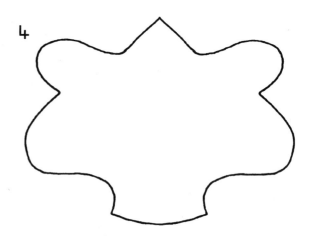

5

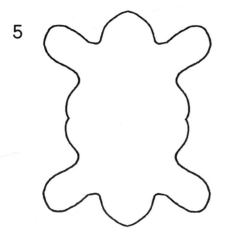

6

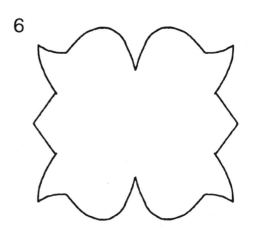

3 Position, movement and symmetry, see page 75

A	B	C	D	E
F	G	H	I	J
K	L	M	N	O
P	Q	R	S	T
U	V	W	X	Y
Z				

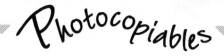

Length, mass and capacity, see page 76

1

▲ Look at the three containers. They are all different shapes and sizes. Find out as much as you can about them by measuring them in different ways.

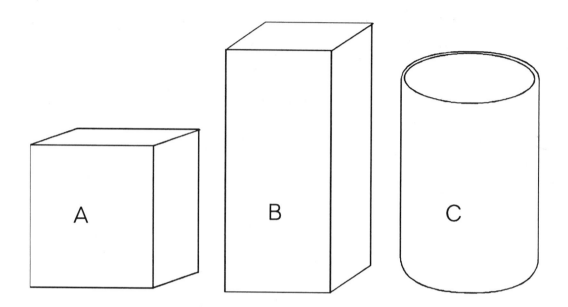

▲ Write down what you find out. You can use the table below but you will need to write in your own headings in the boxes along the top.

Headings						
A						
B						
C						

SHAPE, SPACE
AND MEASURES

1

▲Draw in the big minute hand and write the time under each clock.

a. _____

b. _____

c. _____

d. _____

e. _____

f. _____

▲ The times are written under these clocks. Can you draw in the hands?

a. eight o'clock

b. one o'clock

c. five o'clock

d. half past ten

e. half past seven

f. half past five

SHAPE, SPACE
AND MEASURES

2

▲Write the time under each clock.

a. _____

b. _____

c. _____

d. _____

e. _____

f. _____

▲ The times are written under these clocks. Can you draw in the hands?

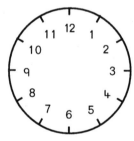

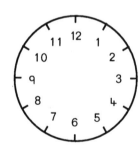

a. quarter past three   b. quarter past six   c. quarter past twelve

d. quarter to one   e. quarter to five   f. quarter to nine

Curriculum Bank
136

SHAPE, SPACE
AND MEASURES

3

▲Write the time under each clock.

a. _____

b. _____

c. _____

d. _____

e. _____

f. _____

▲ The times are written under these clocks. Can you draw in the hands?

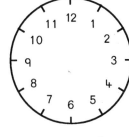

a. five minutes past three

b. twenty-five minutes past six

c. ten minutes past twelve

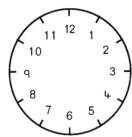

d. five minutes past three

e. twenty-five minutes to nine

f. ten minutes to one

SHAPE, SPACE AND MEASURES

▲ We went out for
a walk at:

We came
back at:

How long were
we out walking?

_____

▲ The television
programme started
at:

The television
programme finished
at:

How long did the
programme last?

_____

▲ I went to
visit my friend
at:

I came home at:

How long did my
visit last?

_____

▲ Our PE lesson
started at:

Our PE lesson
finished at:

How long did
our PE lesson
last?

_____

SHAPE, SPACE
AND MEASURES

USING AND APPLYING MATHEMATICS

This section of the programme of study should be set in the context of the other sections. It is very important that the children are given opportunities to use and apply mathematics in practical activities, in real-life problems and within mathematics itself. Using and applying mathematics can only occur in relation to the knowledge and understanding of other aspects of the curriculum. It is an approach and not a body of knowledge in itself. Children should be given the opportunity to explain their thinking to support the development of their reasoning. Aspects of the using and applying approach are included within almost all the activities in this book. The table on pages 140 and 141 shows where there may be opportunities for the teacher to incorporate using and applying mathematics into activities.

The programme of study for using and applying

mathematics is divided into three main subsections: making and monitoring decisions to solve problems; developing mathematical language and communication; and developing mathematical reasoning. Each subsection is further sub-divided into three or four separate aspects.

The 'using and applying' aspects of the mathematics National Curriculum provide the context within which the content of the curriculum is taught and learned. There has to be a balance between those activities which develop knowledge, skills and understanding, and those which develop the ability to tackle practical problems. The processes involved in the 'using and applying' dimension enable pupils to make use of and communicate their mathematical knowledge; for many pupils this is the main point in learning mathematics.

The diagram below shows the context, content and process dimensions of mathematics teaching.

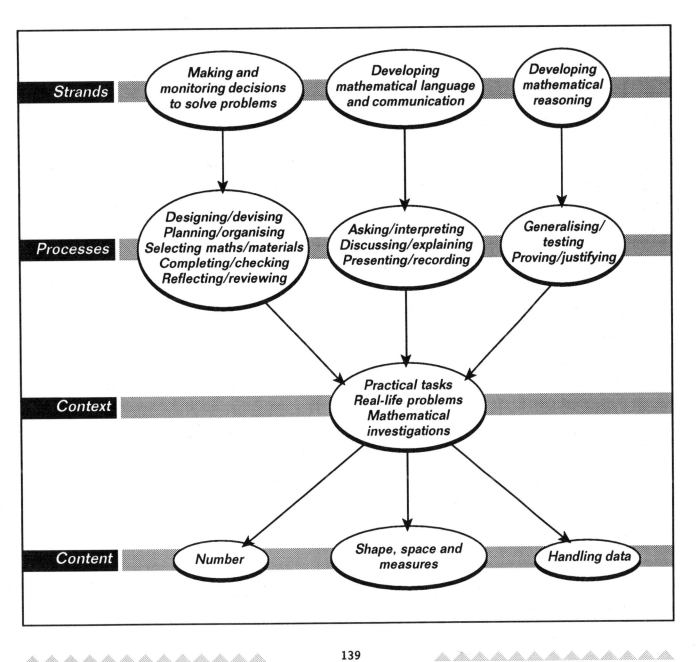

SHAPE, SPACE AND MEASURES

ACTIVITIES	SOLVING PROBLEMS				COMMUNICATION				LOGICAL REASONING		
	Pupils select and use the appropriate mathematics.	Pupils select and use mathematical equipment and materials.	Pupils develop different mathematical approaches and look for ways to overcome difficulties.	Pupils organise and check their work.	Pupils understand the language of number properties of shapes and comparatives.	Pupils relate numerals and other mathematical symbols to a range of situations.	Pupils discuss their work, responding to and asking mathematical questions.	Pupils use a variety of forms of mathematical presentation.	Pupils ask questions including 'What would happen if...?' and 'Why?'	Pupils recognise simple patterns and relationships and make related predictions about them.	Pupils understand general statements and investigate whether particular cases match them.
	a	b	c	d	a	b	c	d	a	b	c
Three-dimensional shape											
Unpacking the shopping	●		●		●	●	●				
Making shapes		●	●		●		●				
Buildings	●	●	●	●	●		●		●		
Paint a face	●	●	●		●	●			●	●	
Sorting solids	●	●	●	●	●	●	●		●		●
Guess the clue	●	●	●	●	●		●	●	●	●	●
Two-dimensional shape											
Shapes around the classroom	●	●			●		●	●		●	
Mosaics	●	●	●	●	●				●	●	
Four in a row	●				●	●			●	●	●
Triangles	●	●	●	●	●				●	●	●
Repeating patterns	●	●	●	●	●	●	●	●	●	●	●
Sock patterns	●	●	●		●		●	●	●	●	●
Position and movement											
Hide and hunt					●		●		●		
Mazes	●	●	●	●	●	●	●	●	●		
Posting letters	●	●	●	●	●		●	●	●	●	●
Round the village green	●	●	●	●	●		●	●	●	●	
Filling shelves	●				●			●		●	●
Circles and squares	●	●	●	●	●	●	●	●		●	●

SHAPE, SPACE AND MEASURES

ACTIVITIES	SOLVING PROBLEMS				COMMUNICATION				LOGICAL REASONING		
	Pupils select and use the appropriate mathematics.	Pupils select and use mathematical equipment and materials.	Pupils develop different mathematical approaches and look for ways to overcome difficulties.	Pupils organise and check their work.	Pupils understand the language of number properties of shapes and comparatives.	Pupils relate numerals and other mathematical symbols to a range of situations.	Pupils discuss their work, responding to and asking mathematical questions.	Pupils use a variety of forms of mathematical presentation.	Pupils ask questions including 'What would happen if…?' and 'Why?'	Pupils recognise simple patterns and relationships and make related predictions about them.	Pupils understand general statements and investigate whether particular cases match them.
	a	b	c	d	a	b	c	d	a	b	c
Length											
Big and bigger		⊛	⊛	⊛	⊛		⊛	⊛	⊛	⊛	
Longer and longer	⊛	⊛	⊛	⊛	⊛	⊛	⊛	⊛	⊛	⊛	⊛
Whoppers!		⊛	⊛	⊛	⊛		⊛	⊛	⊛	⊛	
Trains	⊛	⊛	⊛	⊛	⊛	⊛	⊛	⊛	⊛	⊛	⊛
Mass											
Heavier or lighter?		⊛	⊛	⊛	⊛		⊛	⊛	⊛	⊛	
Tubby teddies		⊛	⊛	⊛	⊛	⊛	⊛	⊛	⊛	⊛	
Mystery parcels	⊛	⊛	⊛	⊛	⊛	⊛	⊛	⊛	⊛	⊛	⊛
What a muddle!	⊛	⊛	⊛	⊛	⊛	⊛	⊛	⊛	⊛	⊛	⊛
Capacity											
Which holds more?	⊛	⊛	⊛	⊛	⊛		⊛		⊛	⊛	
Counting cups	⊛	⊛	⊛	⊛	⊛	⊛	⊛	⊛	⊛	⊛	⊛
Teddy bears' picnic	⊛	⊛	⊛	⊛	⊛	⊛	⊛	⊛		⊛	
Guess and test	⊛	⊛	⊛	⊛	⊛	⊛	⊛			⊛	⊛
Time											
Fast fun!		⊛	⊛				⊛			⊛	
How long does it take?	⊛	⊛		⊛	⊛	⊛	⊛	⊛	⊛	⊛	
Am I on time?	⊛	⊛			⊛	⊛	⊛	⊛	⊛		
Race against time	⊛	⊛	⊛	⊛	⊛	⊛	⊛	⊛		⊛	
Assessment											
Sorting three-dimensional shapes	⊛	⊛	⊛	⊛	⊛	⊛	⊛	⊛	⊛	⊛	⊛
Shapes and patterns	⊛	⊛			⊛		⊛				
Position, movement and symmetry	⊛	⊛	⊛	⊛	⊛		⊛		⊛		⊛
Length, mass and capacity	⊛	⊛	⊛	⊛	⊛	⊛	⊛	⊛			⊛
Time	⊛	⊛			⊛	⊛		⊛		⊛	

SHAPE, SPACE AND MEASURES

INFORMATION TECHNOLOGY WITHIN SHAPE, SPACE AND MEASURES AT KS1

The information technology activities outlined in this book can be used to develop and assess children's IT capability as outlined in the National Curriculum. Types of software rather than names of specific programs have been mentioned to enable you to use ideas regardless of the computers used.

Main IT Focus

The main emphasis for the development of IT capability within these activities is on control and information handling. However, within mathematics there is a wide range of software available to support children's learning, and teachers may still want to include specific software which runs on their computer and which addresses the content and understanding of the subject being taught. The activities in this book are very practically based and give children opportunities to use concrete materials and resources to develop mathematical understanding. Content specific software should not be used to replace such experiences and should be used to develop or reinforce understanding only after initial practical work. Teachers should also be aware that although such software may assist pupils in their learning of mathematics, it may add little to the development of the pupils IT capability.

Using programmable toys for developing mathematics

Most schools now have access to one of a range of programmable floor robots. The first to be developed were floor Turtles which are connected to the computer by a cable or an infrared transmitter connected to the computer and a receiver on the Turtle (similar to the remote control on the television). There are advantages and disadvantages to both systems. The cable link can get twisted and can limit the range of the Turtle on the floor. On the other hand, the infrared link requires a direct line between computer and Turtle, and children or furniture in that direct line may affect the signal.

Over the fast few years, programmable toys have become very popular in schools. The first was a toy called 'Big Track', which has now been developed into a more educational variant in the form of Roamer, or PIP. Both devices achieve the same results, are free-standing and do not need the computer. This has the great advantage of releasing the computer for other tasks; there are also no problems with leads or signals.

When floor robots are in constant use, the drain on batteries can be significant. All three types can be purchased with rechargeable batteries and although this increases the initial cost there is a long term saving to be made. If the batteries are charged regularly they will generally be sufficient for a day's use by children, although you may need to recharge them at lunch-time if they are in heavy use all day.

Floor robots can be used in a variety of ways with young children. They will initially enjoy exploring the commands to discover how to make the robot move forward and backwards, or to turn it. The command language used is a variation of the traditional LOGO language and children need to develop an understanding of the need to be precise in their instructions, to estimate the distance to be travelled and the amount of turn required. Courses can be set up and the robot sent around them. When children become more familiar with shapes, they can control the robot to make a square or a triangle. Most devices allow children to attach a pen so that the robot can draw a trail on the floor or paper. A set of command and number cards can also be useful in helping children to plan or record their routes.

The children will also need to be taught how to use other features of the Roamer or PIP. These might include:

- ▲ turning the robot on and off;
- ▲ cleaning the memory of all other commands;
- ▲ moving backwards and forwards;
- ▲ turning to the left and right;
- ▲ making a bleep;
- ▲ pausing for a set time.

However, it is not enough to allow children to experiment without the intervention of an adult who can encourage them, challenge them with new tasks, teach them new facilities and generally assess their understanding of the concepts of turn and distance and the fundamentals of control technology. So try and set up floor robot activities with another adult present for some of the time at least.

The floor robots will arrive with some settings that may not be appropriate for your classroom. The Roamer, for example, moves forward its own length (about 30cm) if given the command FORWARD 1. This can be altered very simply by using the change units command. To set the distance of a unit to 10cm enter ↑ [10].

The angle of turn can also be altered in the same way. This can be useful for young children so that to make a quarter-turn they enter [1] and to turn a right angle they enter turn [4]. To set the angle of turn to 23 degrees enter ⟲ [23]. Roamer cannot deal with half-degrees, but as there will always be some inaccuracy because of the floor surface the extra 2 degrees for a right angle will hardly show. Once changed, these settings will remain in operation until the robot is switched off.

Finally, but of great importance to young children, is the ability to dress or decorate the floor robot to fit the theme of the work. PIP has a LEGO base on its top surface which means that LEGO models can be attached to the top; Roamer users can purchase a plastic cover which can be decorated; and Turtle users often create a soft fabric top to which items can be attached by gluing or sewing. Children enjoy dressing their robot and the work can be included within design and technology activities.

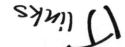

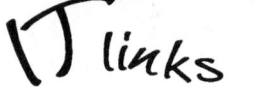

IT links

The grids on this page relate the activities in this book to specific areas of IT and to relevant software resources. Activities are referenced by page number rather than by name. (Bold page numbers indicate activities which have expanded IT content.) The software listed is a selection of programs generally available to primary schools, and is not intended as a recommended list. The software featured should be available from most good educational software retailers.

Area of IT	Type of Software	Activities (page nos.)					
		Chapter 1	Chapter 2	Chapter 3	Chapter 4	Chapter 5	Chapter 6
Communicating Information	Art/graphics	18	**24**, 28, 29				
Communicating Information	Framework		24		42		
Information Handling	Database					**51**	
Information Handling	Branching Database	**14, 21**					
Information Handling	Graphing software				43, 45	55	59
Control	Roamer/PIP/Turtle			33, **35, 36**	43		

Software Type	BBC/Master	RISCOS	Nimbus/186	Windows	Macintosh
Framework		My World		My World	
Art/Graphics	Picture Builder	1st Paint Kid Pix Splash	Picture Builder	Colour Magic Kid Pix 2	Kid Pix 2
Database	Our Facts Grass Datashow	DataSweet Find IT	Our Facts Datashow Information Workshop	Sparks ClarisWorks Grass	ClarisWorks EasyWorks
Branching Database	Branch	ReTreeval	Branch		
Graphing software	Datashow	Pictogram Picture Point DataSweet	Datagraph	Datagraph EasyWorks	EasyWorks
Control	Roamer/PIP/Turtle				

SHAPE, SPACE
AND MEASURES

	ENGLISH	SCIENCE	HISTORY	GEOGRAPHY	D&T	ART	MUSIC	PE
3-D SHAPE	Talking about three-dimensional shapes, both mathematical and everyday. Describing them. Using the correct terminology.	Describing living organisms with reference to their shape. Observing similarities and differences, eg. seeds that are spherical or plants with hollow cylindrical stems.	Describing buildings. Comparing past and present similarities and differences. Constructing castles, Tudor houses, etc. Using straws for skeleton frameworks or junk models.	Describing physical and human features. Making models of physical features from fieldwork activities.	Making models from junk or construction equipment. Using malleable materials to create three-dimensional models.	Using malleable resources to create sculptures, or 3-D media (pasta, pulses, polystyrene, etc) to create depth and texture.		Describing and making shapes in the course of gymnastic activities.
2-D SHAPE	Describing flat shapes in the classroom and around the school. Listening to the description to guess the article being described.	Observing external appearances of living things and materials.	Looking at Victorian tiles, Roman mosaics. Copying and creating patterns which tessellate using flat mathematical shapes.	Making maps and plans of real or imaginary places. Using maps and plans.	Designing models and artefacts using drawing to record early ideas.	Using different tools (brush, rollers, sponges, rubber stamps, vegetables) to create pictures and patterns.		Awareness of pattern in traditional dance (country, square, Morris dancing).
POSITION AND MOVEMENT	Explaining where resources in the classroom belong. Writing instructions for making a simple artefact from constructional equipment.	Describing the movement of familiar things as they speed up or slow down or change direction. Sounds travel and change as they move nearer or further away.	Investigating buildings and the changes over time, particularly the living environment, eg. sleeping/animal quarters. Their original position compared to present day.	Following directions given verbally. Drawing routes around the school. Using maps to find routes from home to school and plan new routes.	Updating drawings during the design process to show new positions of elements. Describing how jointed toys, movable parts change position as they move.	Describing and making repeating patterns. Reflecting and rotating patterns to make images with symmetry.	Recognising and describing pitch – high/ low.	Perform movements, changing positions according to a pattern or an instruction. Respond to a change of direction.
MEASURES	Describing outcomes from measuring using comparative language. Recording results.	Using measurement as part of a scientific enquiry. Explaining outcomes.	Constructing a time line of 'Ourselves'. Using baby photos and recent ones. Sequencing events from birth to present day.	Collecting data on daily temperatures, the amount of rainfall over a month, how many hours the sun shines over a week, etc.	Measuring and estimating when constructing artefacts from a range of materials.		Recognising and describing duration of beat – long/ short and tempo of music – fast/ slow. Make comparisons.	Respond to music through dance. Vary speed related to tempo and make comparisons of distance to travel or time available to travel.

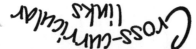
Cross-curricular links

The Living Planet

SALLY MORGAN

KINGfISHER

Contents

KINGFISHER
Kingfisher Publications Plc
New Penderel House
283-288 High Holborn
London WC1V 7HZ
www.kingfisherpub.com

Material in this edition
previously published by
Kingfisher Publications Plc
in the *Young Discoverers*
series
This edition published 2001

10 9 8 7 6 5 4 3 2 1

This concise edition
produced by PAGE*One*

Copyright © Kingfisher
Publications Plc 2001

1TR/0701/WKT/-(MAR)/128MA

A CIP catalogue record for
this book is available from
the British library.

ISBN 0 7534 0638 1

Printed in China

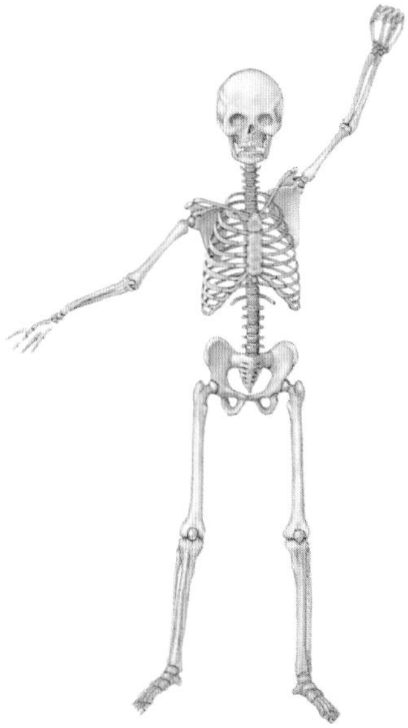

About This Book 4

INSIDE THE BODY 5

What Are We Made Of? 6

The Skeleton 8

Teeth 10

A Healthy Diet 12

Digestion 14

The Waterworks 16

Heart and Circulation 18

Breathing 20

The Nervous System 22

The Senses 24

Keeping Fit 26

ANIMALS IN ACTION 27

The Animal Kingdom 28

Communication 30

The Brain and Nervous System 32

Sight 34

Hearing 36

Smell 40

Taste 42

Touch 44

A Sixth Sense 46

Learning and Instinct 48

MINI-BEASTS IN CLOSE-UP   49

Is it a Minibeast?   50

Growing Up   52

Plant-Eaters   54

Hunters and Trappers   57

Flying Insects   60

Self Defence   62

Friend or Foe?   64

Life in the Water   66

Life under Logs and Stones   69

Living Together   70

PLANT LIFE   71

All Kinds of Plants   72

Making Their Own Food   74

Inside a Plant   78

Plants in the Food Chain   80

Plants as Food   82

Trees   84

Plants in the Desert   87

Flowers   88

Fruit and Seeds   90

Index   93

Acknowledgements   96

About This Book

This book looks at the plant and animal life on Earth.

The first section, *Inside the Body*, looks at how your body works and what it is made of. It explains how exercise and a healthy diet keep your body fit.

Animals in Action explores how different animals are adapted to their environments. It explains how they communicate and use their senses to search for food and to avoid danger.

Minibeasts in Close-Up is all about small animals without backbones, such as worms, spiders and insects.

Plant Life tells you how different plants grow and reproduce and explains how essential plants are to the survival of all living things.

For all the experiments, you should be able to find most things around the home, garden or in a park or nearby woodland. You may have to buy some items at a local garden centre. After an experiment, return any wild creatures to where you found them. Do not collect flowers or plants from the wild, even if there are lots of them.

Remember: Be a Smart Scientist

- Before you begin an experiment, read the instructions carefully and collect all the things you need.

- Put on some old clothes or wear an overall.

- When you have finished, clear everything away, especially sharp things like knives and scissors, and wash your hands.

- Keep a record of what you do and what you find out.

- If your results are not quite the same as those in this book, do not worry. See if you can work out what has happened, and why.

INSIDE
THE
BODY

What Are We Made Of?

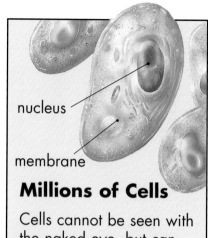

Your body is two-thirds water. The rest is made up of about 50,000 million tiny cells – the basic building blocks of life – which vary in shape and size and carry out different jobs. For example, red blood cells carry oxygen, and nerve cells pass messages to and from the brain. Cells have only a limited lifetime, so they have to be repaired or replaced when they wear out. Groups of the same type of cell form body tissue such as skin and muscle. Groups of different types of tissue make up organs such as the heart and the lungs. Each organ has a particular job to do in the body.

nucleus

membrane

Millions of Cells

Cells cannot be seen with the naked eye, but can be examined under a microscope. They have a membrane around the outside and contain a nucleus, or control centre.

Mammals

Humans, like mice, belong to a group of animals called mammals. They share several similar characteristics. They have mammary glands, so the females can produce milk for their young. Mammals have a constant body temperature, which for humans is 37°C, and their skin is covered in hair.

Muscles are attached to bones. When a muscle shortens, it pulls on the bone and moves it. Muscles also make up your heart and surround your gut.

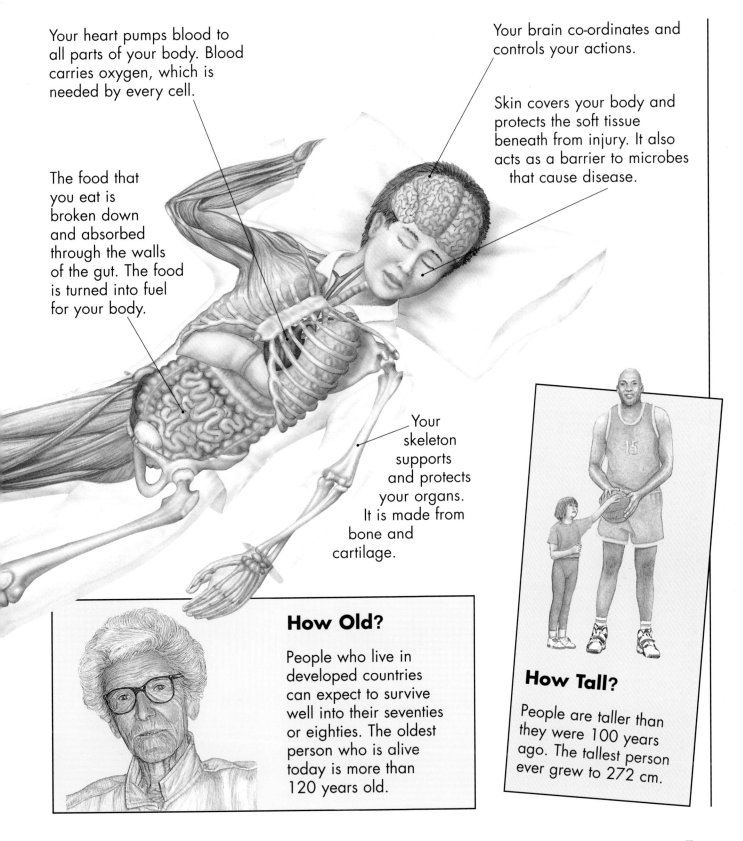

Your heart pumps blood to all parts of your body. Blood carries oxygen, which is needed by every cell.

The food that you eat is broken down and absorbed through the walls of the gut. The food is turned into fuel for your body.

Your brain co-ordinates and controls your actions.

Skin covers your body and protects the soft tissue beneath from injury. It also acts as a barrier to microbes that cause disease.

Your skeleton supports and protects your organs. It is made from bone and cartilage.

How Old?

People who live in developed countries can expect to survive well into their seventies or eighties. The oldest person who is alive today is more than 120 years old.

How Tall?

People are taller than they were 100 years ago. The tallest person ever grew to 272 cm.

The Skeleton

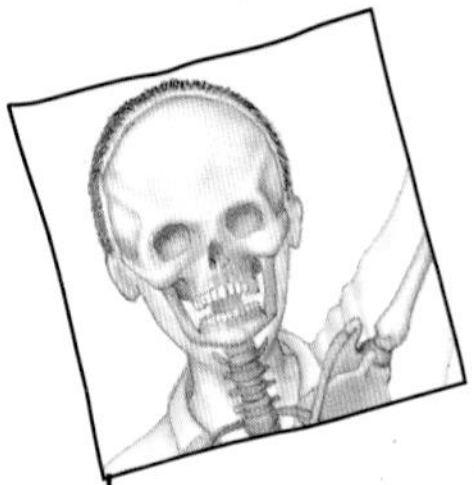

The skeleton is the hardest and strongest part of your body. Without it, you could not stand up, or move. The skeleton protects your organs and the muscles that move your limbs are attached to it. The spine supports your body. It is made up of a column of small bones called vertebrae, separated by small rubbery discs of cartilage that cushion the bones and allow the spine to bend. Joints allow other bones to move.

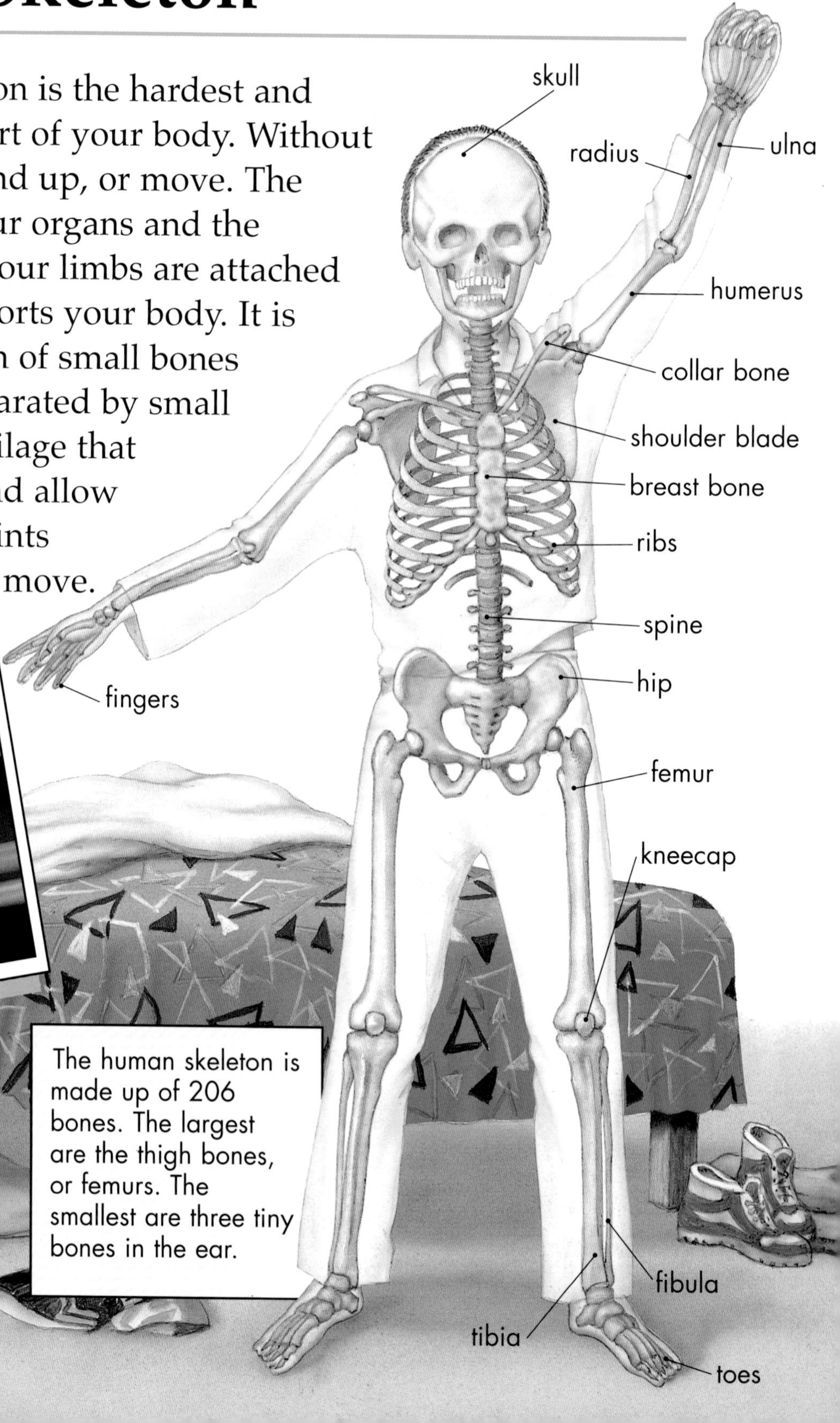

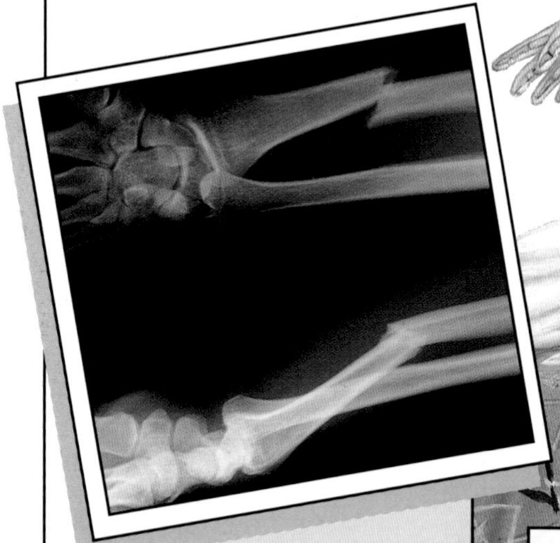

skull

radius

ulna

humerus

collar bone

shoulder blade

breast bone

ribs

spine

hip

femur

kneecap

fingers

fibula

tibia

toes

X-rays

Doctors use X-rays to take photographs of bones inside a patient's body. This X-ray shows a broken arm.

The human skeleton is made up of 206 bones. The largest are the thigh bones, or femurs. The smallest are three tiny bones in the ear.

Do it yourself

Muscles work in pairs. One contracts, or shortens, while the other relaxes, or stretches.

1. Take two lengths of wood. Ask an adult to help you join the ends using a hinge. This will be an elbow.

2 Attach four hooks to the wood in the positions shown. Use short lengths of string to attach rubber bands between the hooks.

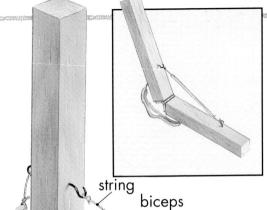

string

biceps band

hinge

triceps band

hook

3. The top band acts as the biceps muscle and the one underneath is the triceps muscle. When you bend the two pieces of wood at the elbow, the triceps muscle is stretched and the biceps shortens.

shoulder

hip

knee

elbow

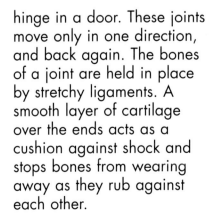

Joints

Shoulder and hip joints are called ball and socket joints because the upper arm bone and the thigh bone end in a smooth ball that swivels in a hollow socket. This type of joint allows movement in all directions. Elbow and knee joints are called hinge joints because they work like the hinge in a door. These joints move only in one direction, and back again. The bones of a joint are held in place by stretchy ligaments. A smooth layer of cartilage over the ends acts as a cushion against shock and stops bones from wearing away as they rub against each other.

9

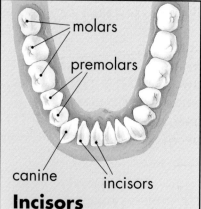

Teeth

The first set of 20 teeth, called milk teeth, start to appear within a few months of birth. Under the milk teeth, deep in the gums, are the permanent teeth. The first permanent teeth appear at about six years of age. They push out the milk teeth as they grow. An adult has 32 teeth. Beneath the tough outer covering of enamel is dentine, which makes up most of the tooth. It is softer than enamel and is easily damaged by decay. Deep in the middle is the pulp cavity, which contains nerves and blood vessels.

Incisors and Molars

The sharp incisors at the front are for cutting food, and the canines next to them are for tearing food. Premolars and molars are the large, flat teeth at the back that are used for chewing food.

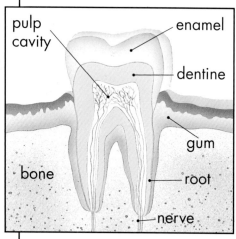

A colourless, sticky layer called plaque forms over your teeth. Unless you brush your teeth properly, it hardens to form tartar, a tough layer that is difficult to remove and eventually leads to gum disease and tooth decay.

Avoid Teeth Like These!

Bacteria in your mouth produce acids that dissolve away the surface of a tooth's enamel and cause dental decay. Toothache starts when decay reaches the nerves. A dentist will remove the decay and replace it with a filling of grey amalgam (a mixture of metals), or white plastic material that blends in better with the tooth.

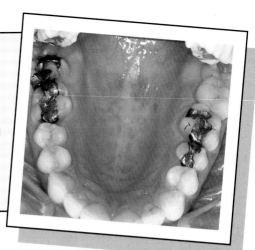

Do it yourself

Some teeth are designed to bite off food, and others are better for chewing. The teeth you use to bite off food have sharp edges. Those for chewing are larger with a flat, ridged surface.

1. Using a mirror, have a good look at the teeth in your mouth. How many teeth have you got? Are they milk teeth or permanent teeth? Can you name them?

2. Bite off a piece of raw carrot and chew it. Which teeth did you use to bite off a piece? Which teeth did you use to chew the carrot? Did your tongue help?

👁 Eye-Spy

How many of your teeth have fillings? Carry out a survey to find out how many fillings your friends have. Which teeth are most usually filled? Do your parents have more or fewer fillings than you?

A Healthy Diet

Your body needs a mixture of foods that contain different nutrients. Carbohydrates and fats produce energy. Bread, potatoes and cereals are rich in carbohydrates. Milk and meat contain fat. You need protein for growth and to repair cells. Meat, eggs and beans provide protein. Your body also needs minerals and vitamins. Calcium, found in milk and cheese, helps build strong teeth and bones. Iron, which is needed for red blood cells, is added to breakfast cereals.

Vitamins

Vitamins are named by letters. Vegetables and fruit are good sources of Vitamin C. Milk and cheese provide vitamins A and D. Rice, cereals, and brown bread provide Vitamin B.

What do you eat for breakfast? Most likely, you have a bowl of cereal with milk, and perhaps some toast. Somebody living in Indonesia might have rice mixed with vegetables and topped with a fried egg. Both meals are a healthy start to the day.

Do it yourself

Try this test to identify foods that contain starch, a carbohydrate found in plant foods.

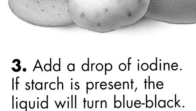

1. Collect a selection of foods such as a biscuit, an apple, cheese, and a potato. Grind up a small sample of one of them.

2. Add a small amount of water and mix well. Leave aside for a few minutes and then pour the liquid into a small container.

3. Add a drop of iodine. If starch is present, the liquid will turn blue-black.

4. Repeat this for each food. Which ones contain starch?

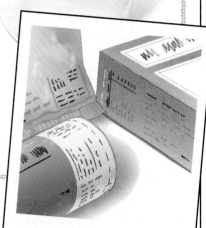

Vegetarians

People who eat a vegetarian diet do not eat meat. Their meals are based on vegetables, especially pulses (beans and peas), often with small amounts of eggs, milk and cheese for protein.

Junk Food

Sweetened drinks, crisps, hamburgers and chips are called 'junk food' because they are convenient and cheap, but not very healthy. They contain a lot of fat and carbohydrate.

👁 Eye-Spy

Look for the list of contents on packaged foods. Some foods contain preservatives, or are given artificial colour and taste. There may also be numbers for energy (calories), fat and protein.

Digestion

Food provides energy for your body and helps you to grow. When you swallow, chewed food mixed with saliva passes to your stomach and intestines. Digestive juices, which contain chemicals called enzymes, surround the food and break it down so that it can pass through the walls of the intestine into the blood system. All that is left, once digestion is complete, is a small quantity of faeces. This contains the bits of food you cannot digest, and it passes out of your body when you go to the toilet.

Salivation

When we see, smell, or think about food, glands under the tongue start to release saliva. This helps to break down food for the digestive process. Animals salivate, too. You may have seen a dog drool when it is given some food.

Do it yourself

Saliva lubricates food so that it is easy to swallow.

1. Chew a small cube of dry bread without swallowing.

2. As the bread becomes mushy, you should start to detect a sweet taste in your mouth.

3. Repeat this with a piece of apple or cheese. Is there any difference?

How It Works

The enzymes in your saliva break down starch into sugar. This produces the sweet taste in your mouth. This only happens with foods such as bread, which contain cooked starch.

Special Stomachs

Plants contain a tough material called cellulose, which cannot be digested by humans. A cow's large stomach contains bacteria that can digest cellulose. To help digestion, the cow brings up the food and chews it a second time.

👁 **Eye-Spy**

Food provides energy for daily activities such as walking and running. Make a list of all the things you do during the day that require your body to use energy.

Your digestive system is about 9 m long. Food passes from your mouth to your stomach, where it is stored for up to four hours. Food may take several days to pass right through the digestive system. Muscles in the walls of the intestines squeeze to push the food along.

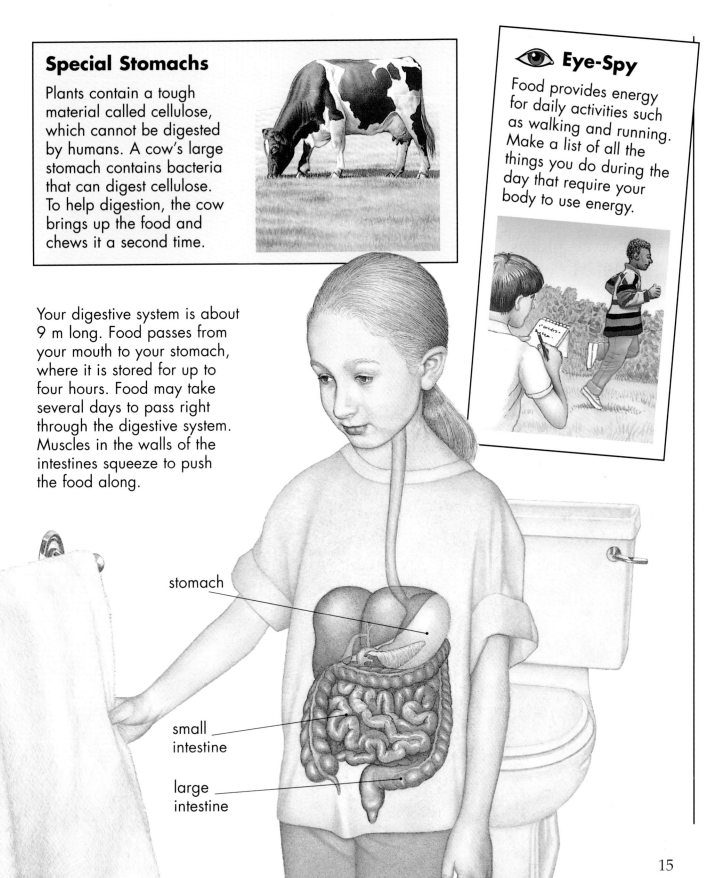

stomach

small intestine

large intestine

15

The Waterworks

Your kidneys filter out wastes and excess water from your blood after food has been digested. The waste materials become a liquid called urine. Urine travels down two tubes called ureters to your bladder, where it is stored. When the sphincter muscle on your bladder relaxes, the urine flows down another tube called the urethra and out of your body. Your kidneys also help to control the amount of fluid in your body. If you drink a lot of water, your body has to get rid of some, so it produces extra urine.

Each of us has two kidneys. Every day, 1,500 litres of blood circulate through your kidneys.

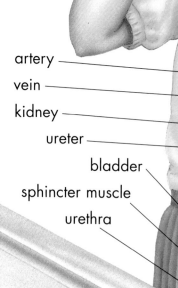

artery
vein
kidney
ureter
bladder
sphincter muscle
urethra

Hot and Thirsty

During exercise, your skin sweats to help keep you cool. This water has to be replaced, so your brain tells you that you need water by making you feel thirsty.

Do it yourself

You can make a very simple filter to show how a kidney works.

1. Use a ready-made coffee filter paper, or fold a piece of kitchen paper into a cone shape. Put the filter into a plastic funnel. Place the funnel in a container.

2. Grind up some chalk and mix the powder in water so that it is very cloudy. Pour the cloudy water into the filter.

3. The water that drips from the filter is much clearer than the water that went into the filter. The filter in your kidney is similar. It lets some of the water and all of the waste through, but keeps back the valuable blood cells.

Why Do Babies Need Nappies?

Babies have no control over the moment when urine passes out of their bladder. They have to learn how to use the sphincter muscle.

Water to Drink

A person can survive for many days without food, but will die within two days without water. In parts of Africa where it is hot and there is not much rain, people often have to travel long distances to find enough clean water to drink. During a severe drought, many thousands of people die.

Heart and Circulation

Blood is circulated all around your body through a system of blood vessels. At the centre of the blood system is your heart – pumping tirelessly day and night. Arteries carry blood from your heart to all parts of your body. Veins bring blood from which oxygen has been removed back to your heart. Blood carries oxygen from the lungs and food from the intestines to the cells, and picks up carbon dioxide and other waste materials from the cells.

Blood Cells

Blood is made up of plasma and blood cells. Red cells carry oxygen and white cells protect your body from disease.

Do it yourself

Your pulse tells how fast your heart is beating.

1. Take your pulse while you are resting. Count the number of pulses, or beats, you can feel in one minute.

2. Now run up and down some stairs.

3. Take your pulse again. By how much has your pulse rate increased?

4. Wait five minutes and measure your pulse again. Has it returned to normal?

How It Works

When you exercise, your muscles need oxygen. Your heart beats more quickly in order to pump blood to the muscles. Your pulse may increase from 60–75 beats to over 100 per minute.

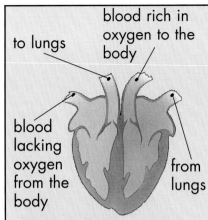

The Heart

Your heart is two pumps working side by side. Blood from your body enters the right side and is pumped to the lungs. Blood from the lungs returns to the left side and is pumped to your body.

blood rich in oxygen to the body

to lungs

blood lacking oxygen from the body

from lungs

Your body has 100,000 km of blood vessels containing about 7 litres of blood. Arteries and veins are linked by tiny capillaries.

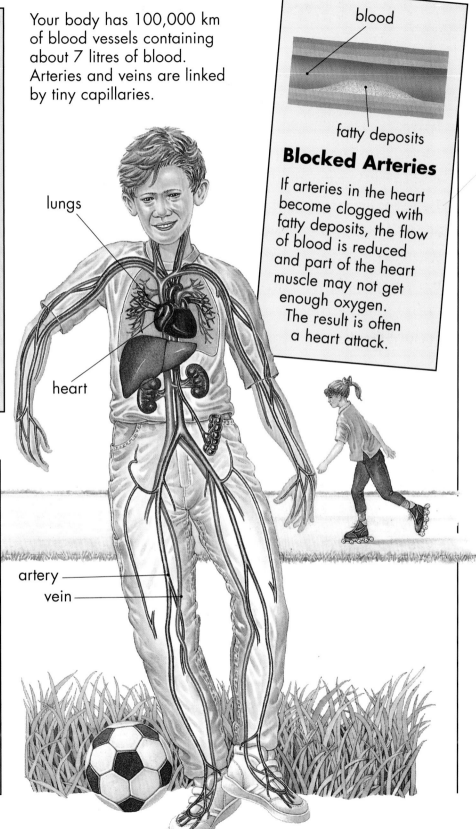

lungs

heart

artery

vein

Blocked Arteries

blood

fatty deposits

If arteries in the heart become clogged with fatty deposits, the flow of blood is reduced and part of the heart muscle may not get enough oxygen. The result is often a heart attack.

Clotting Blood

platelets

red blood cells

If you cut yourself, small cells in your blood called platelets form a network of fibres across the cut. Red blood cells become trapped in the net and harden to form a scab.

19

Breathing

Every four or five seconds, you take a fresh breath of air into your lungs. When you breathe in, your chest expands as your lungs fill with air. Air contains oxygen, which the blood cells need to release the energy locked up in food. The cells produce a waste gas called carbon dioxide. This is picked up by the blood and carried back to your lungs. When you breathe out, the air that leaves your lungs contains much less oxygen, but an increased amount of carbon dioxide.

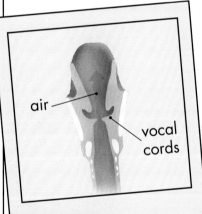

Voice Box

When you speak, muscles bring your vocal cords close together so that air leaving your lungs is forced through a narrow slit. As air rushes through the cords, they vibrate and produce a sound.

The trachea leads from the back of the throat into the chest, and then divides into two narrower tubes called bronchi. These carry air into the lungs. Beneath the lungs there is a muscle called the diaphragm, which moves down when you breathe in, helping to suck air into the lungs, and up when you breathe out again.

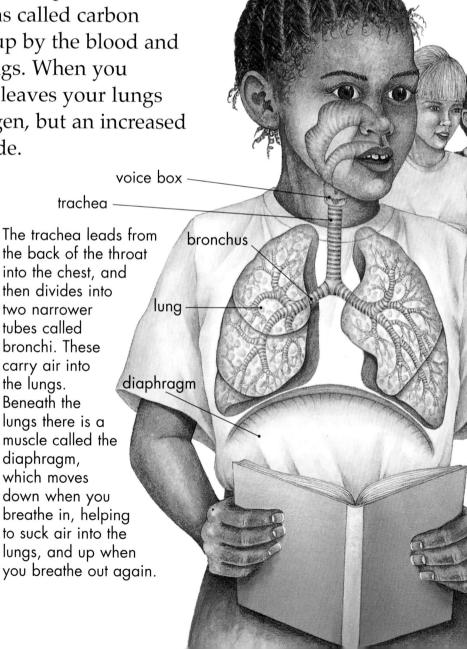

Breathing Under Water

Divers take compressed air with them in a special cylinder. They use a mask and breathing apparatus so that they can breathe normally.

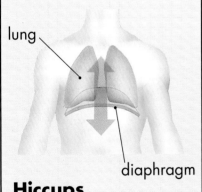

lung

diaphragm

Hiccups

Hiccups are caused when your diaphragm contracts sharply. This stops you breathing in normally and your vocal cords make the familiar 'hic' sound.

Do it yourself

How much air can you expel from your lungs?

1. You will need a large plastic container, rubber tubing and a crayon. Fill the container with water.

2. Fill the sink with water and lower the container into the sink. Quickly turn it upside down without letting in any air. Push one end of the rubber tubing into the container, holding your finger over the other end to block it.

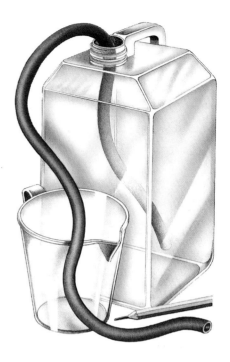

3. Take a deep breath and blow out through the tubing. Mark on the container the water level after you breathed out.

4. Empty the container and then fill it with water up to the mark. This represents the volume of air that you expelled from your lungs.

The Nervous System

Your brain is the control centre of your body. Without it, you could not move, think, or remember anything. Your brain receives information from all over your body, especially from the senses. It uses this information to co-ordinate your actions. The nerves carry messages from your brain to all parts of your body. The information kept in your brain for future reference is called memory. This is a store of all the things you have seen, heard, and done.

The brain and spinal cord make up the central nervous system. Nerves then branch off to the rest of the body. This outer network of nerves is called the peripheral nervous system.

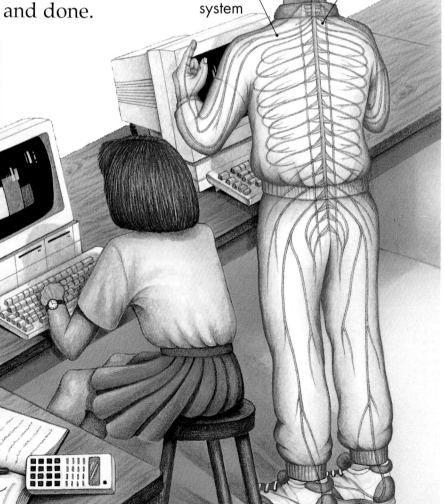

brain

spinal cord

peripheral nervous system

Eye-Spy

Your brain determines whether you use your right or left hand for writing. Most people are right-handed, but may use the left hand for certain jobs. See which hand you use to do a variety of tasks.

Do it yourself

Try this test to see how fast your reflexes are.

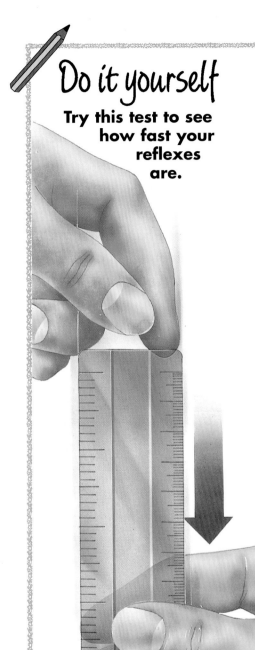

1. Sit down with your friend standing in front of you, holding a ruler vertically by its end.

2. Hold your hand open immediately below the ruler, ready to catch it when it drops. Your friend should let the ruler drop without warning.

3. Grab the ruler as it falls through your open hand. Note how far the ruler has fallen by looking at the scale.

4. Try catching the ruler first with the right hand, and then with the left hand.

Reflexes

Some nerves work without the brain being involved. The message rushes along a nerve to the spinal cord and the reply returns along another nerve, telling the muscle to contract. If you sit with one leg crossed over the other and somebody taps your leg just below the kneecap, the lower part of your leg kicks up. This automatic response is called a reflex.

The Brain

The brain is a soft grey organ with a wrinkled surface, protected by the skull. It weighs about 1.5 kg and contains as many as 10,000 million nerve cells. The spinal cord leads away from the base of the brain.

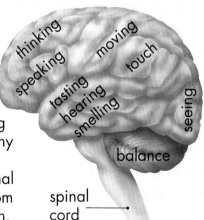

thinking
speaking
moving
touch
tasting
hearing
smelling
seeing
balance
spinal cord

The Senses

The sense organs turn a stimulus, such as a touch or a noise, into an electrical message that is sent along sensory nerves to your brain. Your skin has nerve endings that are sensitive to pressure, touch, heat and pain. Your sense of taste comes from taste buds on the tongue. It is linked to the sense of smell, which comes from sensors in your nose. Your ears hear sound waves that enter the ear and hit the eardrum. You see with your eyes. Light rays enter the front of the eye and produce a picture on the retina at the back. The picture is detected by special sensors called rods and cones.

Balance

Ears help you to keep your balance. Inside your ears there are three tubes filled with fluid. When you move your head, the fluid moves and this sends information to your brain.

Do it yourself

See what happens if you eat food without being able to see or smell it.

Blindfold a friend. Hold a piece of onion under her nose to dull her sense of smell. Now give her some food to eat. Can she tell you what she is eating? Can she tell the difference between two types of bread?

apple

potato

cheese

brown bread

white bread

When you play ball games, your senses are very important. You have to watch the ball and the other players. You have to listen for calls and be ready to move quickly.

Do it yourself

You can see some colours out of the corner of your eye more easily.

1. Ask a friend to sit on a stool. Stand behind her. Take two pens of the same colour, and hold one in each hand. Put your arms out to the side, at your friend's eye level. Slowly move your arms forward, around the front of your friend.

2. Ask your friend to tell you the colour of the pens while keeping her eyes looking to the front.

3. Try with two more pens of a different colour. Which colour does your friend see out of the corner of her eye more easily?

How It Works

Bright colours are more easily seen out of the corner of the eye. This is why emergency vehicles use red and yellow – it helps us to see them coming up behind us.

Braille

Braille is a form of writing using raised dots. A blind person can feel the dots with his fingertips and translate them into words.

Keeping Fit

When you are fit, your body works well and you feel good. You are more energetic and less likely to suffer from illnesses such as colds or flu. Exercise keeps your muscles firm and strengthens your heart and lungs. To stay fit your body needs plenty of exercise each day. Walking, swimming, cycling and playing sports are all good exercise. When you exercise, you use up more energy, so it is important to eat a good balanced diet.

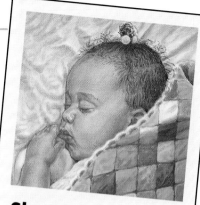

Sleeping

Having enough sleep is essential for staying fit. When you sleep, your heartbeat and breathing slow down and your muscles relax.

👁 Eye-Spy

There are many things you can do during the day to improve your fitness, such as walking to school and taking the stairs rather than the lift. How many other things can you think of?

Unhealthy Lifestyle

Eating junk food and spending hours sitting in front of the television is bad for your health.

Healthy Lifestyle

Eating plenty of fresh fruit and vegetables and exercising regularly is good for your health.

ANIMALS
IN
ACTION

The Animal Kingdom

Animals range in size from tiny creatures that can only be seen under a microscope to the huge blue whale. Although they may look very different from one another, animals have many features in common. Their senses — sight, hearing, smell, taste and touch — allow them to communicate and to be aware of their surroundings. The senses also help animals to find food, which gives them the energy to move, and to find a mate, so that they can reproduce, or give birth to young.

How Many Types?

There are 1.5 million types of living organisms. Animals are the largest group, and they are divided into vertebrates (with backbones) and invertebrates (without backbones). Arthropods are the largest group of invertebrates.

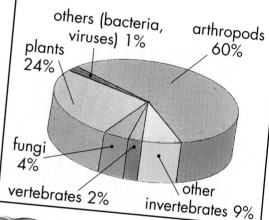

others (bacteria, viruses) 1%
plants 24%
arthropods 60%
fungi 4%
vertebrates 2%
other invertebrates 9%

tiger

snail

rattlesnake

toad

earthworm

tapeworm

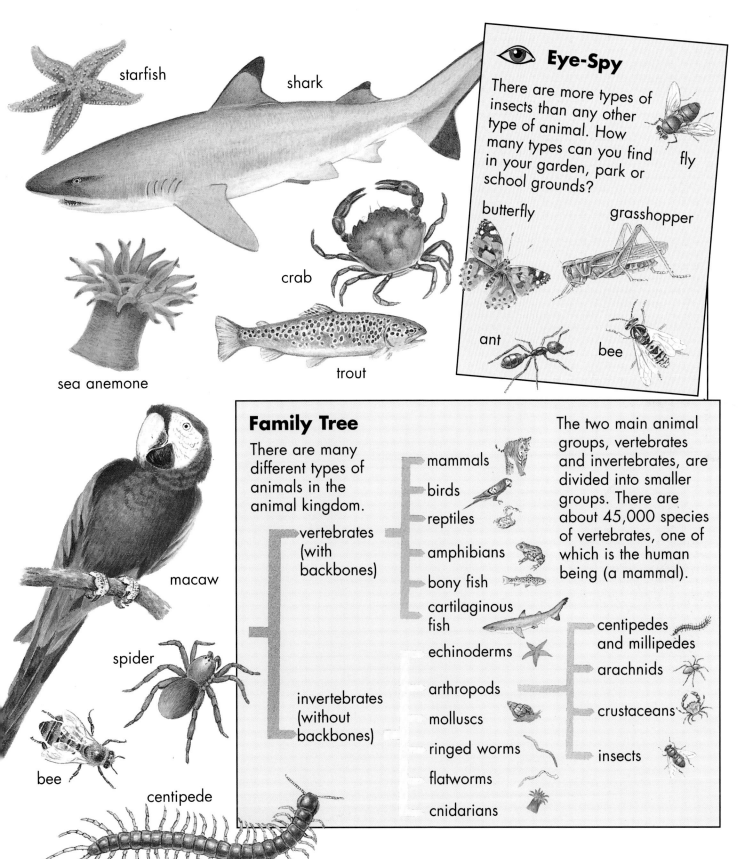

starfish

shark

Eye-Spy

There are more types of insects than any other type of animal. How many types can you find in your garden, park or school grounds?

fly

butterfly

grasshopper

ant

bee

crab

trout

sea anemone

macaw

spider

bee

centipede

Family Tree

There are many different types of animals in the animal kingdom.

The two main animal groups, vertebrates and invertebrates, are divided into smaller groups. There are about 45,000 species of vertebrates, one of which is the human being (a mammal).

vertebrates (with backbones)
- mammals
- birds
- reptiles
- amphibians
- bony fish
- cartilaginous fish

invertebrates (without backbones)
- echinoderms
- arthropods
  - centipedes and millipedes
  - arachnids
  - crustaceans
  - insects
- molluscs
- ringed worms
- flatworms
- cnidarians

29

Communication

Animals communicate by sight, smell, touch, hearing and even electrical signals. They send signals to tell other animals that they have found a new source of food, and they send special alarm signals if they sense danger. One of the most important roles of communication is to bring male and female animals together. Many male birds have brightly-coloured feathers or sing beautiful songs to attract the females.

Making Light

On a summer's night, a female glow-worm climbs a tall grass stem and signals to a male glow-worm with her brightly-lit abdomen.

Colour Talks

A cuttlefish communicates by using colour. It changes the colour of its skin to send messages to other cuttlefish. A red colour indicates anger. This is used by one male to warn off another.

butterfly

jaguar

In the shadowy darkness of the jungle, animals have to advertise their presence with bright colours, or by sounds.

arrow-poison frog

uakari monkey

howler monkey

macaw

toucan

tree frog

Dance of the Honey-bee

A honey-bee tells other bees where to find food by dancing. It performs a waggle dance in a figure of eight. The angle of the central part of the dance tells the bees in which direction to fly.

Do it yourself

Biologists learn a lot about animal communication by observing their behaviour.

Watch your pet and see how it communicates by its behaviour. This cat's fur is bristling because it is frightened of the unfamiliar ball.

31

The Brain and Nervous System

Animals need fast links between their senses and their muscles so that they can move, search for food, and avoid predators. The nervous system connects the senses to the brain, which receives information from all over the body. The brain analyses the information and sends a message back to tell the muscles to move. The largest part of a vertebrate's brain is the forebrain, or cerebrum. Mammals have a much larger cerebrum than any other kind of animal. Different parts of the cerebrum control the senses, memory and intelligence.

Blinking

Blinking is an automatic reflex. Mammals do it without thinking. Each time a mammal blinks, the eyes are washed with a fluid, keeping them free from germs.

👁 Eye-Spy

When you catch a ball, your body reacts quickly because of reflexes. These are automatic responses that you do not have to think about. How many different reflexes do you use during the day?

Large and Small Brains

Stegosaurus was 9 m long and weighed about 1.75 tonnes. Yet this dinosaur's brain was only the size of a walnut, weighing just 70 g. A human brain weighs about 1.4 kg.

brain

Chimpanzees have learned to use a stick as a tool to dig termites from their nest. This method of feeding involves the senses of sight, touch and taste. Their brain co-ordinates the actions.

Do it yourself

Build a maze and see how long it takes your pet mouse or hamster to find some food.

1. To make the walls, cut some corrugated cardboard into strips about 15 cm wide. Hold them in place on a large board with sticky tape or glue.

corrugated cardboard

2. At the centre of the maze, place a little food. Put your pet at the entrance to the maze. It will use the senses of sight and smell to find the food.

food

33

Sight

Sight is the sense that helps animals to observe their environment, find food, and see other animals. Most animals have two eyes, each giving a slightly different image. Predatory mammals have eyes at the front of their head so that both eyes can focus on one object. The brain compares the views from each eye to produce a three-dimensional image that allows the mammal to judge the distance and speed of its prey. Many animals have eyes on the sides of their head, to give good all-round vision that alerts them to attackers.

Compound Eyes

Insects have compound eyes made up of thousands of tiny, separate lenses. The large compound eyes of this dragonfly help it to be an efficient hunter.

vulture

lion

jackal

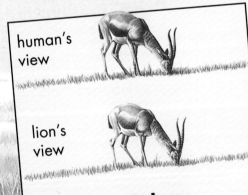

human's view

lion's view

Seeing in Colour

A human looking at a gazelle sees a full colour image. A lion looking at a gazelle sees only shades of black and white.

Do it yourself

Your eyes can play tricks on you. Try this trick to 'behead' a friend!

1. Ask your friend to stand against a wall. Close your right eye. With your left eye focus on a point 1 m to the right of her head.

2. Walk towards your friend and keep looking at the point.

3. All of a sudden, you will notice out of the corner of your eye that your friend's face has disappeared.

How It Works

When you are a certain distance away from your friend, the light from her face falls on the 'blind spot' in your eye. This spot is where the optic nerve leaves the eye, so there are no cells to detect the light. Because the brain receives no information about light falling here, it cannot see the face.

Sharp eyesight is important on the wide open plains of the African savannah. Lions find and chase their prey, while vultures hover above, on the look-out for their next meal.

zebras

hyena

Hearing

Sound is made by something vibrating. The movement creates sound waves that travel through air, water and solid objects. A mammal's ear is more developed than the ear of a fish or bird. It has three parts — the outer, middle and inner ear. The outer ear funnels sound waves into the head. The middle ear has three tiny bones that magnify the sound. The inner ear is filled with a fluid. Sound waves cause the fluid to push on nerve endings and this sends a message along a nerve to the brain.

African guinea fowl can hear the sound of thunder hundreds of kilometres away. This tells them that rain is on the way.

At night in the desert, sound carries well. Animals that come out in the cool of the night have excellent hearing that enables them to find food and to hear predators.

coyote

jack rabbit

Strange Ears

Not all animals have ears on their heads. Crickets have ears on their knees, and cockroaches on their tails. Spiders have no ears at all. Special hairs on their legs and feet can detect sound vibrations.

cricket

cockroach

spider

36

Do it yourself

Having two ears allows us to judge the direction of sounds. See what happens when you use only one ear.

1. Place a blindfold over your eyes and cover one ear.

2. Ask a friend to stand a short distance away and tap a hollow object with a stick. Can you tell from which direction the sound came?

More Things to Try

How good is your hearing? Ask your friend to drop a small object to the ground. Then get them to drop it further away. How far away can you still hear the sound of the object hitting the ground?

kit fox

Large Ears

To improve their hearing, people cup their hands behind their ears. This makes a funnel to catch more sound waves. Rabbits have large ears for the same reason.

Many animals have a hearing range that is greater than our own — they can hear sounds that we cannot. Dog trainers use a whistle that seems to make no sound, but it can be heard by a dog. Sometimes we can hear these sounds by using special sound recorders. We cannot hear the ultra-sonic noises made by bats, but they can be picked up by an electronic bat detector that alters the sound so that we can hear it.

Hearing Under Water

Dolphins produce sound waves that travel through water. The sound waves bounce off fish and this tells the dolphins where to hunt. Fishing boats use sonar in the same way.

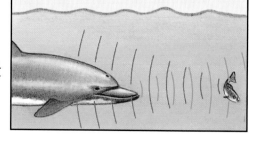

Elephants make loud trumpeting noises, and they also communicate with their stomachs! Their stomachs produce very low growling sounds that humans cannot hear. These sounds travel great distances over the grasslands and can be heard by elephants far away.

Do it yourself

An animal's sense of balance comes from its ears.

Squirrels have to be able to keep their balance when climbing and jumping, or they would fall to the ground.

You can lose your balance if you spin around too quickly. You can prevent this by 'spotting'. Pick an object on the wall and focus on this as you spin. Does this stop you feeling dizzy?

Seeing With Sound

Bats have excellent hearing and use it to navigate and hunt in the dark. A bat emits very high frequency sounds that bounce off walls and other objects, forming an echo. The bat's ears pick up the echoes. The bat can then work out the position of objects, including flying moths.

echo

high frequency sounds

How It Works

Spinning round confuses your sense of balance. By focusing on a fixed spot, your brain receives extra information from your eyes.

39

Smell

When we smell something, we are detecting traces of substances in the air. As we breathe in, the air passes over special sensors in the nose. Humans can distinguish between 10,000 different smells, and dogs can detect even more. Predatory animals rely on their sense of smell to find food. Polar bears can detect the rotting body of a seal on the ice more than 20 kilometres away. Some animals have a sense of smell, but do not have noses. Lizards and snakes use their darting tongue to collect smell samples from the air.

Pheromones

Moths communicate by releasing chemicals called pheromones. Their antennae are so good at detecting pheromones in the air that one moth can follow the scent trail of another over great distances.

Sniffer Dogs

The long shape of a dog's nose encourages air to circulate around the most sensitive parts, giving the dog a good sense of smell. Some dogs are trained to sniff out drugs concealed in luggage.

The giant anteater has an excellent sense of smell which it uses to find its favourite food, termites.

Marking Territory

Deer mark trees and shrubs around the edge of their territory with a scent that lingers for many days. This warns other deer to keep out.

Do it yourself

A scent becomes less noticeable as you get used to it.

1. Dab scent on your arm. You can detect it easily. Can you smell it after an hour?

2. Can your friend smell the scent after an hour? Your smell receptors have become used to the smell and lost their sensitivity to it, but to your friend the scent is new.

41

Taste

The sense of taste comes from taste buds on the tongue, inside the cheek, on the roof of the mouth and in the throat. Humans can only distinguish between four basic tastes — sweet, sour, salty and bitter — but when these are combined with a sense of smell, we can distinguish between many different foods. Animals that live in water often have a particularly well-developed sense of taste. Deep-sea fish have poor sight, and some of them rely on taste-sensitive filaments that hang from their mouths.

Butterflies have special taste sensors on their feet. Female butterflies use them to make sure that they lay their eggs on the right kind of leaf.

Taste Buds

Not all mammals have the same number of taste buds. Pigs have about 15,000 taste buds — almost twice as many as humans.

shark

spiny lobster

Sea anemones and octopuses have taste cells on their tentacles, and sharks have them in their mouth. The spiny lobster has a pair of antennae that can smell and taste rotting flesh.

octopus

Do it yourself

Find out which food the birds in your garden prefer.

1. Put two different foods, such as breadcrumbs and sunflower seeds, into two containers. Place them on a bird-table or on an outside ledge. Hang a bag of peanuts from the table.

2. Record in a notebook which species of birds visit the table and what food they eat. Do they come at a regular time? Do they have a favourite food? You may need a bird watcher's book and a pair of binoculars to help you identify all the different birds.

sunflower seeds

breadcrumbs

peanuts

More Things to Try

Try some more hanging food, such as pine cones with peanut butter smeared between the scales, pine cones filled with suet, or a chain of peanuts in their shells. Other foods that you could put in the containers are meal-worms, small pieces of cheese, or chopped-up apples.

sea anemone

Touch

The sense of touch is triggered by pressure on an animal's skin or outer covering. This stimulates receptors that send messages along the nerves to the brain. A mammal's skin has millions of receptors for light and heavy pressure, hot and cold, and pain. Some areas, such as the fingertips, are more sensitive than others. Fish are very sensitive to changes in water pressure. A line of touch receptors, called the lateral line, runs along their bodies.

Birds have whisker-like feathers on their wing tips that provide information about air currents. This helps them to control their flight.

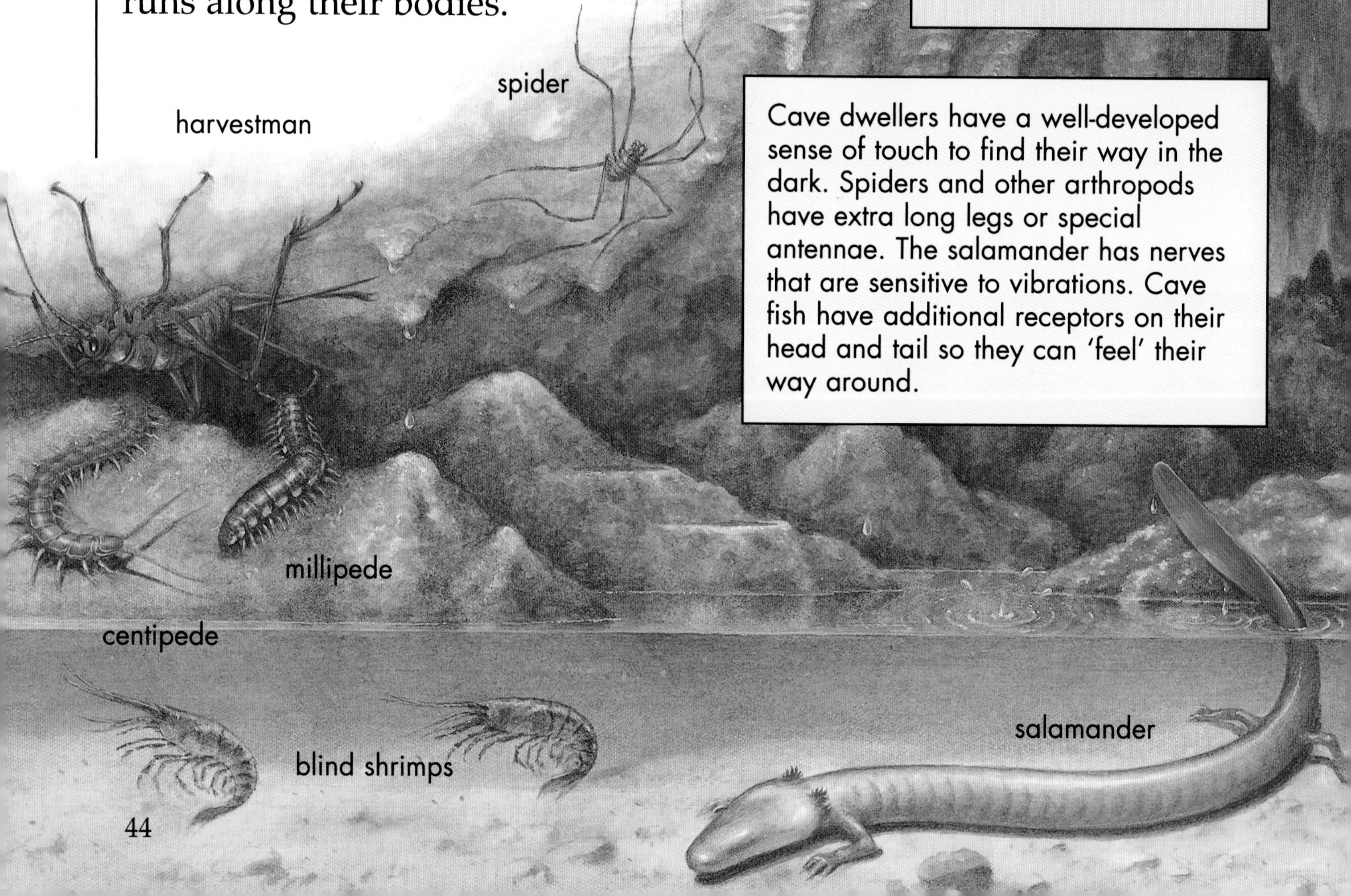

Cave dwellers have a well-developed sense of touch to find their way in the dark. Spiders and other arthropods have extra long legs or special antennae. The salamander has nerves that are sensitive to vibrations. Cave fish have additional receptors on their head and tail so they can 'feel' their way around.

spider

harvestman

millipede

centipede

blind shrimps

salamander

Whiskers

Moles have sensitive whiskers around their mouths. They can even sense a draught of air caused by a wriggling worm. Whiskers on the tail tell a mole about the size and shape of a tunnel.

Discover which part of the skin is the most sensitive.

Blindfold a friend. Hold two pencils with the tips close together. Touch the tips on the skin of the forearm, the back of the arm, the palm and the back of the hand. Can your friend feel one or two pencil tips?

How It Works

An area of skin with touch receptors close together is very sensitive. Two pencils touch two receptors, so the brain detects two tips. If the receptors are fewer and further apart, the skin is less sensitive and one of the tips may not be close enough to a receptor to trigger it.

Fingertips

Gorillas have sensitive fingertips with many touch receptors. These help gorillas to groom each other. Grooming removes fleas and strengthens the bond between parent and offspring.

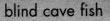

blind cave fish

45

A Sixth Sense

Many animals have senses that we have only just begun to understand. Using these senses, they may view the world very differently from the way we see it. The Earth has an invisible magnetic 'field' that causes a compass to point to north. Some animals can detect this and use the information to navigate. Many fish have special organs that can generate an electrical charge. They use these organs to find their way around and even to stun their prey.

Animals often seem to behave strangely just before a disaster such as an earthquake. Cats carry their kittens to safety, and snakes and rats flee from buildings. These animals can sense changes in the environment that humans are not yet aware of.

Seeing the Heat

The rattlesnake has poor eyesight, but at night it can detect mice moving from several metres away. It has a sense organ on its head that can 'see' the body heat of its prey.

The Platypus

The platypus lives in murky rivers of Australia. It hunts at night, using a special sense organ in its bill to detect the electrical activity produced by the muscles of its prey.

Homing Pigeons

Pigeons are good navigators. If they are released hundreds of kilometres away, they can still find their way home. It is not clear how they navigate, but scientists think that they may be sensitive to the Earth's magnetic field.

47

Learning and Instinct

Animals are born with natural instincts that help them to survive. Newborn foals can get up and run within minutes. Birds instinctively know how to build their first nest and care for their young. But other patterns of behaviour are learned by watching adults or by trying things out. For example, an animal will learn which food is good to eat and where to find it, and which food makes it feel ill.

Young cheetahs learn to hunt by watching their mother and hunting with her. They practise hunting techniques during play with their brothers and sisters.

👁 Eye-Spy

Look out for young animals learning to do something for the first time. It could be young birds taking their first flight, or a kitten playing with a new toy.

MINIBEASTS
IN
CLOSE-UP

Is it a Minibeast?

Minibeasts are small animals that are often too small to be seen with the naked eye. Because there are so many types of animals, zoologists divide them into groups. The two main groups are animals with a backbone (vertebrates) and animals without a backbone (invertebrates). Minibeasts are all invertebrates. Arthropods are the largest group of invertebrates. They include insects, crustaceans, millipedes, centipedes and spiders. Worms are also invertebrates, and so are molluscs, a group that includes snails and slugs. Cnidaria are soft, water-living minibeasts that include sea anemones and jellyfish.

Caught in Amber

Millions of years ago, some insects were caught in sticky resin which oozed from the bark of pine trees. When this hardened and became amber, the insects were preserved inside.

No Backbone

A fish has a backbone, a bony rod running the length of its body. A crab has no backbone. Instead, it has a heavy protective outer covering.

Minibeasts vary in size, shape and colour. Scorpions and spiders have eight legs, while butterflies, bees and fleas have six, and earthworms and sea anemones have no legs at all. The starfish has a spiny covering, and the snail has a coiled shell that protects its soft body.

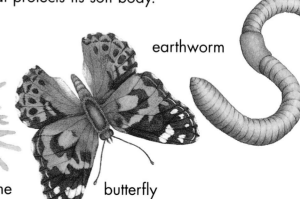

earthworm

sea anemone

butterfly

50

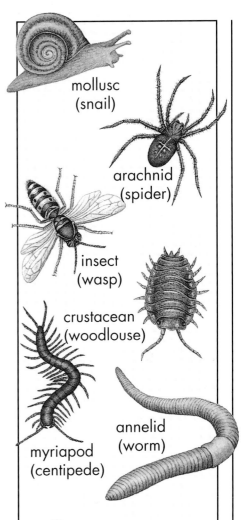

mollusc
(snail)

arachnid
(spider)

insect
(wasp)

crustacean
(woodlouse)

myriapod
(centipede)

annelid
(worm)

Ants

Ants are tiny minibeasts that can only be seen clearly when looked at under a magnifying glass. This photograph of an ant is many times larger than life size.

starfish

bee

spider

flea

snail

scorpion

👁 Eye-Spy

Minibeasts are found everywhere – in the garden, park and school grounds. Try to find an example of a minibeast from each of the main groups. As you try to identify an animal, count the number of legs and look for wings. The pictures above may help you with the identification.

51

Growing Up

Caterpillars and butterflies look very different, but they are actually the same animal at different stages in life. The caterpillar, in the growing stage, eats plants. Once it is fully grown, it enters the pupal stage. This is when the body of the caterpillar is completely reorganized into the body of a butterfly. After a few weeks, the case of the pupa splits open and the adult emerges. This complete change in appearance is called metamorphosis.

Courtship

The male fiddler crab attracts a female by waving his large claw. Different waves have different meanings.

The female butterfly lays her eggs on leaves. The eggs hatch within a few days and the young caterpillars feed on the leaves, growing rapidly. After a few weeks they pupate and undergo their metamorphosis.

1. egg

2. caterpillar

3. pupa

5. adult

4. new adult

Do it yourself

Stick insects are easy to keep as pets.

1. You will need a large plastic container such as an old aquarium, with a lid.

2. Stick insects feed on privet and blackberry leaves, so collect some branches for food. Keep the plants fresh by wrapping tissue paper around the bottom of the stems, and putting them in a small plastic pot of water.

3. Put in another small pot of water, for drinking.

4. The stick insects may start to lay eggs. The eggs are tiny, round and brown, and are easily confused with droppings. Collect the eggs and keep them in a small container until they hatch.

Locust Life Cycle

A locust egg hatches into a small hopper. It looks like an adult, but it is much smaller and lacks wings. The hopper grows rapidly, eating its own body weight in leaves each day. Every few days, it moults its skin to grow larger. At the fifth and final moult, the adult locust appears, complete with a set of wings.

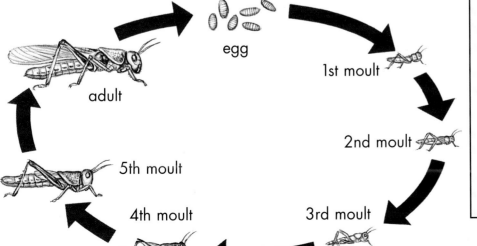

adult — egg — 1st moult — 2nd moult — 3rd moult — 4th moult — 5th moult

👁 Eye-Spy

Female butterflies lay their eggs on the leaves of plants that the caterpillars like to eat. Nettles are popular, and you may find several types of caterpillars feeding on them. Look for caterpillars and make a note of the plants you find them on.

53

Plant-Eaters

Plants are an important source of food for many minibeasts. Minibeasts and other animals that eat only plants are called herbivores. Most herbivores eat a wide range of plant food, especially leaves, but some feed on just fruit, pollen or nectar. Herbivores are the first link in the food chain because they feed only on plants. They, in turn, are eaten by larger animals called carnivores, the meat-eaters.

Honeypot Ants

Honeypot ants store nectar and honeydew in their bodies until they become too fat to move.

Do it yourself

See how many minibeasts you can find in the leaves of a tree.

1. Place a large white sheet under a low branch.

2. Give the branch a good shake. All the minibeasts living on that branch will fall onto your sheet.

3. Examine the animals you have caught. Those with wings will probably fly away, but the others will remain. Some of the more common minibeasts you might find are crab and wolf spiders, lacewings, green caterpillars, fruit flies, gall wasps and weevils. There may also be several different types of beetles.

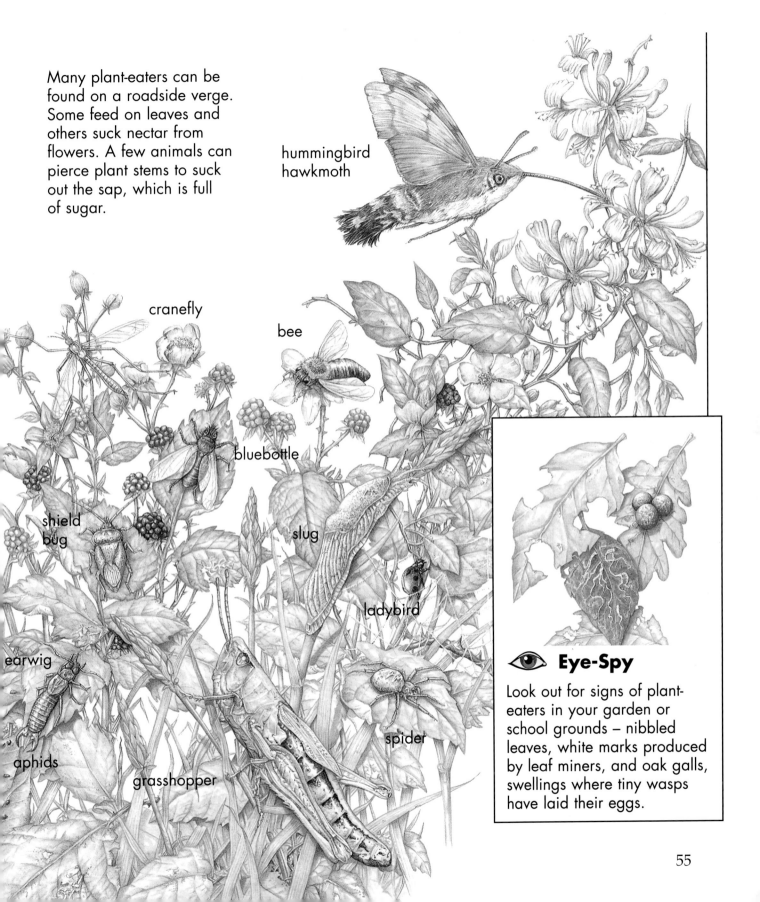

Many plant-eaters can be found on a roadside verge. Some feed on leaves and others suck nectar from flowers. A few animals can pierce plant stems to suck out the sap, which is full of sugar.

hummingbird hawkmoth

cranefly

bee

bluebottle

shield bug

slug

ladybird

earwig

aphids

grasshopper

spider

👁 Eye-Spy

Look out for signs of plant-eaters in your garden or school grounds – nibbled leaves, white marks produced by leaf miners, and oak galls, swellings where tiny wasps have laid their eggs.

55

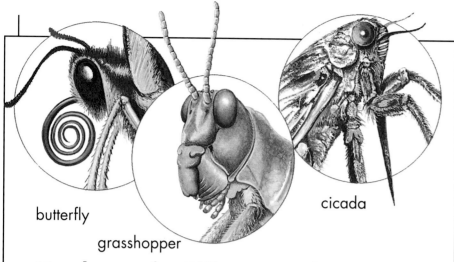

butterfly

grasshopper

cicada

Mouthparts for Different Foods

The mouthparts of insects are suited to their particular type of food. Butterflies uncoil a long thin proboscis to reach into flowers and suck out the nectar. Grasshoppers have strong biting jaws. Cicadas have piercing mouthparts that are used to suck sap from the plant stem.

Grazing Limpets

Limpets have a rough tongue called a radula which they use to scrape algae off rocks.

Do it yourself

At night, moths are attracted to bright lights.

1. On a summer night, hang a white sheet on a washing line.

2. Shine a strong torch through the sheet and watch the moths flying around in silhouette on the other side.

How It Works

Many moths fly at night in search of food. They are distracted by bright lights and come spiralling into them.

Hunters and Trappers

Many minibeasts feed on other minibeasts. These are meat-eaters – the carnivores. They are very powerful for their size and are ferocious hunters. Carnivores can move fast and have good eyesight so that they can spot their prey moving amongst leaves or flying through the air.

Hunters and trappers can be found in nooks and crannies of the woodland floor. Beetles and centipedes lie in wait, ready to jump out and chase their prey. The wolf spider lives up to its name!

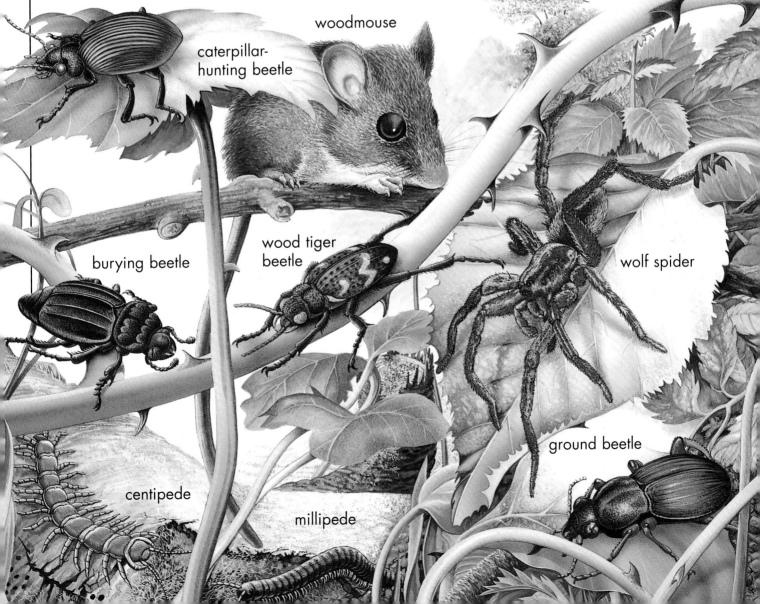

caterpillar-hunting beetle

woodmouse

burying beetle

wood tiger beetle

wolf spider

centipede

millipede

ground beetle

Some carnivorous minibeasts set traps to catch their prey. Spiders spin webs with sticky threads to trap and hold flying insects. When an insect gets trapped, the spider bites it and injects a poison that paralyzes it. Then it bundles the insect in spider silk and injects it with enzymes that break down its body, turning it to a liquid the spider can suck up.

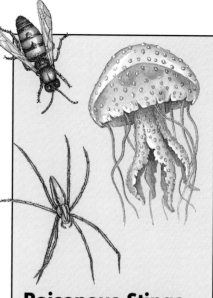

Poisonous Stings

Jellyfish, spiders and hunting wasps kill their prey with a powerful sting. The wasps carry their prey to their nests to feed their larvae.

orb-web spider

mesh-web spider

Spiders' Webs

Orb-web spiders spin large webs to trap flying insects. Mesh-web spiders make webs to trap crawling insects. The nursery-web spider spins a net-like web over a plant to protect the eggs she has laid.

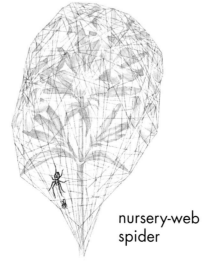

nursery-web spider

Do it yourself

At night, the woods come alive with minibeasts moving about in search of food. You can catch them in a pitfall trap – but make sure you return them to the woodland floor.

1. Find two plastic cups or other small containers and put one inside the other.

👁 Eye-Spy

Crabs are found on rocky shores, in rock pools and under rocks. See how many you can find on the shore. You could try to entice them from their hiding places by dangling a small piece of meat on a piece of string.

Aerial Hunters

Dragonflies have large wings and enormous eyes that help them to hunt efficiently. They fly along stretches of water at speeds up to 48 km per hour, looking for flying insects. Then they pluck their prey out of the air, using their spiky legs as a net.

2. Dig a hole and put both containers in it so that the top of the inside one is level with the ground.

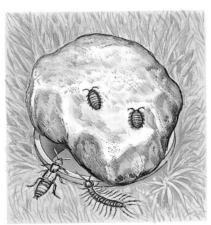

3. Put some meat or fruit in the container. Place a stone across the top, but do not cover it completely.

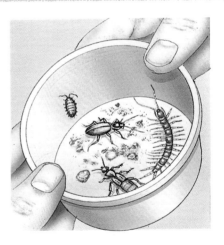

4. Next day, lift out the inside container. Now you can see what you have caught in the trap.

Flying Insects

In the animal kingdom, only birds, bats and insects can fly. Wings allow these animals to travel great distances in search of food. Most flying insects have two pairs of thin, almost see-through wings, but some have just one pair. Beetles have two pairs, but the front pair is hardened to form a tough protective cover for the hind pair, which are folded out of sight. The ladybird has a pair of hard red wings, and underneath are a pair of thin wings used for flight. The fastest fliers are dragonflies, horseflies and hawk moths, which can reach 58 kph.

African giant swallowtail

Largest Wings

The world's biggest butterflies belong to the swallowtail family. The African giant swallowtail has a wingspan of about 23 cm.

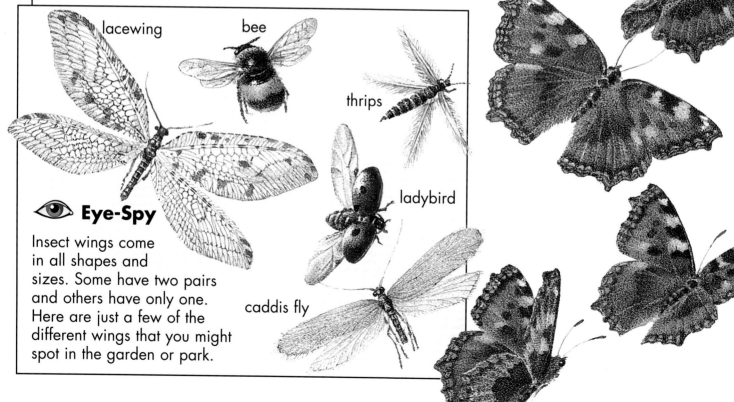

lacewing

bee

thrips

ladybird

caddis fly

👁 Eye-Spy

Insect wings come in all shapes and sizes. Some have two pairs and others have only one. Here are just a few of the different wings that you might spot in the garden or park.

Butterflies have a weak, fluttering flight. Their large wings beat slowly, up and down. The swallowtail butterfly has the slowest wingbeat of any insect, just five wingbeats per second.

Coming in to Land

This high-speed flash photograph of a bee shows how it holds out its wings to reduce speed before coming in to land on the leaf.

Do it yourself

Attract insects to your windowsill by planting flowers that are rich in nectar and have a strong scent.

1. Fill a window box with compost and water it well.

2. Sprinkle flower seeds onto the surface of the compost. Plant nasturtium seeds near the edge so that they trail over the sides as they grow. Others can be sprinkled in groups.

3. Cover the seeds with a thin layer of compost and wait for them to grow. Water whenever the box looks dry.

Self Defence

Minibeasts need to be able to defend themselves against predators. Beetles and woodlice have a heavy armour covering that is difficult to crush. Some insects deter their attackers by spraying them with acid or other chemicals. With clever camouflage, minibeasts can lie concealed and avoid being eaten. Their colouring may make them look like a piece of bark, a leaf or part of a flower.

Warning Colours

The bright colours of the sea slug warn other animals that it is covered in sting cells and should not be eaten.

👁 Eye-Spy

Many minibeasts are hard to spot in the garden because they are so well camouflaged. Caterpillars may be hidden amongst the leaves, camouflaged to look like bits of twig. Moths may have wings that are patterned to match the bark on which they rest. Snails may have shells that blend into their background. How many camouflaged minibeasts can you find in the garden or park?

rhinoceros beetle

Some minibeasts have tough outer skeletons. Others have claws or powerful legs. The silkworm caterpillar has dangerous, stinging bristles and the io moth has eyespots to frighten off predators. The scorpion has a sting.

moth

silkworm
caterpillar

praying
mantis

illipede

scorpion

Do it yourself

Try this experiment to see how camouflage works.

1. Cut out a butterfly shape from a piece of black paper. Make a pattern of white dots on the butterfly and on a large sheet of black paper.

2. Place the animal shape on the sheet of paper. Is it easy to spot? Put your finger on the shape and move it about. Is it easier to spot now?

This caterpillar resembles a shrivelled leaf.

How It Works

Camouflage works best when an animal remains still. The camouflage pattern blends into the background. Movement is easily spotted by any predators, even if the camouflage is perfect.

63

Friend or Foe?

Minibeasts live everywhere, indoors and out. Most are harmless, but a few are pests. Slugs, colorado beetles and locusts damage crops. Leatherjackets, which are the larvae of daddylonglegs, eat the roots of plants, and slugs, snails and caterpillars eat the leaves. Fortunately, there are just as many minibeasts that are useful. Hoverflies and ladybirds help in the garden by eating the aphids that feed on plants. Worm burrows aerate the soil and help water to drain away.

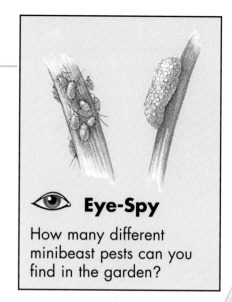

👁 **Eye-Spy**

How many different minibeast pests can you find in the garden?

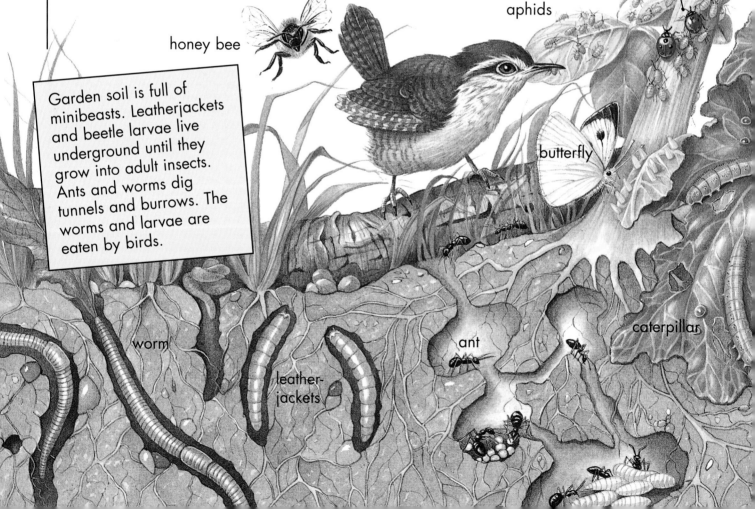

Garden soil is full of minibeasts. Leatherjackets and beetle larvae live underground until they grow into adult insects. Ants and worms dig tunnels and burrows. The worms and larvae are eaten by birds.

honey bee

aphids

ladybird

butterfly

caterpillar

worm

leather-jackets

ant

Colorado Beetles

The yellow and black striped Colorado beetle is not very big, but it is a major pest of the potato crop.

A swarm of locusts can devastate a huge area of crops in just a few hours, stripping the plants of all their leaves.

How It Works

Slugs need moisture, so they prefer places that are dark and damp. The traps create these conditions. The slugs may also try to eat the inside of the grapefruit skin.

Do it yourself

Try these slug traps in your garden.

1. Take half a grapefruit skin, a piece of wood and some black plastic.

2. Place your traps near some vegetables on a warm, wet day when slugs will be active. Leave them overnight.

3. Next morning, see which trap was the most successful. Turn the traps over and leave the slugs for the birds!

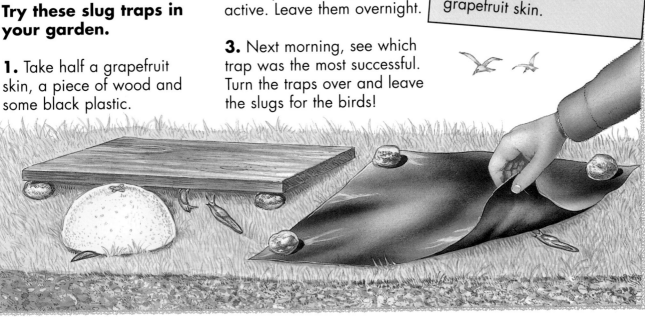

Life in the Water

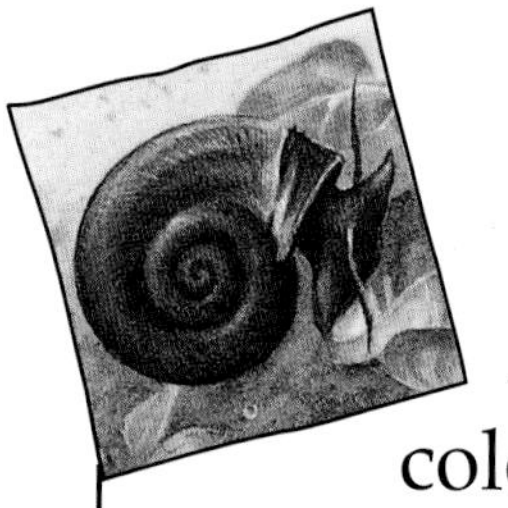

A pool of water is quickly colonized by minibeasts. The first to arrive are the water beetles and mosquitoes, then other insects soon fly in. Ducks may bring the eggs of snails and fish on their feet. Soon the pool is brimming with life. Many microscopic animals swim in the water or live in the mud. In a pond, all the animals and plants live together as a community. The water lilies and other plants provide shelter, and food for the plant-eaters.

A wide variety of animal and plant life can be found in even the smallest pond. Pond weeds and algae are food for plant-eaters such as mussels and snails. The plant-eaters are food for hunters such as backswimmers, water scorpions and beetles.

Water Spider

The water spider spins a balloon-like web that it fills with bubbles of air. It spends most of its time in the air-filled web and darts out to catch prey.

springtails

whirligig beetles

backswimmer

mosquito larvae

damselfly nymph

water mites

water scorpion

mayfly nymph

snail

backswimmer

leech

66

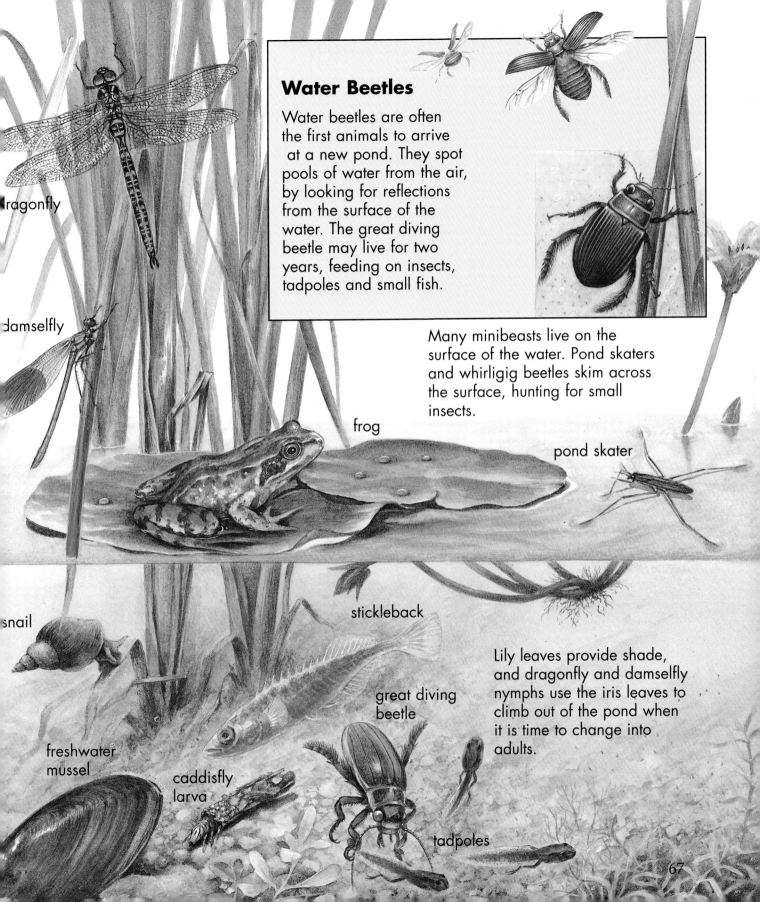

dragonfly

damselfly

Water Beetles

Water beetles are often the first animals to arrive at a new pond. They spot pools of water from the air, by looking for reflections from the surface of the water. The great diving beetle may live for two years, feeding on insects, tadpoles and small fish.

Many minibeasts live on the surface of the water. Pond skaters and whirligig beetles skim across the surface, hunting for small insects.

frog

pond skater

snail

stickleback

freshwater mussel

caddisfly larva

great diving beetle

Lily leaves provide shade, and dragonfly and damselfly nymphs use the iris leaves to climb out of the pond when it is time to change into adults.

tadpoles

Do it yourself

The best way to find out about life in a pond is to go pond dipping.

1. You will need to take a net, a large bowl, some small pots, a magnifying glass and your notebook. You may find a guide book to pond life helpful.

2. Sweep the net through the water to catch the surface minibeasts. Empty the contents into the bowl and examine your catch.

3. You may need to move the animals into the pots to have a close look at them. Try to keep the plant-eaters away from the meat-eaters.

4. Use the magnifying glass to look at the smaller animals. Remember, you may have to count the number of legs to identify an animal.

5. More minibeasts may be found on the pond weed, under lily leaves, or on irises near the edge. Others can be found under stones.

6. Note down what you find. The types of minibeast are a good guide to how clean the water is.

7. Return all the animals to the water when you have finished.

Deep Water Warning

Water is dangerous. Be very careful when working at the edge of the pond. Take an adult with you.

magnifying glass

pots

guide book

net

note book

bowl

Life under Logs and Stones

A pile of logs and dead leaves creates the damp and dark conditions that are ideal for animals such as woodlice and millipedes. These minibeasts play an important role in recycling the nutrients locked up in the remains of dead plants and animals. Beetles, millipedes and woodlice break up leaves into tiny pieces. Other minibeasts eat the rotting wood. Then fungi and bacteria finish the process of decomposition.

Fallen leaves are broken up by small minibeasts and quickly rot down. Amongst the leaves and logs are hunters such as centipedes and false scorpions. Frogs and toads may hunt here, too.

Centipede or Millipede?

A millipede has two pairs of legs on each segment, while a centipede has only one pair per segment.

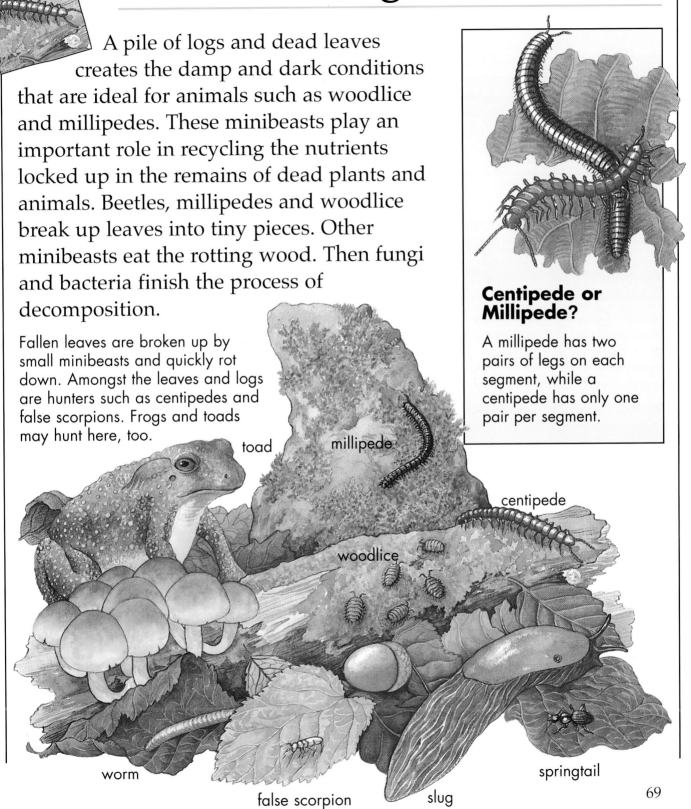

toad

millipede

centipede

woodlice

worm

false scorpion

slug

springtail

69

Living Together

Social insects live together in groups or colonies. The colonies form a community in which adults and young play a role. There is usually only one queen, and she is responsible for laying all the eggs. Most of the individuals are workers. Workers are female, and their jobs include building the home, finding food, keeping the home clean, and looking after the larvae. There are a few males to mate with the queen. Many bees and wasps live like this, and so do all the ants.

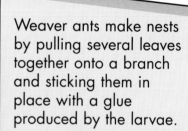

Weaver ants make nests by pulling several leaves together onto a branch and sticking them in place with a glue produced by the larvae.

A wild bees' nest contains more than 80,000 worker bees. There is a single queen bee and a few male drones. The nest is made up of wax combs suspended inside a hollow tree. Each comb contains hundreds of wax cells. The queen lays a single egg in each of the cells. The larvae hatch and are fed with pollen and honey by the workers. They then pupate to become new worker bees.

PLANT
LIFE

All Kinds of Plants

There are over 380,000 different kinds of plants, and they are found in all but the very coldest parts of the earth. There are plants in the oceans, too. We recognize most plants easily, because they are green. The colour comes from green pigment called chlorophyll. Plants range in size from tiny single-celled algae to giant redwoods and Australian eucalyptus trees that reach more than 100 metres. Some plants live for just a few weeks, others live for thousands of years.

Tallest Plants

The giant redwoods of North America are some of the tallest plants in the world, reaching heights of more than 100 m.

Seaweeds

Seaweeds are marine plants. They do not have proper roots and stems. Instead they have a holdfast, a root-like structure that attaches them to rocks, and fronds that bend with the currents.

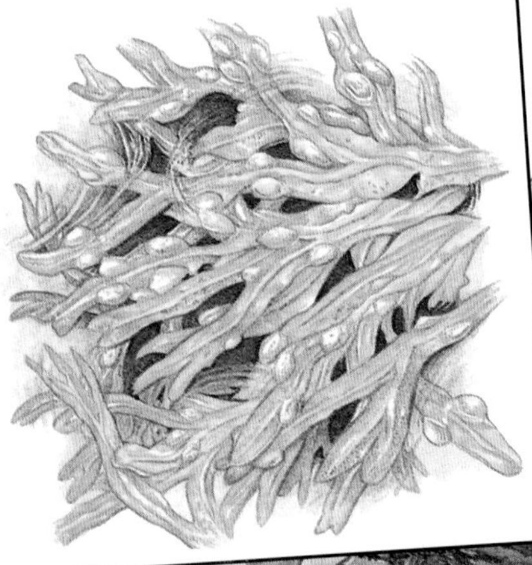

moss

flowering plant

Plants can be divided into groups. Algae, which include seaweeds, are the simplest plants. Mosses and ferns are primitive land plants. Conifers are a group of large, cone-bearing plants. The most advanced plants are the flowering plants. Their flowers produce seeds and fruit. They include the broad-leaved trees.

conifer

broad-leaved tree

👁 Eye-Spy

Many different types of plants can be found in parks and gardens. Try to find an example of a plant from each group.

Parts of a Plant

Each flowering plant has a shoot with stems and leaves, and a root system under the ground. Flowers are produced at certain times of the year and these turn into fruits and seeds.

flower

stem

leaf

root

fern

Making Their Own Food

Plants are different from other living organisms because they make their own food by photosynthesis. This process takes place in the leaves, where there is lots of chlorophyll. Some photosynthesis also takes place in green stems. Plants have many leaves, to trap as much light as possible. During the day the chlorophyll absorbs light energy from the sun. This is used to turn carbon dioxide and water into sugar, which is used to fuel the plant's growth. Sometimes the sugar is stored as starch. The gas oxygen is released into the air. Oxygen is needed by animals and plants.

carbon dioxide

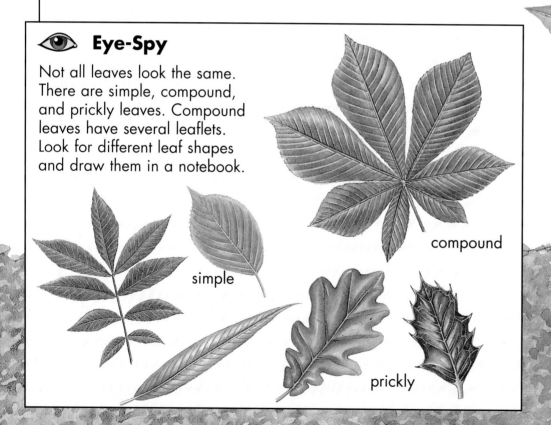

👁 Eye-Spy

Not all leaves look the same. There are simple, compound, and prickly leaves. Compound leaves have several leaflets. Look for different leaf shapes and draw them in a notebook.

compound

simple

prickly

water

74

Largest Leaves

The huge floating leaves of the giant waterlily are the world's largest simple leaves, often reaching 2 m across. They are supported by ribs that radiate from the centre, like spokes on a wheel. The leaves are so strong that they can support the weight of a young child.

sunlight

oxygen

water

Do it yourself

See how a runner bean seeks the light.

1. Put a runner bean seed in a pot of compost. Water the compost and wait for the seed to grow.

lid   shoe box

runner bean plant

shelf

2. Take a shoe box with a lid and cut a hole in one end. Paint the inside of the box and lid with black paint.

3. Using smaller pieces of card, position the 'shelves' as shown in the diagram.

4. Stand the box so that the hole is at the top. Put the young runner bean plant inside and replace the lid.

5. Every few days, open the box and water the plant.

How It Works

The runner bean detects the dim light coming through the hole and grows towards it. Plants make sure that their leaves are in the best position for photosynthesis.

When a fly falls into the liquid inside a pitcher plant, its body is dissolved and this releases nutrients for the plant.

When an insect lands on the sticky leaf of the Venus fly trap, it struggles to get free. The leaf then snaps shut and traps the insect inside.

Light is essential for plants – without it they would become yellow and have stunted growth. They also need nutrients from the soil, especially nitrogen, phosphorus and potassium. Farmers make sure that plants get sufficient nutrients by adding fertilizers to the soil. Fertilizers contain balanced amounts of nutrients, to get the best possible growth from the crops.

One way to make sure that plants get enough nutrients is to add decaying plant matter or manure to the soil. This is mixed into the soil so that the roots can absorb the nutrients.

Eye-Spy

Not all leaves are green. Make a note of the different coloured leaves of pot plants in your home. Some plants from tropical countries have red pigments as protection against the strong sun.

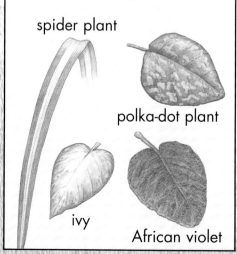

spider plant

polka-dot plant

ivy

African violet

76

Leaf Mosaics

The leaves of a tree are carefully arranged in a mosaic pattern, so that they do not shade each other.

Changing Colour

In the autumn the leaves of deciduous trees change colour from green to shades of yellow and red as the chlorophyll breaks down. Finally, the leaves fall. New green leaves form from buds in the spring.

Do it yourself

Discover how important nutrients are to the growth of plants.

1. Fill a small margarine tub with sand. Fill another tub with sand mixed with a teaspoonful of slow-release fertilizer. Firm the sand in each tub with your hand. Water both tubs.

2. Sprinkle grass seed evenly and cover with a thin layer of sand. Place the tubs on a sunny window ledge and water them regularly if they dry out.

3. Measure the height of the grass each week and compare the colour of the leaves.

tub with sand

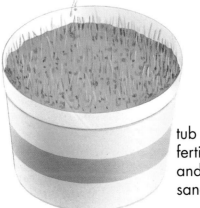

tub with fertilizer and sand

How It Works

Sand on its own does not contain nutrients, so the grass growing in just sand will not grow well. The leaves will be yellow and short. Fertilizer provides the grass with nutrients, so it will grow taller and the leaves will be a healthy green.

Inside a Plant

Plants have to be able to move water and food from the roots to the leaves, and from the leaves to the growing tips. Inside a plant there is a system of tubes. Water is absorbed by the roots and is moved through the tubes up the stem to the leaves. When the water reaches the leaves, some is used in photosynthesis, but most evaporates from the surface of the leaves. This process is called transpiration. Sugar is carried in phloem tubes from the leaves to wherever it is needed for growth. Sugar can be moved both up and down the plant, whereas water moves only one way.

sugar

water

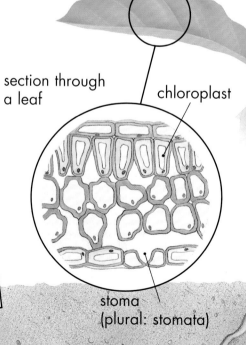

section through a leaf

chloroplast

stoma
(plural: stomata)

Transpiration

If a plant loses too much water, it wilts. A beech leaf loses far more water than a laurel leaf which has a waxy, waterproof upper surface.

laurel

beech

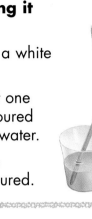

During the day, water evaporates from the surfaces of leaves. Trees have thousands of leaves, and the largest trees can lose as much as 1,000 litres of water each day.

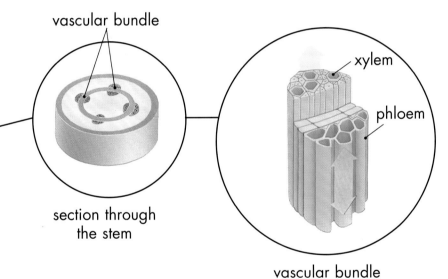

vascular bundle

xylem

phloem

section through the stem

vascular bundle

A complex network of tubes connects all the parts of the plant. In the stem, the phloem and xylem are found close together in a vascular bundle. The vascular bundles form the veins, which can be clearly seen in leaves. When water reaches the leaves, some may enter the choloroplast to be used in photosynthesis, but most of the water evaporates from the surface of the leaves. Water from the xylem vessels moves through the air spaces in the leaves and out through holes called stomata.

Plants in the Food Chain

Plants are essential to the survival of all living things. They are producers, because they are responsible for making food. Animals are consumers, because they eat plants. Some animals, called herbivores, eat only plants. Other animals, called carnivores, eat the herbivores. In this way, plants and animals form food chains. If anything happened to the plants, there would not be enough food for the herbivores and they would starve. So would the carnivores.

Plants have ways of protecting themselves from herbivores. Just a touch of this poison ivy may cause a nasty skin rash. Some trees have thorns, and nettles are protected by stinging leaves.

Do it yourself

Dead leaves and plant matter can be broken down into compost.

1. Make some wire netting into a circle and support it with canes.

2. Line the bin with sheets of newspaper. Place your kitchen and garden waste in the compost bin.

3. Cover the top with a piece of old carpet and leave for a few months.

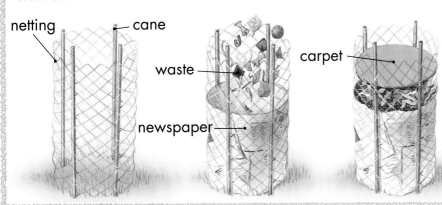

netting — cane

waste

newspaper

carpet

How It Works

As micro-organisms start to break down the plant material, they release a lot of heat. The carpet and newspaper help to trap the heat, speeding up the breaking down process. After a few months, you should have a rich organic compost that can be put back into the soil.

Death and Decay

Plants need nutrients for healthy growth. Fortunately, these nutrients are recycled, so they never run out. The remains of plants and animals are broken down by bacteria and fungi and the nutrients are returned to the soil.

Plants as Food

Plants are an important source of food, and they make up a large part of our diet. The three most important plants are rice, maize and wheat. These plants are large grasses and they are called cereals. Cereals are useful plants, because they produce seeds that contain the starch and protein that we need. Wheat seeds are ground up to make flour, while rice and maize can be cooked as they are. In many parts of the world, people survive on a totally vegetarian diet that contains only plants, with no animal food at all.

Most of the world's richest soils are used for growing cereal crops. Cereals are often grown in huge fields with no hedgerows. The crops are collected by enormous combine harvesters.

rice

wheat

barley

millet

rye

maize

Medicinal Plants

For thousands of years plants have been used to reduce pain, heal wounds and cure illness. The bark of the cinchona tree produces quinine, which is used to treat malaria. Digitalis made from foxgloves may be used to treat heart disease. Rheumatism may be treated with drugs made from the autumn crocus, and leukaemia with drugs from the periwinkle.

periwinkle

cinchona

autumn crocus

foxglove

Scientists look for better ways of growing crops. These tomatoes receive a mixture of nutrients to ensure maximum growth.

Do it yourself

Potatoes are good to eat because they are full of starch, which provides energy.

1. In spring, dig over a patch of ground and plant a potato tuber that has begun to sprout.

2. When the shoot is about 15 cm tall, pile up earth around the stem. Continue to do this as the plant grows.

3. Late in summer, the plant will begin to die back and you can dig up the new potatoes. Use a fork, but be careful not to spike any potatoes.

pile of earth

potato tuber

83

Trees

Forests are very important to the atmosphere, because trees use up carbon dioxide and produce oxygen. Unfortunately, many forests have been felled for their wood, and many types of trees are in danger of dying out. Wood is a versatile material that is used for fuel, timber and furniture. Two of the most prized woods for furniture-making, teak and mahogany, come from the rainforests.

👁 Eye-Spy

Many household items are made of wood. How many examples can you find? Look at the colour and the grain of the wood. Can you guess what type of tree it came from?

Oldest Trees

Some of the oldest trees in the world are the ancient bristlecone pines which are found in the United States. They may be as much as 5,000 years old.

What Type of Tree?

Conifers produce cones and have needle-like leaves that stay on the trees all year round. Deciduous trees usually have broad leaves and drop them in the autumn.

conifer

deciduous tree

Trees form a green canopy high above the rainforest floor, shading the plants and the ground below. Climbing plants form a tangled mass of 'ropes' around the trees, and orchids and bromeliads grow on the branches.

Do it yourself

You can learn a lot about a tree by taking a few measurements.

1. Wrap a tape measure round the trunk of the tree about 1.5 m above the ground.

Annual Rings

When you look at a tree stump, you can see growth rings. There is one for each year of the tree's life. By counting the rings, you can work out the age of the tree. In a good year, a tree will lay down a wider ring than in a poor year. By studying the rings, biologists can work out what the weather was like in the past.

2. Make a note of the measurement in centimetres. This is the circumference. Divide the circumference by 2.5. This gives you the age of the tree in years.

3. Look for girdle scars on a twig of the tree. The distance between two girdle scars is the amount of growth produced by the tree in any one year.

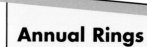

girdle scar

amount of growth in one year

Plants in the Desert

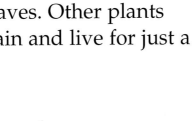

Deserts are dry places that receive very little rain. Daytime temperatures can soar to 30°C, but at night the lack of clouds means that the temperature may fall to 0°C. Few plants can survive such harsh conditions – those that do are specially adapted. Cacti have thick, fleshy stems and spines instead of leaves. Other plants appear if there is rain and live for just a few weeks.

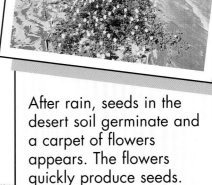

After rain, seeds in the desert soil germinate and a carpet of flowers appears. The flowers quickly produce seeds.

saguaro cactus

paloverde tree

Do it yourself

cholla

2. Plant your cacti and finish off with a layer of gravel. Give your cacti a little water and place the bowl near a sunny window.

— compost

— pebbles

Cacti are easy to grow and you can keep several types in a small bowl.

1. Put a layer of pebbles or gravel at the bottom of a bowl, then fill it with sandy compost.

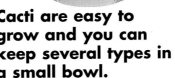

creosote bush

87

Flowers

Flowers contain a plant's male and female reproductive organs. Most plants have both male and female organs in the same flower, but a few have separate male and female flowers. Male organs, or stamens, make a powdery yellow dust called pollen. Female organs include the stigma and ovary. To make a seed, pollen has to travel to the female stigma in another flower. This process is called pollination.

Many garden flowers have been bred from wild flowers. The wild pansy has a small flower, but the garden pansy produces large, brightly-coloured flowers.

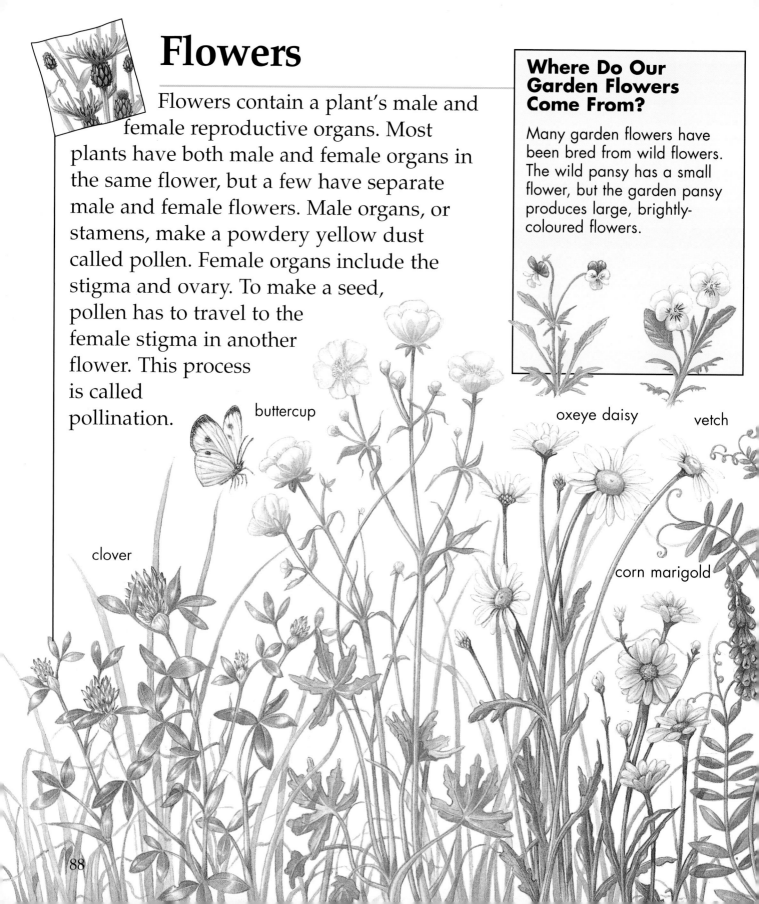

oxeye daisy

vetch

buttercup

clover

corn marigold

petal
stigma
stamen

poppy

knapweed

Largest Flower

The rafflesia plant has the largest and smelliest flower of all! For pollination it attracts flies by creating the smell of rotting flesh.

Do it yourself

Pressed flowers are great for greetings cards.

1. Lay a sheet of blotting paper on a piece of wood or thick cardboard. Position the flowers on the paper so that they do not touch. Put a second piece of blotting paper on top, and then another piece of wood and some heavy books.

2. Leave the flowers for several weeks until they are completely dry. Carefully lift the flowers from the blotting paper.

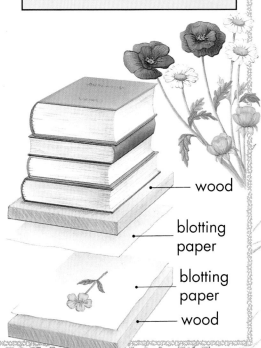

wood

blotting paper

blotting paper

wood

Fruits and Seeds

Once a flower has been pollinated, it can make seeds. First, the petals and stamens wither and drop off. Then the ovary swells in size and starts to change into a fruit. The seeds develop inside the fruit. A seed is a dry structure, with a hard outer covering called the testa. Inside there is a food store and an embryo which will grow into a new plant.

Cones

Conifers produce cones instead of flowers. The cones contain seeds. As the cone dries out, the scales open and the seeds are blown away.

Eye-Spy

A fruit contains seeds while a vegetable comes from the leaves, roots or stem. How many of each can you think of?

In autumn some plants produce colourful berries that are eaten by birds. Others produce light fruit with fluffy hairs that can float away on the wind.

blackberry

clematis

hawthorn

elderberry

rowan

rosehip

Do it yourself

Cones make attractive Christmas decorations.

1. Collect some cones. Make sure they are dry.

2. Dab a little glue on each cone. Sprinkle it with silver or gold glitter, or spray it with silver or gold paint.

3. Tie some string round the cone and hang it fom the Christmas tree. To make a larger decoration, hang three or four cones together.

4. You can also make table decorations using cones, holly, and red ribbon.

The Biggest Seed

The fruit of the coco de mer weighs up to 18 kg and contains just one seed. The seed can take nearly 10 years to develop.

91

Plants have many clever ways of making sure that their seeds are distributed far and wide. Some plants produce fruits with hairy parachutes, which carry the seeds on the wind. Others have pods that act like slings, catapulting seeds away from the parent plant. Spiky fruits get tangled in animal fur. Brightly-coloured fruits are very tasty, so they are eaten by mammals and birds.

Broom and vetch pods dry and split open, popping out the seeds. The burdock relies on animals to pick up its prickly burrs. The seeds of the dandelion, clematis and sycamore are blown by the wind.

Coconut trees are a common sight on tropical beaches. Their fruits drop into the water and are carried by ocean currents to other shores. There they germinate and grow into trees.

Edible fruits

Brightly-coloured fruits are sweet-tasting, so that they will be eaten by animals. The seeds are passed out in the animal's droppings and dispersed over a large area.

broom

clematis

vetch

burdock

aandelion

Index

A

age 7
algae 66
algae, single-celled 72
amalgam 11
amphibians 29
animal kingdom 28-29
animals 36, 66
animals, young 48
annual rings 86
antennae 43, 44
ants 51
armour 62
arteries 18, 19
arthropods 28, 29, 50
artificial additives 13

B

babies 17
backbones 50
bacteria 69
balance 24, 39
balance, testing 39

ball and socket joints 9
beetles 60
biceps muscles 9
birds 29
bladders 16
blind spots 35
blinking 32
blood cells 6, 18
blood clots 19
body temperature 6
bones 8
bony fish 29
braille 25
brains 7, 22, 23, 32
breathing 20-21
bronchi 20

C

cacti 87
cacti, growing 87
calcium 12
calories 13
camouflage 62-63
canines 10

carbohydrates 12
carbon dioxide 18, 74, 84
carnivores 54, 57, 80
cartilage 8, 9
caterpillars 52, 53
cellulose 15
cereals 82
chlorophyll 72, 74
circulation 18-19
cnidaria 29, 50
colonies 70
colour vision 34
colours 25, 30, 77
communication 30, 31
compost, making 81
compound eyes 34
cones 24, 90, 91
conifers 73, 85, 90
courtship 52

D

danger, sensing 46
decay 81
deciduous trees 85

dentine 10
diaphragms 20
diet 12-13, 26
digestion 7, 14, 15
dogs, sniffer 40

E

ear, types of 36
echinoderms 29
electrical signals 30
energy 15, 74
enzymes 14
exercise 26

F

family trees 29
fats 12
feathers 44
ferns 73
fertilizers 76
fillings 11
fingertips 45
fitness 26
flatworms 29

flight patterns 61
flowers 79, 88, 89
food 82, 83
food chains 80, 81
food store 90
fruits 90, 91, 92
fungi 28, 69
furniture, wooden 84

G

glow-worms 30
growing up 52-53

H

healthy diet 12-13
hearing 3-39
hearts 7, 18, 19
height 7
herbivores 54, 80
hiccoughs 21
hinge joints 9
homing pigeons 47
honey bees, dance 31
hunters 57

I

incisors 10
inner ear 36
insects 29, 50, 60, 61, 70
instinct 48
intestines 15
invertebrates 28, 50
iron 12

J

joints 9
junk food 13, 26

K

kidneys 16, 17

L

lateral lines 44
leaf mosaics 77
leaf sizes 75
learning 48
left-handedness 22

life cycles 53
lifestyles 26
lungs 20, 21

M

magnetic fields 46
mammals 6, 29, 34
mammary glands 6
metamorphosis 52
micro-organisms 81
middle ear 36
milk teeth 10
millipedes 69
minibeasts, finding 51, 54, 58
molars 10
molluscs 29, 50
mosses 73
moths, attracting 56
mouth parts 56
muscles 6, 9

N

nectar 55

nerve cells 23
nervous system 22-23, 32
nitrogen 76
nutrients, recycling 81
nutrients, testing 77

O

optic nerves 35
outer ear 36
ovaries 90
oxygen 6, 7, 18, 74, 84

P

perspiration 16
petals 90
pheromones 40
phloem tubes 79
phosphorus 76
photosynthesis 74, 79
plant eaters 54-55
plant protection 80
plant types 72-73
plants 28, 73, 76, 78, 83, 85, 87

plants, parts of 73
plaque 10
plasma 18
poison 58
pollen 88
pollination 88
pond life 66, 67, 68
potassium 76
premolars 10
preservatives 13
pulse, testing your 18
pupal stages 52

R

receptors 44, 45
reflexes 32
reptiles 29
right-handedness 22
rods 24

S

saliva 14
scents 41
seaweed 72

seed distribution 92

seed germination 87

seeds 90-91

self defence 62-63

senses 24, ,25, 28, 32, 33, 46, 47

sensitivity, testing 45

sight 24, 34, 35

skeletons 7, 8, 9, 62

skin 7

sleeping 26

smell 24, 40, 41

soil nutrients 76

sound waves 24, 38

spines 8

stamens 88, 90

starch 13, 74

stigma 88

stomachs 15

sweat 16

T

taste 24, 42, 43

teeth 10-11

temperature, body 6

tentacles 43

toothache 11

touch 24, 44, 45

trachea 20

transpiration 78

trappers 57

trees 84, 85, 86

triceps muscles 9

U

urine 16

V

vegetarians 13, 82

veins 18

vertebrae 8

vertebrates 28, 50

vitamins 12

vocal cords 20

W

waste material 16, 18

water, drinking 17

water evaporation 79

water life 66-67

whiskers 45

wing patterns 62

wing shapes 60

wingspan 60

wood, types of 84

woodlice 69

worms 50

X

x-rays 8

xylem 79

Photographs:
BBC Natural History Unit (Niall Benvie); Michael Chinery; Bruce Coleman (Jane Burton, J. Brackenbury, Fred Bruemmer, Alain Compost, Eric Crichton, Jack Dermid, Jeff Foott, Carol Hughes, Hans Peter Merten, John Murray, Eckart Pott, Hans Reinhard); Ecoscene (Alexandra Jones); National Slide Bank; Nature Photographers Ltd (Michael Gore, Paul Sterry); NHPA (Anthony Bannister, G.J. Cambridge, Stephen Dalton, Manfred Danegger, George Gainsburgh, E.A. Jones, R & D Keller, Michael Leach, Ivan Polunin); Panos (Jenny Hartley, Wang Gang Feng, David Watts); Science Photo Library (Aaron Polliack); Supersport (Eileen Langley); ZEFA